Reorganize
for
Resilience

Reorganize for Resilience

Putting Customers at the

Center of Your Business

Ranjay Gulati

HARVARD BUSINESS PRESS
BOSTON, MASSACHUSETTS

Library of Congress Cataloging-in-Publication Data

Gulati, Ranjay.

  Reorganize for resilience : putting customers at the center of your business /
Ranjay Gulati.

    p. cm.

  Includes bibliographical references and index.

  ISBN 978-1-4221-1721-7 (hardcover : alk. paper) 1.   Customer services.
2.   Customer relations. 3.   Organizational change. I.   Title.

  HF5415.5.G85 2010

  658.8'12–dc22

2009033706

In Memoriam

To those who taught me and are no longer with us:
Sushma Gulati
Deepak Gera
Aage Sorensen
Manmohan Dayal

Contents

Introduction

Resilience in Turbulent Markets

From Inside-out to Outside-in

MANAGERS EVERYWHERE FACE the most turbulent market conditions since the Great Depression. Global competition has accelerated, and excess capacity worldwide will likely persist as desperate competitors slug it out for increasingly demanding customers who treat goods and services as commodities where price is the only differentiator.

If you face maturing markets and shrinking product life cycles, then your traditional avenues for winning through product or service innovation are receding. You might try to control the purchase equation while cutting costs for short-term relief. Simultaneously, you might curb investment in innovation as product life cycles shorten. But these measures can't effectively tackle a market where customers have more choices, more information, and are themselves being squeezed in a challenging market. Faced by eroding pricing power, managers find themselves in a vicious cycle of declining output, prices, and profits.

1

What's more, in a marketplace where price erosion seems the norm, the goal of driving volume and margin growth simultaneously is almost inevitably elusive. To grow margin, firms must cut costs and maintain, or even increase, prices. However, a strategy of raising prices risks growing per-unit margins at the expense of reduced sales volume. When firms cut prices to gain top-line growth, growth often comes directly at the expense of margins, which can erode rapidly. All in all, it's a "growth trap" that companies today are desperate to avoid.

This monumental market adversity has triggered survival instincts in most firms. The lofty goals of yesterday to grow and expand businesses have been replaced by efforts to stabilize sales and price declines while at the same time make draconian cuts in costs. The natural response of most business leaders is to look at such turbulence as a period of shakeout in which some will survive and others not and the key differentiator will be those who have honed their survival instincts and acted upon them most effectively. A recent study I conducted with a colleague found some interesting trends that cut across the last three recessions: approximately 60 percent of companies survive through drastic downturns while the remaining 40 percent don't, with some variation across different recessions.[1] Furthermore, the survivors themselves come in two very distinct forms. The first are those that set their sights on survival as their primary goal. They hunker down, conserve resources, slash costs drastically, and wait for the storm to pass before surfacing from their bunkers to pick up where they left off. All endeavors to drive growth are shelved and the focus is on conservation and preservation. They expect to come out of the economic downturn albeit with a nasty hangover from which they anticipate they will recover. The second group, constituting 5 to 10 percent (variance across recessions) out of the survivors, came out of adverse markets not only mere survivors, but actually having leveraged adverse markets to catapult themselves far ahead of their competitors. These firms find ways to embrace downturns that turn adversity into opportunity: they survive and thrive at the same time.

My research uncovered that some companies have circum-navigated the challenges posed by turbulent markets. Few tradi-tional businesses are prospering as I write, but some smart ones are holding their own—even as they nicely position themselves for breakaway success when the roiling seas finally recede. How have they managed it?

By looking at company strategies starting in the last downturn in 2000 and continuing into this one, I found that those compa-nies built around an *inside-out* mind-set—those pushing out prod-ucts and services to the marketplace based on a narrow viewpoint of their customers that looks at them only through the narrow lens of their products—are less resilient in turbulent times than those organized around an *outside-in* mind-set that starts with the marketplace, then looks to deliver creatively on market opportu-nities. Outside-in orientation maximizes *customer* value—and pro-duces more supple organizations.[2]

Embracing an *outside-in* perspective—focusing on creatively delivering something of value to customers instead of obsessing over pushing your product portfolio—builds an inherent flexibil-ity into organizations. While this perspective is beneficial under all market conditions, its advantages become particularly acute in adverse and turbulent markets, making you inherently more responsive to market shifts, a competence that's especially impor-tant in markets where firms must radically alter what they produce, what they sell, and how they sell it. Rallying around customer problems thus results in the resilience that protects businesses from economic storms.

A recent study by Richard Ellsworth offers even broader evi-dence of the bottom- and top-line power of fostering resilience through a customer-centered outside-in approach. While the study primarily compared organizations that shared a common purpose with those that didn't, it also examined whether the actual purpose they pursued mattered. Among purpose-driven companies, *customer-driven* companies were significantly more successful than *shareholder-driven* ones, providing a 36 percent advantage in shareholder returns, compared with their industry median; shareholder-aligned organizations provided only a 17 percent advantage.[3] In sports terms, that's a rout.

Is Your Company Resilient? The Four Levels of Organizational Resilience

All organizations like to think of themselves as resilient. They want to see the world as their customers see it, to partner with customers to solve their problems, which in turn allows them to be nimble and responsive to market shifts. Such customer-centricity that is a key enabler of organizational resilience is, however, easier said than done. The vast bulk of enterprises talk the customer talk while failing consistently to walk the customer walk. This failure results from not only how companies understand (or don't understand) customers externally, but also—far more importantly—how they *structure their internal organization*. Without organizational flexibility, a company will never be truly resilient, a grave risk in turbulent times. Which is your enterprise—resilient or rigid?

In my research, I've observed what I call the four levels of organizational resilience. Where does your business fit in?

Level 1

Level 1 firms are quick to assure customers that they are the center of the universe, but they guarantee a high level of rigidity by continuing to view the marketplace entirely through the lens of their own goods and services. The motto of level 1 companies is simple: we make, you take. For some, the customers become incidental to the entire enterprise. That's how many GE executives described a stagnant GE when Jack Welch took over as CEO in 1981: "[GE is a company] . . . with its face to the CEO and its ass to the customer."[4]

Level 2

Level 2 firms have more than a veneer of pliancy. They systematically gather customer information and channel it to the appropriate units. They thoroughly understand their heterogeneous customer base, and can thus distinguish precise customer segments and needs and can tailor their products accordingly.

Intellectually and emotionally, though, level 2 enterprises step only partially toward resiliency. Though they understand customer needs, they still focus on their products, viewing their customers through the lens of the company's offerings, focusing on customers' experience with their purchase while ignoring the larger problems that customers may be trying to solve. Structurally, level 2 enterprises remain organized by product or geography, and gaining insight into customers remains the province of separate staff units like marketing. These firms will bend in a storm, but only so far.

Dept/Cc

CSR-Sales

Level 3

Level 3 firms are a quantum leap beyond their level 2 competitors when it comes to pliancy. They focus first on the problems their customers are trying to solve, and only then turn to their products, configuring their offerings to address those problems. Further, they conserve resources by allocating them only to those tasks that will help customers most. Whether premium providers of a differentiated offering or low-cost leaders, level 3 firms filter all resource allocation decisions through the lens of deep customer awareness, turning encounters with select customers from transactional to relational. Authentic empathy with customers and their issues becomes paramount as these firms continually evolve their offerings to meet those issues.

Intellectually, level 3 firms have achieved resilience at the highest plane. Moreover, they have the structural elements to become, in Zen terms, one with their customers. They have mechanisms to foster greater integration between their disparate units. Sometimes they even bust those units apart, replacing them with structures more closely aligned with their customers.

What, then, holds level 3 back from maximum resilience? Two things: At an emotional level, these firms are not yet ready to sever the final ties to their old product- or service-centric corporate identity. While they see through the prism of customer problems, they continue trying to match what customers want with what they themselves produce. Hence, their evolution to full resilience remains incomplete. More important, at a structural level, they are unwilling to eradicate the final rigidity that holds them back: their own borders. They think outside the box but live inside one.

Level 4

The most resilient companies—level 4 firms—go well beyond their competitors in attuning goods or services to customers' needs and even beyond redefining themselves in terms of the customer problems they want to solve. A level 4 firm is more attached to producing solutions to those problems than it is to the products and services it offers. This intellectual, structural, *and* emotional transition means that it is no longer concerned whether the inputs it uses to solve customers' problems are its own or assembled through a network of partners.

Successfully dealing with their own organizational barriers ultimately differentiates level 4 firms. Unlike lower-level peers, they understand that they cannot become deeply and profitably resilient without an organizational architecture that enables and encourages the entire company to understand and respond to customer needs. The entire firm reorients around a common axis: the customer. Without these fundamental organizational adjustments, all the other activities to improve customer understanding—market research, activating and monitoring customer communities, open innovation, and more—will never deliver their full potential.

Structurally, level 4 firms foster permeable boundaries not only between their disparate internal units, but also between themselves and external partners that may now produce key elements of their offering. Level 4 firms might have stumbled their way into authentic resilience, but once they get there, they embrace living inside their customers' wants and needs and make that part of their deliberate strategy. Their borders are their customers' borders, even if that means that some boundaries are dissolved into partnerships and third-party arrangements.

Apple's phenomenally successful iPhone is a case in point. Apple partnered with AT&T, granting the carrier five years of exclusivity as the only iPhone-compatible U.S. carrier, approximately 10 percent of iPhone sales in AT&T stores, and a small piece of Apple's iTunes revenues.[5] In return, AT&T developed iPhone features like visual voice mail, which provides enhanced information about received messages and a touch-screen interface for calling back or deleting them, and streamlined the in-store sign-up process. And while Apple wrote its own operating system, it partnered with multiple firms to produce a wide range of applications. Some are free, like the preloaded Google Maps; others are sold through its online store. Other partners produce a vast array of accessories, sold in Apple and other retail stores.

That partnering is only on the outside. When industry analyst iSuppli Corporation examined the iPhone's innards, it found a global catalog of third-party companies. German semiconductor producer Infineon supplied much of the phone's core communication capability; National Semiconductor provided the chip that connects the display to the graphics controller; Balda AG provided the display module. The touch screen included components from Epson Imaging Devices, Sharp, and Toshiba Matsushita Display Technology. Samsung provided at least three crucial components, and a host of other suppliers for other components were also represented.[6] iSuppli estimated the cost of these inputs and calculated that the margins for Apple likely exceeded 50 percent.

Take note—not all companies must emulate Apple or, for that matter, can gain by enhancing their resilience from level 3 to level 4. Apple itself is now trying to pull some of its outsourcing back in-house. The level to aspire to is largely determined by how exposed a company is to the raging commoditization wars and other market dynamics. What's important to keep in mind is that achieving full organizational resilience requires a companywide commitment—because the process is likely to reveal that the company itself is the biggest impediment on this journey.

How Can You Become Resilient?

Over the last decade, long before economic circumstances made resilience such a vital survival skill, I have interviewed over five hundred executives, from CEOs to division heads and line managers, and analyzed close to a dozen enterprises, searching for the secrets of resilient organizations. I began my research during the 1999–2000 recession, when I was looking at strategies companies used to survive and thrive, and have continued to track the same firms and some others through the post-2000 upswing until the present. My research has revealed a four-part path that many of these companies are following.

- First, they have changed the conversation with their customers from one that focuses only on product specifications and price—the underpinning for inside-out thinking—to one that is more outside-in, focused on how they can help address customer-articulated needs. They have also sought to discover customer needs that may not be fully articulated.

- Second, they no longer conceive of themselves as *selling to* customers, but rather as *solving problems with and for* customers. Their corporate souls are shaped not by *making* or even *being* but by *solving*. Developing real and deep customer empathy has become a key imperative.

- Third, many have developed a salutary indifference to whether their own key inputs or even outputs are produced by themselves or someone else. As customer-centric companies focus on the set of customer problems they want to solve, they become less concerned with the means and more focused on the ends. Thus, these resilient enterprises are defined not by the stalwartness of their boundaries but rather by their permeability. Where once corporate boundaries were marked by defensive fortifications, these firms are strong enough to invite their former enemies inside.

- Finally, and most important, for these resilient firms, *customer centricity* and related outside-in thinking isn't a shopworn mantra; it's their way of life. Their CEOs and top management see the business from the outside in—immersed in the broad customer experience, not constricted to the narrow lens of product or service—and build an organizational architecture that preserves that perspective and allows the company to bend the customers' way—the more so, the worse the economic climate. Under dire commoditization pressures, these companies have hacked down not costs but the old structures that held them in a product-centric world. They have not simply sharpened or redefined their strategy—the normal nostrums—nor was effective marketing alone the key.

Most managers understand *why* they need to be resilient, and many have figured out *what* customers want and *what* their companies should offer, but few appreciate the huge *organizational* barriers that prevent them from delivering on the suppleness they so fervently desire. While building customer centricity and outside-in thinking can make for great mission statements, most companies find it also spawns operational chaos and job confusion because they are not set up to execute on the promise.

Virtually all organizations have traditionally been built around stand-alone "silos" that revolve around a set of functions, products, services, or geographies, guarded by fortified boundaries that resist the intellectual, structural, and emotional changes that cooperation and coordination around a customer axis require. This organizational architecture has dictated strategic focus, which was by necessity inside-out (*from* the product or service *to* the customer), and, in turn, the customer interface, which was oriented toward selling products or services rather than toward customers and the problems they are trying to solve with those products or services.

These legacy boundaries are the final and often most resistant barrier to organizational elasticity. Even in a networked age, organizational boundaries have an extraordinary and endemic capacity to impede new growth initiatives by creating blind spots to fresh opportunities that may reside between silos or that can only come about through cross-silo collaboration. Altering such core elements is not easy—but it can be done. In fact, as readers will discover, some companies have done so very successfully, and many more could.[7]

Building resilience into an organization can involve a complete restructuring, or require the bridging of existing product, geographic, or functional lines, and processes that have created barriers. But busting up organizational silos does not always equal obliteration, nor should it. Boundaries are often crucial to innovation and the development of deep product and marketing expertise—not to mention corporate identity—so managers must find ways to maintain those benefits while harnessing the aggregate strengths of the company's silos to develop and improve customer-centric offerings.

How This Book Evolved

This book grows out of a decade of research. The role of outside-in thinking and action in fostering resilience is exemplified by

FIGURE I-1

Firms included in study

Business-to-consumer (B2C)	Business-to-consumer (B2C) and Business-to-business (B2B)	Business-to-business (B2B)
Harley-Davidson	Tribune	Jones Lang LaSalle
Starbucks	Best Buy	Lafarge
Target	Cisco	GE Healthcare

the nine companies I tracked over the course of this study (see figure I-1).[8] The companies include firms that sell products, services, and both (GE Healthcare). Some are large multinational corporations (e.g., Lafarge). Some are technology intensive (Cisco), and some are not (Starbucks). One (the Tribune Company) ultimately stumbled—though for reasons that had to do with external industry factors, not its thinking.

What all nine companies had in common when I picked them in 1999 and 2000 was their passion and commitment to look for innovative ways to survive and thrive through a recession. All had focused on achieving authentic resilience as a key to their success and made a serious effort to achieve that goal, and collectively, they strongly outperformed the S&P 500. Their total shareholder return over the 2001–2007 time frame of my study was a whopping 150 percent, compared with the S&P 500 at 14 percent. Only two companies in my sample, Tribune and Cisco, underperformed the S&P composite, mirroring problems in their specific industries. Over the same time period, these nine companies, which worked so diligently to achieve deep and meaningful resiliency, reported an astonishing average increase of 134 percent in sales growth, compared with a 53 percent average increase for the S&P 500.

What makes their stories even more significant is that the relatively good news has continued into the current sharp downturn that began in early 2008. While most of them have suffered along with others in their sectors, most have done better than their immediate competitors. Over the twelve-month period starting January 31, 2008, Best Buy's major rival, Circuit City, filed for bankruptcy first and then, ultimately, liquidation. During the same time period, Jones Lang LaSalle gained ground on its major rival, CB Richard Ellis, which is reflected in its relative market capitalization: CB Richard Ellis's market capitalization has gone from being 2.2 times that of Jones Lang LaSalle to 1.6 times at the end of January 2009. Similarly, Lafarge's market capitalization is down 1 percent in this time period, while that of its major rival, Cemex, has dropped 22 percent.[9]

I also relied on a number of other sources for some of the ideas that went into this book. Before I began my fieldwork, I conducted an exploratory survey-based study of *Fortune* 500 CEOs to explore their key strategic and organizational challenges coming out of the last recession in 2000.

A final source of data was my MBA and executive MBA students to whom I was teaching the cases I'd written on these companies. As a teaching device, I also asked several hundred of my executive MBA students from North America, Europe, and Asia to discover and document cases of companies that had faced the kinds of implementation challenges associated with becoming customer centric in turbulent markets. These stories further sharpened my thinking.

The Path of This Book

This book is primarily about implementation: the managerial processes that firms use to build resilient organizations by prying open the internal boundaries that separate the firm's units and the external boundaries that separate the organization and its partners. The many pitfalls on the road to resilience will be covered at length throughout this book, but so too will the pathways, as I explore the underpinnings of success and failure in firms' quest for the deep customer centricity that is so crucial today. I will also demonstrate the importance of companies' making their internal and external boundaries more permeable and adaptive. Getting there, I will show, requires turning the inside-out mind-set and organizational architecture outside in.

Chapter 1 starts off by addressing the question of *how* an organization can recognize and shift internal barriers to move toward resiliency, tracing one company's journey to customer centricity as an example. This chapter also introduces the five levers—coordination, cooperation, clout, capability, and connection. Used together, these key organizational levers carry a company from *why* to *what* and *how*, and lead it to building a resilient organization. Chapters 2 through 6 examine each of these levers in depth, providing a tool kit that you can use to dissolve silos and replace them with a resilient organizational architecture. Finally, the conclusion considers these five levers in the context of the four levels of resilience, and describes the way these can work together to achieve the truly supple organization, one that dances with its customers rather than dictating to them.

Now let's start on our journey.

1

Building a Resilient Organization

The Process and the Tools for Systemic Integration

SINCE THE 1980S, bagged salad—that staple of every grocery store's produce section—has risen from nonexistence to a $2.5 billion-a-year industry.[1] Yet developing and delivering bagged salad was not a simple matter of packaging. Rather, it was the result of a revolutionary shift to outside-in thinking that never could have been achieved without a pliant mind-set and supportive organizational architecture.

The creative leap that allowed companies like Fresh Express and others to turn a commodity product into a growth juggernaut required looking beyond the traditional questions that most companies ask about their customers: What do they like and not like about my product? How much did they pay for it? Where do they prefer to buy it? While valid, these product-centric questions provide a distorted understanding of the marketplace. To gain a more holistic picture, companies must view the marketplace through the lens of their customers, where the real transactional power lies

15

(+)

today. The question is not how much the customers will pay and what kind of lettuce they like, but rather how the making and consumption of salad relates to their busy lifestyle. Ask *those* questions, and you will see that what busy customers truly want is for you to *make the whole salad* for them.

Answers like that one are almost impossible to uncover when the inquiry is inside-out—when the questions start with the product and *then* move to the customer. The leap becomes harder still when each of a firm's units has a distinct view of the customer, in many instances, resembling the proverbial six blind men touching different parts of an elephant and trying unsuccessfully to discern what the animal really is.

What resilient firms have discovered is that offering real customer solutions requires an enterprisewide effort to develop deep new kinds of knowledge about customers—the underlying problems customers are trying to solve with a product or service and how customers may actually use the product or service.[2] This approach may lead organizations to explore adjacent unmet customer needs that lie outside of the company's core offerings.[3] In the case of bagged salad, health-conscious customers were simply too busy to make a decent mixed salad. In fact, it turned out that the prospect of this task was the biggest impediment to their purchase and consumption of lettuce. This is not, in and of itself, a huge insight, but getting to it required a deep, authentic empathy for the plight of the customer. It meant lifting the product- and service-centric veil that many firms have worn all their lives. When Fresh Express and others did lift it, what they found sitting right in front of them was a humble bag of greens waiting to launch a multibillion-dollar market. In an economic climate characterized by virtually cost-free duplication, zero-plus profit margins, almost infinite choice, *and* constantly shifting thresholds as to what constitutes a maximum shopping experience, elevating customer value as the primary goal can be and often is the difference between survival and extinction.

Which company is going to get there first—the one that couldn't see beyond its product to bagged salad in the first place, or the one that is already working with its customers to add maximum value to its products? Which is even going to know that customer tastes have shifted, as they always do?

Gaining deep customer insight is complicated enough; acting on it is even more challenging. There are dozens of stories of organizations that overlooked brilliant ideas in their laboratories or the minds of their employees, recognizing them only when someone else emerged a market winner with the very same idea. Building outside-in oriented resilient organizations is about both insight *and* action. Action requires overcoming internal organizational barriers—moving from the *what* of customer empathy to the *how* of organizational integration. Bagged salad could never have come to market without the *insight* about real customer needs and the *action* of disparate silos both enabling this insight and coming up with the most desirable mixes and the systems to deliver them. It is this greater collaboration between an organization's disparate units that creates the pliancy and elasticity that will ultimately allow outside-in thinking—and resiliency—to flourish.

Outside-in thinking *does not mean blindly following what customers tell a company to do.*[4] Customers themselves may not be able to articulate their needs precisely. Instead, the approach involves a creative process driven by a deep and holistic understanding of the problems of the organization's existing and desired customers, together with a careful consideration of the possibilities given the organization's technological, service, and manufacturing capabilities—a combination, in short, of technology push and customer pull. The goal isn't merely to *serve* customers. The goal is to *immerse* yourself in customer problems so you can offer up unique solutions.

While the example of bagged salad suggests how customer centricity may lead to a premium, differentiated offering, this orientation is equally appropriate for companies offering low-cost products and services. A common misconception is that firms that operate as low-cost leaders are not customer centric. In fact, such firms are equally beholden to customers' needs. They, too, can give customers what they want and are willing to pay for, while eliminating those elements that customers don't desire and so are not willing to pay for. The success of Wal-Mart is a vivid example; in the face of an economic downturn, it has sought to further reduce its costs and prices by pulling back in areas that don't deliver customer value. In sum, when you are either adding or subtracting elements in your offering, both sets of decisions should be made through the prism of customer problems.

Even as the traditional strategic choice to focus on product leadership, operational excellence (low cost), or customer intimacy starts to blur in today's competitive and demanding marketplace, it is becoming clear that each of these approaches must still be anchored in outside-in thinking. True, some firms operating in emerging industries and/or with novel technologies that provide meaningful advantages over competitors might spend less time on their customer-facing activities, but even these firms must drive their innovation efforts by a deep understanding of what their customers want in the first place. And those firms striving for operational excellence must still align their points of excellence with their customers' desires, so that they introduce suppleness into the very core of the enterprise, no matter what they are offering.

Critical Important

How to Build a Resilient Organization: Systemic Integration at Best Buy

As the new century dawned, the maelstrom of market conditions that IBM's Lou Gerstner once described as "commodity hell" was all too real for consumer electronics giant Best Buy.[5] While U.S. consumer electronics sales were showing steady growth, retailing these products was an ever-increasing challenge. Historically, manufacturers had sold their wares through consumer electronics retail chains such as Best Buy and Circuit City, and through high-end specialty retailers like Tweeter Home Entertainment Group. Wal-Mart, though, was threatening to break that model wide open. Known for its low-price merchandising, the world's largest retailer had used its significant economies of scale to make an aggressive push into Best Buy's territory. By 2004, Wal-Mart was generating

$17 billion in electronics revenue.[6] And although it had captured the number-two spot in the U.S. consumer electronics market, Wal-Mart was not the only threat on the retail horizon. Online retailers such as Amazon and Dell had also pushed into this market, as had alternative-format warehouse retailers like Costco.

In this fiercely competitive climate, Best Buy was worried about remaining profitable and retaining its leadership position. Becoming a low-cost leader like Wal-Mart was not a realistic strategy. Best Buy produced nothing, so product innovation was also out of the question. Even if it had been an option, ease of imitation and low-cost competition from around the globe would likely have decreased margins even further.

What's more, in the competitive consumer electronics retail sector, where price erosion seems to be the de facto norm, the goal of driving volume and margin growth simultaneously seemed elusive. To grow margin, firms like Best Buy had to find ways to cut costs and maintain, or even increase, prices. However, pursuing the latter tactic ran the risk of growing per-unit margins at the expense of reduced sales volume. And if these firms cut prices to gain top-line growth, they would find that this came directly at the expense of their margins, which could erode rapidly.

These factors together create a "growth trap" of choosing between revenue or margin, and Best Buy ought to have been caught too. Yet Best Buy enjoyed double-digit growth in sales and total return for the first seven years of the decade. Indeed, in the third quarter of 2008, Best Buy's earnings per share, while drastically reduced, nonetheless exceeded analysts' expectations by an average of 46 percent. Things are likely to continue to get worse for consumer electronics, but in this rapidly shrinking sector, Best Buy remains one of the few still standing, while others, notably rival Circuit City and even Tweeter, have folded.

Why? Why is Best Buy still standing while the graveyard of consumer electronics retailers is littered with new tombstones? What did the company undertake that its competitors failed to pick up on? The easiest explanation is that Best Buy embraced the imperative of outside-in thinking, but the company never could have done that without first busting apart an organization that couldn't get out of the way of its own rigidities and building in a new pliancy from the store floors to the corner suites.

Overcoming the Organization

As early as 2000, during the last recession, Best Buy realized that in a consumer electronics marketplace characterized by heightened competition, margin erosion, maturing product lines, shrinking product life cycles, and a drastic customer pullback inspired in large part by a paucity of credit, customer buying behaviors had become increasingly transactional. The onus was no longer on customers to choose from the products placed before them, but on the supplier to demonstrate how its product or service could add value for customers. By refocusing itself around its customers, Best Buy hoped to create precious differentiation between itself and its competition, driving top- and bottom-line growth, and thus enhancing its own chances not just for survival but for success. According to an internal document, "Wal-Mart and Dell . . . would always be better at a purely logistical game; we had to learn to see customers' faces, to understand what they want . . . and win *with* customers."

Winning with customers, in turn, required the internal integration of Best Buy's disparate units around a common agenda of driving customer value. Building this customer axis is far more revolutionary than a structural reorganization—reorganizations happen all the time. It involves a change of mission from serving up products and services to solving a discrete set of customer problems and integrating a firm's disparate silos to do so.

Facing the Crisis

Best Buy understood that in the context of rising customer expectations, achieving meaningful internal integration and developing true solutions required not only a more comprehensive under-standing of select customers and their needs, but also having (1) the ability to utilize that information internally to develop the integrated bundles of products and services those customers wanted, and (2) the ability to deliver and sell those solutions in a way that built strong connections with those customers. But unlike most other firms that dream the dream of customer cen-tricity, Best Buy had a well-thought-out implementation plan, and by 2004, CEO Brad Anderson was ready to roll it out.

In October 2004, Anderson first made public a new operating model that the company had been incubating since February 2002. According to a Best Buy director, the company's old model involved "buying products from vendors, teaching associates how to sell the product, and then the customer gets whatever we buy." As late as 2002, this inside-out strategy appeared to be successful: Best Buy was enjoying record-breaking profits and dominating competitors. But that fall, then-new CEO Anderson dampened company officers' enthusiasm with a video documentary that fea-tured interviews with customers who had left Best Buy without buying anything. When asked why, the customers expressed anger and disgust with the store's service and apathy about Best Buy generally. Best Buy would have to change that.

Best Buy, in short, was what it sold, or maybe more accurately (and ominously), what its merchandizing unit bought to put in the stores, since Best Buy itself made nothing at all. As chief mar-keting officer Barry Judge explained, "Lots of retailers make prod-ucts. Banana Republic makes products. Williams-Sonoma and Target make products. Part of their differentiation and image comes from stuff you can't get anywhere else. Best Buy doesn't really have unique products." Achieving Anderson's vision entailed a 180-degree shift in perspective—from inside-out to outside-in and from a product axis to a customer axis. As Shari Ballard, executive vice president of human resources, legal and entertainment, put it, "The anchor point of customer-centricity is understanding how customers are intending to use this in their life and then solving that problem for them. So, it's a customer-backed solution rather than a product- or organization-out solution." Best Buy's point of differentiation would no longer be the goods on the shelves but the overall customer experience. Instead of living inside the boxes in the storeroom and the display models on the floor (Buy me! Buy me!), the company would have to start living inside the minds of shoppers (Help me! Help me!), a very different proposition indeed.

The Beginning of the Journey: Differentiating Customers, Not Products

A lot had already happened in the years preceding Brad Anderson's formal pronouncement. Best Buy's journey toward resiliency in a threatening world had begun when it first started using customer data to identify target customer segments, determine their needs, and position products and services to meet them. The company had identified five groups:

- *Tech fanatics*. Tech-savvy, young adults looking for the newest gadgets or the latest video games, movies, and music

- *Home theater connoisseurs*. Affluent and busy professionals looking for the best technology and a high level of expertise and service

- *Family men*. Male buyers looking for long-lasting and affordable products for use by their families

- *Busy moms*. Suburban mothers seeking products to make life easier and enrich the lives of their children

- *Small-business customers*. Professionals looking for the right technology solutions to run and grow their small businesses

Some of the findings were eye-opening for company executives. Women, for instance, purchased 55 percent of all consumer electronics and also influenced approximately 75 percent of all such purchases. Yet most retailers, including Best Buy, had historically tailored their marketing and store concepts around the interests and purchasing patterns of male consumers. If Best Buy was going to become truly customer centric, it would have to listen to what the research was telling it.

From Insight to Action: Reconfiguring the Architecture

When Best Buy started its transformation journey, all major decisions were driven by the products it sold, the latest available technologies, and operational efficiency. The company's two vertical organizations, retail (focused on store operations) and merchandising (focused on individual products), used these drivers to achieve company goals. Merchandising, in particular, was responsible for managing the profitability of different product categories. Consequently, it owned all product-marketing strategies, product-pricing decisions, and inventory management. It was further charged with understanding technology trends and profit opportunities and using those insights to craft in-store product assortments, placement, and displays that would maximize Best Buy's financial performance while also supporting the firm's brand image.

Buyers were grouped around product categories, such as printers and digital cameras. Category managers' incentive compensation was largely driven by their category's financial performance as measured by revenue, EVA contribution, and return on invested capital.[7] Because Best Buy's operating profit percentage, like that of most other retailers, was typically in the mid single digits, one of the merchandizing organization's biggest priorities was to capture increased economies of scale in purchasing to help drive down costs.

Given that neither retail nor merchandizing naturally catered to distinct customer segments and needs that spanned across a range of products, inflexibility and blind spots were endemic to the organization. Anderson took the first steps toward resiliency by establishing a permanent cross-functional group that could focus on the development and implementation of segment-specific strategies. Five segment teams were formed—one for each target customer group. Each team comprised a segment lead (vice president or director level) and two other members. The role of each team was to spearhead efforts to understand and incorporate customer needs into all aspects of Best Buy's value-delivery system.

Segment leads had oversight responsibility for how changes to in-store operations were deployed across the company to support these strategies. They were also responsible for the development and management of a disciplined experimentation process to identify levers for tailoring Best Buy's sales, marketing, and merchandising efforts. Finally, they were charged with managing the financial performance of their respective customer segments as a business. This entailed understanding business opportunities and identifying where to invest company resources to win with their segment on a national basis.

Segment teams starting testing their strategies in June 2003 at six lab prototype stores located in Washington, D.C., and Baltimore. Lab stores implemented a new store operating model: serving all Best Buy customers, but focusing on the needs of the largest and most profitable customer segment(s) that shopped at that store. Segment teams and store employees tested the effects of elements such as lighting, store layout, product assortment, and employee service models on a given segment's purchasing behavior. Importantly, the segment teams did not have any authority over the merchandising or store operations units. Rather, they served as staff support groups that collaborated with those units.

To better understand the needs of one of the segments, management conducted a series of focus groups. These were not the traditional product-centric focus groups in which customers are asked about the firm's existing products. Rather, they focused on

Perfor~ focus groups on

larger customer problems. The busy moms team, for instance, focused on women's needs as consumers of electronics, and learned that busy moms didn't like the in-store sales experience. As Brad Anderson explained, "What they didn't like is that when they came into the store with their kids, their kids would scatter to the entertaining things we had in the store for them . . . When they went to talk about the things they were interested in, such as the purchase of a digital camera so they could share pictures of their kids with a sister in another city . . . our associate would immediately talk about how many pixels you want your digital camera to have. It would drive them crazy. They became even more upset if they came in with a [male friend or] husband because we would talk to him instead of her."

As Nancy Brooks, one of the members of the busy moms segment team, put it, "A male consumer . . . is excited and interested in the technology—just for technology's sake. For them, technology is really exciting and fun. They love to come in and browse just because they want to see what is new. That is not how females are wired in this space. They've got to see the end-benefit of the technology to get the same energy and enthusiasm for the technology." In other words, men shop on Mars, women shop on Venus. And because many senior managers were men, their understanding of female buying behavior was not normally as extensive as their understanding of male consumers. So the busy moms segment team worked with them to shape new ways to connect with these customers.

For instance, the busy moms segment team sought to offer a more tailored assortment of merchandise that included digital imaging and scrapbooking products.[8] It also recommended an expanded selection of home appliances. Other changes included the provision of play areas for children, softer lighting, improved signage, and in-store music that included a greater selection of songs from such artists as James Taylor and Mariah Carey. New express checkout lines were also instituted.

The segment team successfully identified five value propositions that resonated with female customers:

- Personal shopping assistants

- Just-for-kids displays

- Kitchen/laundry zone

- Practical signage

- Inspiring atmosphere

Perhaps the most significant change was the introduction of personal shopping assistants, specially trained consultants who offered busy moms one-on-one service and guidance. In contrast to Best Buy's traditional sales associates, who worked only within a single department, personal shopping assistants were trained to accompany customers throughout their visit and assist them with their purchase decisions on any product. Customers could use these assistants on a drop-in basis, but they could also set up specific appointment times, an added convenience.

Just-for-kids displays also brought together in one spot gaming and software products that catered to children, such as LeapPad learning products and Disney consumer electronics. The kitchen/laundry zone showcased home appliances in complete kitchen and laundry room settings. Lifestyle photos, a color-coded department layout, bright colors, and other changes all helped make the environment more comfortable for target customers.

Scaling Up: Building Bridges Across the Enterprise

Segment teams rolled the successful segment strategies and store operating model out to thirty-two pilot stores across the United States in September 2003. Employees in the lab and pilot stores underwent extensive training on the segment strategies and how to best serve each segment's needs. By April 2004, pilot stores were realizing increases in gross profit rates and year-over-year sales, while employee turnover decreased. Encouraged by these positive results, Best Buy decided to roll out the new store operating model nationally, starting with sixty-eight stores in California. The new segmented stores, along with the original lab stores and pilots, had better financial statistics than the traditional product-oriented stores—9 percentage points higher on average. Because of the performance of the segment-focused stores, Best Buy decided to convert all its stores to the customer-centric operating model by 2009.

Throughout this conceptualization and rollout process, segment teams created end-to-end strategies to win more customers and revenues. As noted earlier, the teams had limited formal authority over merchandising and store operations, but in most cases, they were ahead of the rest of the organization in terms of customer insight. Bringing the other parts of the company along to ensure that their ideas were turned into action required bridge building across the disparate silos within the Best Buy organization.

Inevitably, one of the hardest bridges to build was to the merchandising organization, yet cooperation was critical. Segment teams needed the merchandisers to provide appropriate product assortments for the target segments that shopped most frequently in their stores. Not only did this necessary reform have the potential to reduce Best Buy's overall purchasing power, as it would potentially have to shift away from buying large quantities of a narrower array of products, but it also created significant operational complexity. As Michael Mohan, a member of the merchandising organization, explained, "Our first cut for assortment must be on store size. We have stores that are half the size of other stores, and they can't carry the same assortment. The next cut happens to be where the stores are in the country . . . So, if I solely cut my assortment based on segment, I would actually under-optimize where the consumers are ready to purchase and spend money."

The merchandising organization was also challenged by the change it was being asked to make in its core processes and objectives. Its strategies to date had been focused on maximizing product velocity (i.e., product unit and sales volumes) and product profitability—subject to various strategic considerations. Now merchandising was being asked to explicitly consider how well product assortments were meeting the needs of specific customers and to develop solutions that were driven by the needs of those customers rather than simply by trends in technology or general buying patterns. Like the rest of the company, it would have to learn to dance with the customers, but of necessity, merchandising also had to help lead the change.

From mid-2003 to mid-2004, when the segment teams were operating in isolation from the rest of the company, early product assortment decisions for lab stores were made with minimal involvement from merchandising. Following Brad Anderson's formal internal communication about the customer-centricity strategy in May 2004, however, product assortment decisions became a shared responsibility. Soon, both groups were holding monthly "strategy meetings" to foster increased communication and collaboration. During these meetings, senior buyers would meet with the segment teams to discuss tailored product assortment opportunities.

Building on the positive experience with merchandising, the segment teams began bringing nonmerchandizing units into the fold. One such group was the company's experience design group, responsible for designing the look and feel of Best Buy stores, including layout, lighting, colors, and signage. Because busy moms had said they were put off by the loud music, sharply contrasting colors, and complex layouts characteristic of most Best Buy stores, the busy moms segment team worked closely with the experience design group to design lab stores with softer colors, more open space, and different visual cues. As a result of positive customer feedback, many of these changes were later incorporated into the first pilot stores targeting these customers and later rolled out more broadly.

Strengthening the Front Line

Customer segment teams also had to work closely with the store operations and frontline employees to raise awareness about the importance of customer centricity for the organization. In April 2004, the company hosted a special Retail Road Show in Las Vegas for every regional, district, and store manager in the U.S. retail organization—close to 2,500 people—as well as the company's corporate officers. Over three days, attendees were given a general overview of the customer-centricity strategy and toured demonstration store environments designed to target specific customers. Segment teams were on hand to answer questions. As part of its general effort to introduce greater resilience into the organization, Best Buy further instituted a Customer Centricity University training program that was primarily focused on corporate employees.

Best Buy also sought to bring greater power to the front line by preparing retail associates for an expanded role in store decision making. As one executive put it, the intent was to "engage their heads and not just their hands." As a first step, the company developed a training program to better acquaint its sales associates with the company's target customers. Company executives worked alongside store managers to train retail employees to understand basic financial performance measures; this helped the sales associates understand how serving target customers directly affected store performance, and strengthened their sense of ownership over the company's profitability. This feeling of ownership, in turn, helped associates transcend a long-standing silo mentality that one associate described as this: "The front line is responsible for fulfilling customers' in-store needs. The corporate office is in charge of watching the bottom line."

The company also gave employees greater freedom to tinker with product assortment, placement, and promotion strategies. Employees who wanted to experiment could submit to their store manager a business case defining the perceived problem, presenting a hypothesis about how to address the problem, and proposing a way to test the hypothesis. Employees who received management approval ran the proposed tests. If the results proved positive, managers considered implementing the idea more broadly in the organization.

Given greater clout, these front liners deepened their understanding of customers and began reaching across functions and levels as needed to serve them. In return, real rewards—a million-dollar fund provided "chairman awards" for employee innovation—and psychological rewards flowed back to the front lines.

Extending Resilience Across the Enterprise

In December 2004, Best Buy's customer-centric initiative was accelerated by a reorganization that created a new customer business group that organized all the segment teams; marketing, advertising, and communications functions; customer call centers; and the internal design group under one executive. Up to this point, the customer-centricity strategy had largely been implemented via authoritative dictates from senior management and the persuasive skills of the segment teams to motivate organizational support. This new group was to continue the work already under way by working collaboratively with the company's different functional organizations to determine how each group could best support the new effort.

Since Best Buy's functional organizations had always operated with a high degree of independence, management knew that it would take time for the full effects of this collaborative approach to be realized. Nevertheless, these efforts began to bear fruit, and by December 2005 the company had implemented the customer-centric operating model in 284 stores, with an end goal to convert all stores by 2009.

Top managers believe that the next step is creating tighter horizontal linkages across the company's internal organizations. In new-CEO Brian Dunn's words, "We have been a very strong vertical company. What I mean by that . . . is that we have a strong retail field organization, a strong merchant group, and a strong support group. So, our current task is to create more integrated operating groups where a merchant, a marketer, a field operator, and an HR specialist are clustered around a customer segment and understand it end-to-end."

Although the mechanism for achieving this vision continues to be refined at the time of this writing, senior management remains committed to this course and confident about the company's prospects for the future. As former CEO Brad Anderson had explained, "We saw ourselves . . . as being the leading agent that helped bring the product from manufacturers like Sony and Panasonic . . . to the customer's home . . . We've now begun a change to seeing ourselves as a customer-centric company, one whose focus is on customers' needs in the lifetime application of the product that we sell, as opposed to an agent that efficiently distributes the product. And that's a very profound change with tremendous ramifications."[9]

Best Buy became a company that looked at itself from the outside in, rather than seeing the marketplace from the inside out, migrating its brand from being a company offering all the consumer electronics a customer could want to one that would do everything possible to match individual customers up with uniquely tailored solutions. The earlier brand had tethered Best Buy to its products. The new brand tethers it to the customers and their problems—a far more elastic and portable concept. This new resiliency might not be the sole factor explaining Best Buy's continuing success in the face of recession, but resilience does seem to be its greatest point of differentiation from Circuit City, which dug itself into a product-centric trench and did not survive.

The Implementation Imperative:
From Simple to Systemic
Organizational Integration

It is harder today than ever to develop an outside-in orientation. Why?

Part of the answer is complexity. Customers have become progressively more empowered and demanding; at the same time, some business-to-business sectors have become much more complicated as customers themselves have grown to become multibusiness enterprises. As that has happened, the very definition of *outside-in* or *customer centricity*, has evolved.[10] The speed with which organizations are able to adapt to fast-changing customer needs is another factor. Organizations today have trouble moving as fast as their customers are changing. Behind these inertial elements are a firm's entrenched silos and their inherent resistance to realignment. There are other human elements: employees build their identities around existing hierarchies, and their entire careers are launched and developed along these well-worn tracks. Any change to these structures means upending career trajectory, a daunting prospect even in more stable times.

Making organizational boundaries more porous and the consequent integration challenges have been enduring organizational themes. However, they are exacerbated today by decades of firm-specialization efforts—efforts to develop a deeper expertise and greater efficiency around functional, product, and technology areas. Now, in an ironic twist, the farther firms may have advanced along the specialization continuum during previous eras, the harder it may be for them to propel themselves toward outside-in collaborative organization.[11]

The fundamental shifts needed to align divisions around a customer axis are rarely self-evident, and most firms don't get it right the first time. The delivery of integrated and seamless offerings to customers requires what I refer to as *systemic integration*. As we've seen, true integration requires internal units to work together in totally new ways. Yet internal groups often have no or only very minimal connections. Such intraorganizational barriers are no longer just slowing things down: they make true, systemic integration virtually impossible. Thus, the challenge of developing a customer axis usually means overcoming a company's organizational history, as the Best Buy story demonstrates.

The underpinning for all integration work begins with the division of labor and the concomitant interdependence among units within a firm. *Interdependence*—the relationship among the units or divisions of an organization or system—is integral to all organizational architectures, since every unit depends on one or more other groups to accomplish the overall work of the system.[12]

But the more complex the interdependence, the more sophisticated the integration efforts required. When companies first pursued the division of labor, interdependence among units was relatively simple. Work was usually handed from one unit to the next in a sequential fashion, as on an assembly line. As the twentieth century progressed, integration efforts became increasingly difficult to accomplish.[13] This resulted from the expanded complexity of everything—products, services, relationships, and processes.[14] In the past decade, this interdependence has become even more dynamic: always in a state of change and, increasingly, *unpredictable*. The activities that management must integrate can't always be identified in advance and may not even be fully understood before they are undertaken. Why? Because the interdependencies are no longer completely confined within the company itself. They involve interactions with customers, suppliers, and strategic partners. In addition, dynamic interdependencies often unfold in no typical sequence and must be achieved essentially in real time.[15] Thus, the need for organizational resilience is itself greater than ever. In a rapidly evolving, unpredictable, and always complex competitive environment, firms that can't bend are likely to break. Achieving systemic integration in such a dynamic context requires new activities and orientations that are summarized in figure 1-1. They include:

- *Taking expeditions toward resilience without maps.*[16] As firms' quests to become more outside-in in their orientation involve more disparate parts of the organization, the definition of their tasks tends to become broader and more amorphous. It is like going on an expedition into difficult territory without a map. In fact, a task may not be well articulated or even completely understood by *anybody* involved, and in that case, must sometimes be defined, designed, and executed in real time as the units learn about or anticipate customers' precise needs—in a word, improvised. Remember how Best Buy's segment

FIGURE 1-1

Keys to systemic integration

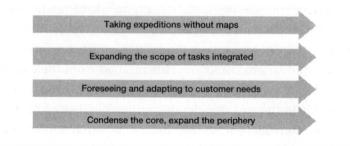

Taking expeditions without maps

Expanding the scope of tasks integrated

Foreseeing and adapting to customer needs

Condense the core, expand the periphery

teams had to tackle interdependence with a whole array of units. The strategies and realignments could be discovered only once the effort was under way. There was no way to know what bridges would have to be built across diverse units that previously had no formal linkages.

- *Expanding the scope of tasks to be integrated.* Achieving systemic integration in the organization involves determining how to produce and distribute more effectively, how to assemble solutions of the highest value, and how to use these solutions to develop long-term customer partnerships within target segments—simultaneously. This necessitates bringing together very disparate functional, product, or geographic groups, those that sit close to the marketplace (e.g., sales and customer service) and those that don't (e.g., product development and R&D). At Best Buy, segment teams had to learn to work with merchandising, store operations, the CIO organization, the experience design team, and ultimately the employees that staff each of their hundreds of stores.

- *Foreseeing and adapting continuously to customer needs.* The nature of integration varies not only from customer to customer but also over time and across projects. Even if a company is initially successful in developing high-value customer solutions, it still must adapt them continually and develop new ones to address shifts in customer needs. Thus, the most resilient companies become adept at monitoring fluctuations in customer needs and customizing solutions in real time, eventually scaling up the solutions to be available firmwide. Ultimately, firms must learn not just how to seamlessly respond to, but also how to anticipate, changing customer needs and offer value-based solutions *before* customers can articulate them. This forces the company to find ways to manage interdependence around a predictable workflow as well as one that changes unpredictably. Once again, Best Buy illustrates how interdependence can shift across time and space, necessitating continued and relentless efforts to keep the bridges standing.

- *Condensing the core and expanding the periphery.* As firms shift their focus from narrow product or service domains to customer fulfillment domains, they rely increasingly on a network of partners to codeliver certain elements. So companies must extend their integration efforts beyond their own boundaries. In a turbulent twenty-first-century market with limited access to credit, partnering becomes an attractive route for multiple firms to cross-leverage each other's assets. Systemically integrated organizations often break down the corporate silo by *condensing their cores*: focusing on their high-competency activities and offerings and outsourcing more tasks to trusted suppliers. They also *expand their peripheries* by partnering with allies that offer complementary products and services. In all partner relationships, companies climb a *ladder of integration* with increasing levels of commitment, trust, and collaboration. In the process of simultaneously condensing their core and expanding their periphery, the focus of attention shifts from transcending internal boundaries to building more permeable external boundaries.

Tools for Resilience: Throwing the
Right Organizational Levers

Today's customers expect solutions to their consumption problems, and they are utterly agnostic as to where those solutions
come from. To meet these customers where they are, companies,
in turn, must become less focused on what they themselves produce and more focused on their customers' most pressing needs—
even when that carries them well beyond their own borders, even
indeed when that means in essence dissolving themselves into
broader partnerships. They must ensure that their organizational
silos have been reconfigured, leveled, or spanned sufficiently to
guarantee an unimpeded line of sight to the customer. Most
important, they must also guarantee precisely the reverse: that the
line of sight from the customer into the organization is equally
unimpeded, and in a final twist that the companies *see themselves*
from the outside, with their customers, so that they can help
wherever the customers are, in their hours of greatest need.

An important factor in Best Buy's resilience has been its recognition that information from across functions must be integrated
for a more valuable view of the business. With this approach, customer information and insight is placed in a holistic context, then
turned into action which in turn necessitates an enterprisewide
effort, across relevant domains ranging from marketing, merchandising, and store operations. With a shared view of the business, information users can more effectively drive collaboration.

Best Buy didn't embed an outside-in mind-set deeply into its
organization overnight. Nor did it topple and bridge its existing
silos through executive fiat, although CEO Brad Anderson certainly
got the company turned in the right direction. Moving up the four
levels of resilience and building systemic integration into the architecture was accomplished one hard step at a time. For any organization, getting there necessitates paying minute attention to the
five levers—coordination, cooperation, clout, capability, and connection—delineated in figure 1-2.[17]

FIGURE 1-2

The resilience tool kit: The five levers

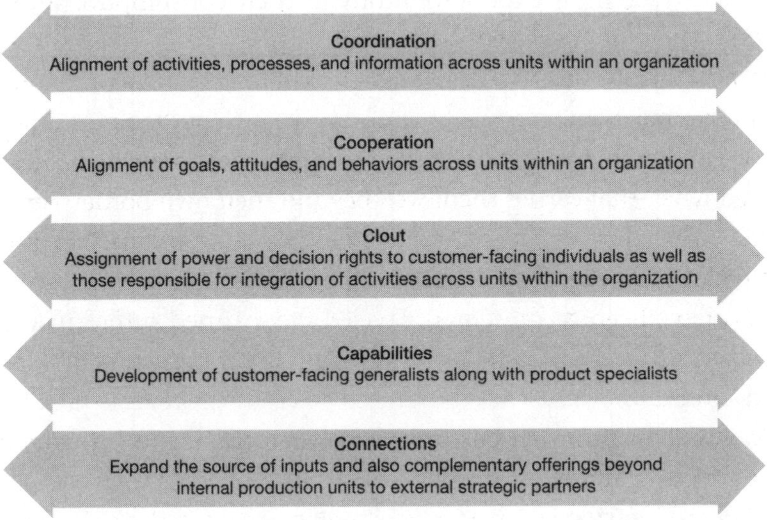

Coordination
Alignment of activities, processes, and information across units within an organization

Cooperation
Alignment of goals, attitudes, and behaviors across units within an organization

Clout
Assignment of power and decision rights to customer-facing individuals as well as those responsible for integration of activities across units within the organization

Capabilities
Development of customer-facing generalists along with product specialists

Connections
Expand the source of inputs and also complementary offerings beyond internal production units to external strategic partners

Coordination aligns tasks and information around a customer axis but doesn't necessarily lead to a collaborative environment, a hallmark of systemic integration. That requires the lever of *cooperation*—the alignment of goals. When members of disparate or competing silos cooperate around a common set of goals, they make adjustments more quickly and at lower cost than in organizations in which the needs of the silo come first. Cooperation, in turn, does not solve the inevitable problems associated with the redistribution of power. To make systemic integration work, *clout* must be in the right hands, and the *capability* to develop new, organization-spanning skills must be fostered and strengthened so frustrated managers don't fall back on their own silo-protecting skills.

Last, the capstone of all this work, and the point where the need for resilience is greatest and the greatest resilience is achieved, is *connection*: shrinking the core and expanding the

FIGURE 1-3

The five C's: Your resilience tool kit

	Inside-out	Outside-in	Barriers	Enablers	Typical pitfalls
Coordination	Intra-product-unit coordination	Cross-enterprise coordination	• Entrenched silos • Lack of sharing of information and tasks across silos • Absence of collaborative mind-set • Lack of authority among individuals assigned to foster coordination	• Informal mechanisms: social networks, individual transcenders • Semiformal mechanisms: boundary spanners, process overlays, task forces, customer segment teams • Formal mechanisms: silo swapping	Overreliance on overlays (task forces, customer segment groups)
Cooperation	Incentive-based cooperation	Values-based cooperation	• Employees' identification with their own units • Limited interaction and collaboration among disparate units	• Redefining corporate values as a way of fostering greater cooperation • Reaffirming the importance of cooperation • Attract right people, give meaning to the importance of cooperation, build metrics and provide monetary and nonmonetary incentives	Overreliance on incentives
Clout	Product leader drives decisions	Customer-owner drives collaboration	• Entrenched power brokers • Localized information • Absence of authority for boundary spanners • Lack of understanding of rationale for outside-in changes and how it impacts individuals	• Shifting resources and recognition to customer-facing, silo-traversing individuals and groups • Delineate customer ownership • Foster greater sharing of customer information	Big positions, small people: creating integrator positions without clout

Organizational levers

	Inside-out	Outside-in	Barriers	Enablers	Typical pitfalls
Capability	Product innovation	Customer solution innovation	• Clinging to old operating principles (role residue) • Maintaining emphasis on developing specialists	• Cultivating and developing multidomain, boundary-spanning generalists with clear roles, career pathways, and incentives • Reallocating clout to boundary spanners and customer-facing individuals • Activate informal social networks across silos	Knowledgeable to none: Jack of all trades
Connection	Protect the core	Shrink the core, expand the periphery	• Rigid mind-set on what is core • Control mind-set with external partnerships	• Redefining boundaries as porous • Build a collaborative mind-set • Enable coordination and cooperation in partnerships	Hollowed out with no center

Organizational levers

periphery to join seamlessly with external partners to identify and solve customer problems. The first four levers are the tactics for integration that rebuild an organization around a customer axis. Connection is what finally busts down the silo of the company itself. Only when that is completed to an appropriate degree—at the intellectual level, the enterprise level, *and* the emotional level—do firms achieve the shape-shifting holy grail of outside-in actions. And in achieving that, they achieve the responsiveness and nimbleness that enable survival in the roughest of oceans. Figure 1-3 outlines all the five levers and shows how they operate in inside-out and outside-in organizations.

We'll now turn to examining coordination, the first lever, in detail.

2

Lever 1: Coordination

*Aligning Activities and Information
Around the Customer Axis*

MERGERS AND ACQUISITIONS can be dangerous liaisons. On paper, they seem to add depth and breadth to an organization. In practice, they often introduce new stumbling blocks to overall resilience. The top brass on both sides might be on the same page, but warfare down the ranks can create paralysis from top to bottom. Yet for business leaders, M&A often proves an irresistible attraction, and sometimes a fatal one. Jones Lang LaSalle (JLL), one of the largest global real estate management firms, was very nearly a case in point.[1]

Established in 1968 as U.S.-based LaSalle Partners, the company had enjoyed years of growth, culminating in a successful 1997 public offering. Its 1999 merger with London-based Jones Lang Wootton seemed both a natural extension of each company's reach and a marriage made in real estate heaven. With more than six thousand people employed in thirty-four countries, the combined company offered a complete array of real estate services—from leasing sales to property management for investor owners to any array of services for corporate occupiers—and

41

a suite of fund management products. Its managers' expertise meant that it could command top prices. In 2000, its first full year of merged existence, JLL recorded revenues of more than $900 million worldwide and was managing more than 680 million square feet of property and more than $20 billion in real estate funds.

But what had looked liked endless love was already beginning to resemble a bad match. The real estate services market had been contracting with the collapse of the information technology sector. Now, the worldwide economy took a nosedive. Competitors merged and consolidated. Price wars raged, margins collapsed. While JLL's annual revenues were impressive, the larger financial picture was increasingly dismal: from 1998 to 2000, revenue had grown at 4.5 percent, while EBITDA had only grown at 1.7 percent, and profit margins had plummeted from 30 to 7 percent. Something had to be done.

JLL thought it had an answer. Rather than focusing on its existing set of stand-alone services, it had begun capitalizing on an emerging trend in corporate real estate services: outsourcing. Large clients that typically had significant in-house staff to manage their global real estate needs were increasingly seeking to farm out their real estate operations to providers who could deliver integrated services. These complex contracts were potentially lucrative because they could be priced at a premium to individual services. In many instances, JLL could provide those services not just more efficiently than the client could, but also more effectively through synergies generated by its disparate offerings. This allowed both JLL and the client to feel as if they were coming out ahead. What's more, JLL could develop stronger and more durable bonds with clients, which often meant greater revenue generation and healthier, long-term relationships.

Yet while the merger had given JLL the global reach and broad array of service offerings required to remain competitive, the corporate marriage had not produced a harmonious union of geographically dispersed, independent business units. How to get them working together? How could the sum of the parts add up to more than the parts provided to clients independently?

JLL's three regional divisions—Americas, Europe, and Asia—operated autonomously with only limited collaboration across regions as well as within regions, mostly on an ad hoc basis. In Europe and Asia, unique cultural and business requirements across borders further fragmented the business into country operations. Postmerger, operations within the regions continued virtually unchanged except for the addition of regional CEOs.

Strong inertial forces also impeded the necessary changes. The independent business-unit model within regions that had worked so well for LaSalle had not only survived the merger but grown even stronger at JLL. Its corporate real estate operations in each of its regions were organized into three service-focused units: corporate property services handled occupier facility management. Tenant representation managed space procurement and renewal. Project development services focused on the project management of facilities fitout and development projects. Each unit had profit and loss authority, determined its own offerings and pricing, and managed its own client relationships. And each was focused on becoming the best in its respective business. As a result, knowledge about the company's customers, while often deep, was scattered across business units with no holistic understanding of customers, their needs, or their relative profitability to JLL. By early 2001, the company's market capitalization had slumped below the premerger valuation of the two predecessor firms.

Far worse, one of JLL's biggest customers was threatening to walk. With 4,500 retail branches in 21 states, a presence in nearly 40 countries, more than 142,000 employees, and more than $57 billion, Bank of America represented huge business. JLL was one of five providers handling the bank's real estate work across the United States, Europe, and Asia. In December 2000, however, the bank announced its intention to reduce its real estate service providers from five to two, and invited JLL, like the others, to submit a proposal. Although JLL had reduced the bank's real estate operating expenses, the bank had previously expressed concerns about service; now, with the looming prospect of losing its largest North American customer, those concerns sent shock waves throughout JLL.

In the nervous months that followed, JLL management moved quickly to reform hiring and promotion protocols, incentive programs, the balance of power among its units, and ultimately its formal structure to provide the products that would keep its client in the fold. At the same time, it recognized that Bank of America was part of a growing number of global multinational firms that would be attracted by coordinated services. JLL's multiyear journey to internal coordination wasn't just about saving one major customer; it was about looking into the future and seeing where its customers would be waiting and what they would want.

Like Best Buy, JLL was faced with the challenge of turning an inside-out perspective outside-in; and like Best Buy, it was running up against its silos, in this case complicated by the lingering effects of its merger. Not only were JLL's business units independent minded *within* each region, let alone across regions; unit heads also worried that the introduction of multiple services might damage client relationships: if one unit were to make a misstep, the client's relationship with *all* of JLL's businesses could go sour. Thus there was little desire to engage in cross-selling efforts, in which, as one executive put it, "someone else [could mess up] up the relationship."

The separate-unit structure had worked well when JLL needed to deliver discrete services quickly and at the lowest-possible cost. But now JLL needed to deliver seamless integrated service bundles across geographies and businesses. To get where it knew it had to go, JLL needed to overcome the problem posed by its organizational architecture. It needed to *coordinate its operations* to meet corporate clients' desire to procure space, get it fitted out, and have it managed day to day—in an integrated and seamless way.

The Coordination Lever

What is coordination? Simply put, *coordination* is the alignment of activities, processes, and information among interdependent units or groups in an organization. Coordination is universal in organizations but has a special meaning here. Customer-centric coordination means that all of these activities are *aligned around a customer axis.*

Coordination that is meant to bring about customer centricity may reach all the way across enterprises. Imagine, for example, two service units that provide very different, although complementary offerings. Both units supply the same customer, who works with both simultaneously. If one unit makes a change or improvement to its services, that may very likely affect the other unit's offering. Consequently, the units need to be sure that their services are always complementary and interoperable. To ensure that resilience trumps inertia, the units need to coordinate their actions, their development plans, and more. As figure 2-1

FIGURE 2-1

The first lever in your resilience tool kit: Coordination

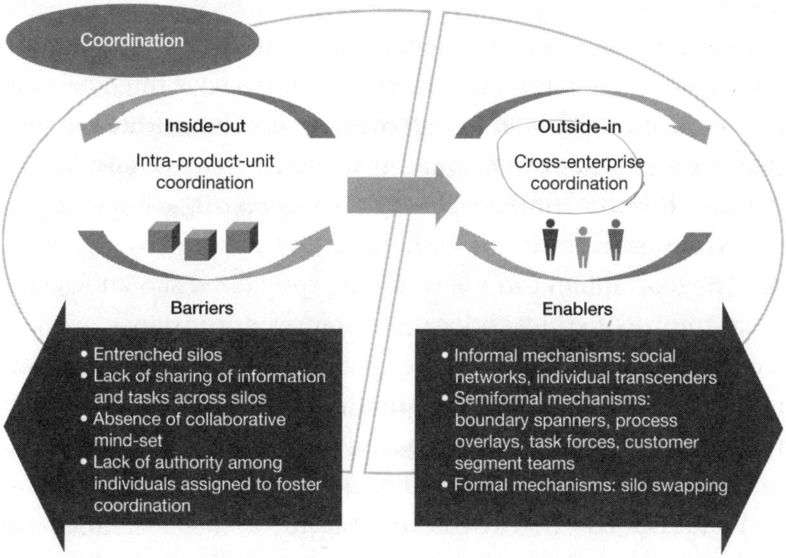

Coordination	
Inside-out	**Outside-in**
Intra-product-unit coordination	Cross-enterprise coordination
Barriers	**Enablers**
• Entrenched silos • Lack of sharing of information and tasks across silos • Absence of collaborative mind-set • Lack of authority among individuals assigned to foster coordination	• Informal mechanisms: social networks, individual transcenders • Semiformal mechanisms: boundary spanners, process overlays, task forces, customer segment teams • Formal mechanisms: silo swapping

summarizes, the need for coordination increases dramatically as an organization goes from inside-out to an outside-in orientation.

JLL's work with the Bank of America–Hong Kong is a case in point. The bank needed to dispose of rapidly aging premises and lease new offices that would enhance its profile as a world-class financial institution. In January 2004, the bank instructed JLL to market the owner-occupied space and search for and secure suitable new premises. Both projects had to occur concurrently and within a tight timeline. Jones Lang LaSalle immediately formed a strong and multidisciplined project team from its tenant representation, investment, and project and development services departments, providing a seamless platform that delivered the ideal customer solution—the old premises sold at 15 percent above book value; the new premises delivered far greater efficiency, technical capability, and prestige; and the deals were coordinated to give the bank a comfortable window during which to move house despite the time constraints.

Coordination Versus Cooperation = Ability Versus Willingness

The greater the interdependence among units and groups, the more coordination is required. Yet these units have often become legacy silos, and in order to improve coordination, either the silos must be reshaped or some other managerial systems must be put in place. It is sometimes necessary to blow up silos—but doing so indiscriminately is extremely short sighted. A company organized around geographies can use its highly specialized silo knowledge to customize offerings to local preferences, for instance, while a technology-centric firm can be quick to market with technical innovations. Specialization, in short, is not the enemy; the enemy is the tunnel vision, insularity, and knowledge hoarding that so often are found in highly siloed organizations.

One distinction needs to be made again: *coordination*, which will be discussed here, is often confused with *cooperation* (to be discussed in chapter 3), but they are not at all the same. As summarized in

FIGURE 2-2

Coordination versus cooperation

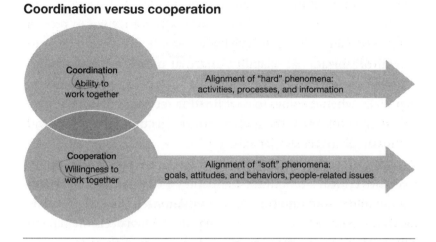

figure 2-2, coordination is about the alignment of "hard" phenom-ena—activities, processes, and information. Cooperation involves the alignment of goals, attitudes, and behaviors—"soft," people-related issues. Thus, cooperation is about ensuring the *willingness* of silos to work together, while coordination is more focused on the *ability* of silos to work together—the structures that allow them to do so.[2]

My colleague Scott Snook has documented the failure of coor-dination that led to the worst incidence of friendly fire since World War II. On April 14, 1994, two U.S. Air Force F-15 Eagle fighters shot down two U.S. Army Black Hawk helicopters over northern Iraq's no-fly zone, killing all twenty-six peacekeepers on board.[3] An inquiry revealed that the tragedy resulted from a series of coordination failures: misidentification of the army helicopters by the air force fighter pilots, failure of the crew of AWACS planes in the region to intervene in a timely manner, lack of integration of the army helicopters into the task force that oversaw opera-tions, and a failure of the technical system that identified friend or foe (IFF). On that day, the helicopters entered the area earlier than planned, the F-15 pilots were unaware of their impending arrival, the helicopters squawked the wrong IFF code, and the fighter and helicopter pilots were unable to speak to each other—a perfect storm of mis- and failed coordination.

Businesses don't risk human capital when they fail to provide their own silos with the capacity to work together, but they do impair organizational pliability, and that ultimately places at risk revenue, profits, shareholder equity, and even their own existence—especially when it comes to coordinating service of customer needs across silos that may themselves not be customer-centric or even sympathetic to a customer axis.

As firms embark on improving their coordination, fine-tuning becomes critical. Sometimes companies go too far in their coordination efforts and find that they have damaged their effectiveness by creating unnecessary overlays that slow down decision making. Others don't go far enough and end up accomplishing very little. But achieving the optimal level of coordination can bring many benefits, including better customer targeting, more customer-focused product development, more effective product delivery, better identification of new or overlooked opportunities, sharper pricing practices, and optimized sales efforts.[4]

As we saw in the cases of Best Buy and JLL, there are many roadblocks to coordination of silos (see "Barriers to Coordination"). Unit leaders, fearing a loss of autonomy, may resist coordinating their activities with those of other units. Sharing information across units that have not exchanged information before may cause more confusion than enlightenment.[5] Most inside-out organizations have silos built around discrete product (or service line) categories: product specialist units operating like corporate islands work toward their own product-centric goals and may not speak the same "language" as other silos. Some units rely on customer feedback in designing their products; others do not. Regardless, there is sometimes limited understanding of customer problems within a silo, and certainly incomplete information when it comes to customer solutions that may span product categories.

The biggest barriers to greater customer-centric coordination come from individual silos' inherent tendency to guard their

autonomy, the font of virtually all organizational rigidity. To skirt
this problem, companies usually start small and create a patchwork of overlays linking different silos through task forces, job
rotation across units, and even the creation of a common overseeing body or individual tasked with ensuring that the units work
together. This is a good place to start, but not an end in itself—the
ultimate goal is an organizational architecture that truly yields an
outside-in perspective.[6]

Better coordination can be achieved through a number of mechanisms, some loosely defined and relatively informal, and others
very formal and clearly delineated (see figure 2-3). When deciding
which ones to employ, leaders must consider a number of factors:

- *Degree of permanence.* If the required coordination is
  related to a time-limited project or issue, coordination can
  be managed through an ad hoc group such as an interunit
  task force that can be disbanded when the project is
  complete. When the coordination need must be more
  systemic or longer-term, a more permanent mechanism
  may be required, such as a standing committee or a new
  unit or position.

- *Depth of legacy issues.* When existing silos need to be
  only slightly reconfigured, coordination efforts can usually
  be informal. However, if the silos have been in place for
  some time, are deeply rooted in the organization, and are
  to be seriously reshaped or reconfigured—or abandoned
  altogether—a more formal approach is necessary.

- *Amount of interdependence.* When there is only moderate
  interdependence between units, the necessary coordination may be accomplished through a few informal mechanisms. When the interdependence involves many units,
  over longer periods of time—and especially if it is
  dynamic—a combination of formal and informal mechanisms is indicated.

Barriers to Coordination

Whatever their cause, barriers to the execution of any change are certain to be raised. By understanding and anticipating them, executives stand a better chance of reducing opposition when selecting and implementing coordination mechanisms.

- *The authority gap.* Sometimes informal and semiformal mechanisms of coordination don't provide the key individuals involved in coordination work with enough authority to accomplish their goals. Transcenders such as designated customer-segment teams might be tasked with relaying customer-related information across functional borders but lack the authority to mandate collaborative behavior from front- or back-end managers. When that happens, transcenders are getting blown by the winds, not bending with them.

- *The mind-set gap.* People who work in front- and back-end units often have different mind-sets and priorities. Owing to the physical and psychological distance between them in large organizations, they seldom have the opportunity to meet or share ideas. They also operate on different time horizons: for example, R&D teams may take a long time to develop products; the customer-facing teams complain that they can't respond quickly to shifting market needs.

- *The incentive gap.* The incentives of front- and back-end units are rarely aligned to promote information sharing across units. For example, people working in back-end units are typically motivated by productivity-related incentives, such as the number of new products developed, manufacturing yield, and many others. Sales and marketing people are often rewarded on the basis of revenue or profits. This is where coordination and cooperation (the focus of chapter 3) become closely intertwined and impact each other.

- *Protectionist behavior.* People naturally want to protect the relationships they've carefully cultivated with customers. They may resist new customer-focused strategies such as cross-selling because they don't want to give up control over those relationships or risk losing commissions, bonuses, or other rewards that they have traditionally earned from such bonds.

- *Uneven profitability.* Another barrier to coordination is disparity in profitability across business units. Units that are more profitable may balk at collaborating with other units because they fear having to share revenues and profits.

- *Historical precedent.* A company's long-standing operating practices often reinforce the sense of autonomy that many unit managers feel. Units that have long dealt with customers directly and independently may be very reluctant to share leads with people in other units.

- *Cost.* Even if unit managers are willing and able to coordinate to better serve customers, managers may still question the cost of establishing coordination mechanisms. As one manager at a company I studied explained to me, "We found that we were always doing as much internal selling of our ideas as we were selling products externally, because we always wanted or needed something from somebody inside to create integrated solutions for external customers." Not surprisingly, such internal-selling efforts take time and are therefore costly.

FIGURE 2-3

Continuum of coordination mechanisms

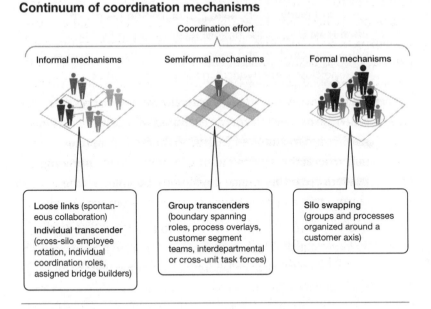

Coordination effort

Informal mechanisms   Semiformal mechanisms   Formal mechanisms

Loose links (spontan-
eous collaboration)
Individual transcender
(cross-silo employee
rotation, individual
coordination roles,
assigned bridge builders)

Group transcenders
(boundary spanning
roles, process overlays,
customer segment
teams, interdepartmental
or cross-unit task forces)

Silo swapping
(groups and processes
organized around a
customer axis)

The greater the amount of coordination required, the more formal the coordination mechanisms must be—but keep in mind that formal mechanisms by their very nature tend to be more difficult and time-consuming to design and implement than informal ones and often are likely to meet the greatest resistance.

Informal Mechanisms

In some organizations, customer-focused cross-unit coordination occurs largely through voluntary processes, known as *loose links*.[7] These occur when people from different parts of the company naturally work together to solve customers' problems, regardless of their job descriptions or reporting relationships. Some organizations are fortunate enough to have a culture in which employees naturally engage in this kind of spontaneous collaboration—usually thanks to a proclivity for cooperation. However, most companies have to work hard to nurture these informal coordination mechanisms.[8]

Loose links, which can occur anywhere in the organization, often lead to the creation of new ideas, products, services, and solutions. At Best Buy, for example, in casual conversation, two managers noted that some home electronics buyers would comparison shop at Best Buy and at nearby high-end electronics retailers. These chance remarks led to the Magnolia Home Theater concept, a store-within-a-store where customers can try out high-end branded home entertainment equipment. Random connections like this are difficult to institutionalize, but managers can foster such interactions by removing barriers or by allowing for more connections at the intersections of units—places where they have some physical or procedural contact. For example, executives can co-locate employees from different businesses or sponsor regular cross-unit events, such as the all-employee "coffee talks" hosted by Agilent Technologies' senior management.[9] The aim is to encourage people to cultivate the personal networks essential for informal coordination. The more elastic the internal borders, the more likely loose links are to happen.

Individual Transcenders

Some firms step up the formality just a bit by explicitly enlisting individual employees to facilitate customer-focused coordination across business units. This type of cross-unit coordination includes (1) the cross-silo rotation of employees and (2) the assignment of bridge builders within independent business units.

Companies often require new hires to spend weeks or months working in several different units before settling into a specific product or functional division. This experience exposes the new employees to the full array of the company's activities and influential people. With their broadened knowledge and networks, these employees can then serve as "lubricants" for interunit collaboration.

Designating cross-organizational *bridge builders* is another useful practice. These people usually operate within a specific function or business unit, and are charged with coordinating the exchange of information or work to sharpen the customer centricity across units.

Inevitably, these informal coordination mechanisms are difficult to manage. They're hard to define, predict, and measure, and almost impossible to control. In addition, it's hard to quantify their costs and therefore determine whether results are worth the expenditure. And they don't have the clout to effect the changes necessary when complex coordination across organizational boundaries is demanded.

For these reasons, many companies opt for more formal coordination mechanisms.

Semiformal Mechanisms: Group Transcenders

When customers' needs are very diverse or ambiguous—for example, when it's difficult to align customer segments with specific products—executives can use a "semiformal" coordination mechanism that I call a *transcender*.[10] These groups operate at the intersections between legacy silos to ensure that there is coordination instead of friction. As a result, they enhance the collective customer centricity of the silos while retaining the benefits that non-customer-centric structures deliver, such as deep product knowledge or economies of scale.

An example: In 2002 Jones Lang LaSalle gathered its three corporate real estate units—corporate property services, tenant representation, and project development services—under a single umbrella organization called corporate solutions. It then created a formal function—account management—to integrate the three units' offerings and deliver full-service solutions to large corporate customers. JLL staffed the new transcender function with high-level officers who had broad experience within the different business units and empowered them to negotiate multiservice contracts and to solve customer problems on their own. Account managers who supported the firm's largest corporate clients resided outside the company's service line organizations. Smaller accounts were still handled by individuals who continued to work within one of the three corporate real estate units and took on the new role as an additional responsibility. JLL positioned the account managers as "trusted advisers" who could both coordinate delivery of the firm's services and help clients with long-term planning and strategy. The three units retained autonomy in that they did not report to the account managers who served more in a support function. Figures 2-4 and 2-5 summarize this shift in structure.

The first customer to benefit from JLL's new organization was the one that had jump-started the firm's drive for greater customer centricity: Bank of America. By providing the bank with a single point of contact—a dedicated high-level account manager—JLL ultimately became one of the two outsourced services providers for the 65 million square feet of real estate in Bank of America's U.S. holdings. From 2001 to 2005, thanks largely to the account management model, JLL won new or expanded contracts with other giants, including Microsoft, Procter & Gamble, Kaiser Permanente, Coca-Cola, BP, Pfizer, and Lenovo. It had gone from a threatened firm to a resilient organization.

FIGURE 2-4

Structure prior to restructuring

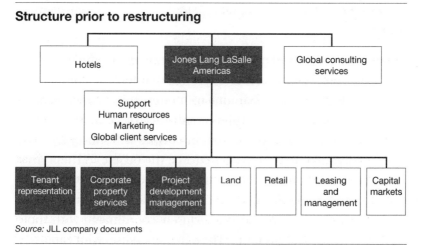

Source: JLL company documents

FIGURE 2-5

Structure after the restructuring

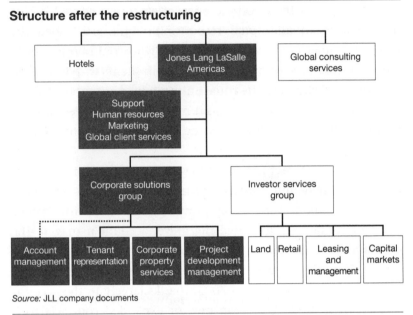

Source: JLL company documents

To put a transcender in place does not require drastic changes
to a company's organizational architecture, so it can be relatively
quick and easy to install one. Transcenders can take several forms,
including boundary-spanning roles (as JLL's did), process overlays,
cross-unit or interdepartmental task forces, and customer-segment
teams.

- *Boundary-spanning roles and organizations.* Companies
  developing products and services that include components from more than one unit often create permanent
  boundary-spanning roles or entities to coordinate across
  divisions. When these roles or entities will subsume
  individual divisions' sales efforts, the people in them must
  possess extensive knowledge of each division's operations
  and a strong outside-in focus. Boundary spanners have to
  ensure that their efforts are closely coordinated with those
  of the individual units. They are generalists who can

seamlessly present the full breadth of a company's offerings to a customer's most senior decision makers while
permitting representatives from individual business units
to maintain lower-level relationships with actual users of
the company's products and services. Inevitably, boundary spanners are resilience agents, but they must also deal
with the inevitable conflicts of interest that arise across
disparate units.[11]

- *Process overlays.* Process overlays are new business
  processes or routinized interactions that facilitate coordination across an organization's parts.[12] They can entail
  standardizing information flows and preplanning interactions among disparate units or the creation of interdepartmental task forces to handle the more complex challenges
  that span silos. Some companies will explicitly create
  cross-functional teams built around each of their customer
  segments. Process overlays can overcome both cross-
  product and cross-geographical gaps but may also encompass cross-functional ones as well, say, connecting the
  customer-facing parts of the organization with the
  research and development side.

- *Customer-information dissemination.* In most firms, customer information is scattered across units. Purchasing
  information may reside with sales, service request history
  with customer service, and preferred channel information
  with marketing. Moreover, many unit leaders, fearing loss
  of authority, hoard their information. In either case,
  companies find it difficult (if not impossible) to "shake
  loose" the information they need to serve customers. To
  promote more democratic access to information and
  thus more flexible use of it, companies must encourage
  and reward the sharing of important information
  between units—but institutionalized information sharing
  requires coordination, particularly the centralization

[handwritten margin note: We even have multiple charts for clients]

docs scanning ?
closely eclipsys plays a role
+ eclipsys plays a role

of customer-related information and the creation of well-defined guidelines for accessing and using it.[13]

Advantages and Disadvantages of Transcenders

Semiformal mechanisms, as we have seen, can harmonize cross-silo operating issues and thereby improve a company's ability to develop and deliver customer-focused solutions, even if the firm is structured around something other than customers. They can simplify interactions by establishing a single point of contact to which customers can turn for multiple products and services. At the same time, they can stimulate improvements in offerings of units that are still organized around their distinct products and services.

However, transcenders also present challenges. Customers may balk at paying a premium for coordinated services. Business customers may themselves be siloed by product or service and prefer to deal with companies that have similar structures, believing that a close organizational match creates maximum efficiencies. Internally, dedicated intermediaries can get caught in the cross-fire between business units. Transcenders must also deal with the inherent tension between establishing autonomy and seeking out ways to interconnect with the operations of other units within the firm. Transcenders often require new reporting and data analysis tools, which cost money and take time to master. What's more, other units may be reluctant to share profits or resources with transcenders. Nevertheless, they are probably the mechanism companies seeking complex coordination should look to first.

Formal Mechanisms: Silo Swapping

Companies facing the deepest challenges—those whose customers' demands supercede any others for ensuring survival—require an extensive, formal restructuring of the organizational architecture to achieve top-level systemic integration around the customer. For example, traditional business units or functions might be replaced with profit centers focused on specific customer segments.[14] I call this *silo swapping*. Rather than reorganizing old silos under a new name or executive, or layering a customer-focused process or team over them, a company obliterates the old units and creates entirely new ones. Silo swapping may be in order when customers' needs are shifting or when a company lacks clarity about which tasks are needed to serve customers, who "owns" which customers, and how decisions regarding customers should be made.

As I have already stressed, silo swapping should not be undertaken lightly because it is a rare case when an existing silo is delivering absolutely no benefit to the organization. Before busting silos, you should ask how the benefits you seek might be delivered in some other way. Organizations undertaking such a change must examine and accept the inevitable trade-offs.

Silo Swapping at JLL

Let's look at one of the more dramatic examples of silo swapping: the case of Jones Lang LaSalle in the Americas.

After creating its corporate solutions organization in 2001, JLL was better able to meet customer demands. The new provider of integrated real estate services contributed to significant top-line growth between 2001 and 2005. Between 2002 and 2004, corporate solutions enjoyed an almost 100 percent increase in annual adjusted gross margin.

But rival firms were also targeting multiservice opportunities—and scoring significant successes. At the same time, JLL had yet to fully leverage its global platform; most coordination efforts were still occurring within specific geographies—the Americas, Europe, and Asia—rather than across broad regional boundaries. Although clients were asking for global best practices, JLL's existing best practice–sharing mechanisms across regions were, according to one manager, "Band-Aids" at best. Furthermore, while JLL had done a fine job of building integrative capacity, it still needed to ensure that it had adequate presence in key local markets—the relevant pieces had to be in place to integrate when needed. On this issue, JLL still lagged behind a major competitor. While JLL offered strongly coordinated centralized sales and marketing, single-transaction customers wanted to see more experts "on the ground" in the markets where they needed JLL's services. Even its large corporate customers had begun to question the firm's ability to execute major multimarket transactions that required a strong local presence. Thus, even though JLL had executed a successful reorganization, it was not enough. It was time to reorganize a second time. As bold as it had seemed at the time, corporate solutions was not nearly bold enough.

Peter Roberts, then CEO of JLL's Americas region, charged a team of senior managers to develop a plan for achieving three key objectives:

- *Increased penetration* of key geographic markets

- *Increased leverage* of single-service client relationships to sell multiple services

- *Seamless and consistent delivery* of integrated global services through best practice sharing

In late 2005, after reviewing the team's proposals, Roberts announced a sweeping transformation that would dissolve the corporate solutions organization and the three service units within it and instead create two new organizations: *clients* and *markets*. In other words, the old silos and the transcender organization put in place to coordinate them were to be blown up and replaced by these two new silos. People who had built their careers and professional identities around doing business a certain way were being asked to accept big changes driven by new client-centric demands. This was a bold move indeed.

JLL's new clients organization was charged with managing the firm's relationships with large, multiservice customers. Rather than operating within one of three independent business units, its product specialists were permanently assigned to client account teams, with no link to any particular service line. However, unlike the old account management function within corporate solutions, these new account teams were considered profit centers, with hiring and firing authority. This blending of the transcenders and service providers into one organization forged tighter coordination among account team members who were now responsible for addressing the full spectrum of corporate client needs.

While the clients organization focused on interfacing with its corporate clients, ultimately those clients' needs had to be fulfilled locally. The markets organization fulfilled those commitments. It also focused on maintaining JLL's local market presence, handled one-off transactions in those markets, and represented JLL's full range of offerings to those customers. This unit provided services for corporations that had relationships with the clients organization, fulfilling commitments to corporate clients for their local market needs. At its core was the old leasing and management unit, which had historically been organized around local and regional markets. The organization also included employees from the former tenant representation unit who had not been working on specific client accounts. By setting up the markets organization, JLL hoped to focus simultaneously on both single- and multimarket real estate transactions while avoiding conflict over which unit should retain sales responsibility and credit for different transaction types. Instead of warring silos, the company got a markets organization that could sway with the breeze.

The new architecture enabled greater coordination within the clients organization around key accounts as well as greater coordination within markets on how to tackle the needs of local market customers. At the same time, JLL created mechanisms by which the clients and markets organizations would coordinate activities. As Bill Thummel, a senior JLL executive, explained, "In the past, when two teams arrived at an intersection of markets, too often the issue was, 'Is this my client or your client?' Now we sought to create a mind-set that embraces the intersections."

Another executive affirmed the importance of actively managing these intersections: "Everybody gets on the phone every Monday, and we call the plays so there are no collisions."

JLL also sought to ensure greater coordination between the customer-facing and back-end-facing sides of the organization by giving back-end people more client contact. As Thummell recalled, "These back-office managers are too good [to keep hidden]. We had to get them out in front and let the clients see who is leading our human resources and our IT departments. The client loved it. The back-office managers liked it because, although they know they're never going to make as much money as a key transactor, at least their names were getting mentioned." By putting back-end managers in front of the client, JLL facilitated the communication of customer needs from front- to back-end groups. The pride that came with exposure to clients also gave back-end employees more incentive to do what was best for customers.

The new structure enabled JLL to optimize its internal division of labor while ensuring that there was adequate coordination across the divisions: account managers in the clients organization would generate much of the transaction activity (for example, by exploring leads and working with clients to identify new needs), and local managers in markets would execute it by delivering what their colleagues in the clients organization had sold. As one manager pointed out, "Those people know the most about the markets. To give the clients the best execution, you want to get it done by those who know the market best." In short, the new structure would allow JLL to present a single face to local and global customers alike. In another executive's words, "We won't go to market as the 'leasing and management' group or the 'tenant representation' group. We'll go to market as Jones Lang LaSalle."

But there were trade-offs. How could JLL preserve its product and service expertise after it had swapped out its product- and service-based structure? In the push to achieve an outside-in perspective, companies can't lose sight of the benefits accrued in their inside-out days. According to one executive, "We have terrific project management, facilities management, and transaction products. And we knew that we could not—for a second—lose focus on those." So JLL embedded product specialists within the account teams in the clients and markets organizations and created a product management team within the clients organization. This team took responsibility for managing the costs of selling and delivering all JLL offerings and shared responsibility for new-product development with a separate group outside the clients organization.

JLL also took steps to manage the new intersections created by the reorganization. It established six "intersection task forces" to deal with issues cropping up between clients and markets. These teams were expected to help members of both organizations think on an enterprise level, especially with regard to customer service. The task forces were also charged with smoothing the day-to-day problems and ongoing policy issues arising from the reorganization. From the start, these teams were expected to be temporary. In fact, within a year, five of the six were disbanded, in part to avoid creating new internal silos. The sixth, the account markets leadership team, was retained as a permanent committee and given responsibility for helping the broad organization to maintain deeper customer centricity, and to promote the resolution of cross-unit issues such as revenue sharing.

At the time of writing, JLL is continuing to evolve the new organization, largely by using a variety of additional cross-unit coordination mechanisms to satisfy ever-shifting customer needs at the segment, geographic market, and global levels. As the market has evolved from a single-service business to one where clients are multiservice and multigeography, JLL has moved to become an organization capable of addressing those needs. It has achieved this resilience by focusing on those customers—comprehending where the market was going and thus how to respond to it. Figure 2-6 shows how the journey of JLL over the past decade exemplifies how an organization may first start with informal, then semiformal, and ultimately formal mechanisms for coordination.

FIGURE 2-6

Jones Lang LaSalle's coordination journey

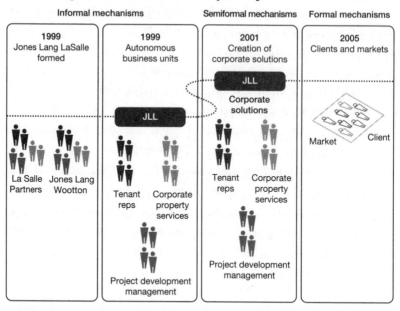

Informal mechanisms   Semiformal mechanisms   Formal mechanisms

1999
Jones Lang LaSalle
formed

La Salle   Jones Lang
Partners   Wootton

1999
Autonomous
business units

JLL

Tenant   Corporate
reps   property
            services

Project development
management

2001
Creation of
corporate solutions

JLL

Corporate
solutions

Tenant   Corporate
reps   property
            services

Project development
management

2005
Clients and markets

Market   Client

Unintended Consequences and Benefits of Formal Coordination Mechanisms

Restructuring an organization's silos and building resilience around the customer axis can stimulate coordination between individuals who previously resided in separate business units. Formal coordination mechanisms such as silo swapping also can help new customer-dedicated units recruit and develop generalists who can orchestrate the sale and delivery of multiple offerings. Yet while a reengineering of silos has its advantages, it is not always superior to the "patchwork" of informal mechanisms discussed earlier.

New silos organized around customers, for example, create a need for other mechanisms to preserve product and service capabilities that span the enterprise. As we saw, JLL did this by embedding service specialists in the clients and markets organizations and creating a product management team within the clients group that took responsibility for managing costs. In each of the two organizations, JLL also designated a tenant representation lead, a corporate property services lead, and a project and development lead responsible for driving best practices and developing innovative offerings. But it would be unwise to emulate this model without recognizing the potential loss of economies of scale that comes from duplicating functions in each customer unit instead of locating them all under one umbrella.

A final challenge is managers' and employees' difficulty in embracing new customer-focused silos. Initially, a more resilient, less border-defined organization can seem a more threatening one. Not surprisingly, many people will ask, "How will this affect me?" rather than "How will the new structure make things better for customers?" JLL was not immune to this, but most managers eventually saw the value of the new structure, their roles in it, and the increased flexibility that came with increased coordination. According to one executive, "The great thing about the new organization is that we can create innovative solutions for clients to address ever more complex issues." JLL has reinforced this positive attitude by establishing "all hands" meetings in several major offices that serve as forums for clients, markets, and support staff to share insights. The exchange of information during these gatherings has resulted in several new or enhanced deals, results that make it very difficult for people to argue against the benefits of silo swapping.

From Coordination to Cooperation

Improving coordination across functions and units is a critical element in shifting to a more resilient, customer-centric organization. Especially in industries where customers' needs and market realities are complex and fast-changing—that is, most businesses today—companies must ensure that people in their various units have access to knowledge about the customers and opportunities and the chance to use that knowledge to better serve the marketplace.

Customers will always be ahead of the product or service you are offering as long as you continue to view the customer and market-place through a product or service lens. To stay with the curve, much less get ahead of it, you have to foster the mechanisms that will allow your business to anticipate—across its entire spectrum—where the customer will be.

That's why coordination is such an important lever. It provides employees with the ability to cross-pollinate an enterprise. Yet even the most elegant mechanisms for customer-focused coordination will fail if people in an organization aren't motivated to cooperate with one another. Unlike small children, companies aren't by nature pliant. Even small entrepreneurial organizations must work diligently to provide the motivation to cooperate, by reinforcing their coordination mechanisms—whether formal or informal—with the appropriate performance metrics, incentives, and cultural adjustments. We take up those in the next chapter.

3

Lever 2: Cooperation

Ensuring Attitudes and Behaviors
Are Customer Focused

IN 1986, LEONARD BOSACK and Sandy Lerner, a husband-and-wife team who managed computer networks at Stanford University, began assembling routers and other computer components in the kitchen of their San Francisco home. The young company—named Cisco, after the city where it was founded—attempted to interest a professor at the University of Washington with a new "translator" device. But because he used a computer system that was incompatible with the two handled by Cisco's translator, the device was useless to him. His network "spoke a different language" from either of the two supported by Cisco's initial translator device.[1] And so he rejected it.

That should have been the end of it. Instead, Cisco went back to the drawing board and developed the multiprotocol router, which became the company's first core product.

That early experience left a visceral understanding—Cisco's success would be built not solely on cutting-edge technology but on making technology suited to the customer and a consistent willingness to alter its organizational architecture as necessary to meet that goal. Its flexible response to a customer's needs was the first step on the path to extraordinary growth. In 2001, Cisco, a worldwide leader in Internet networking equipment, was briefly ranked as the most valuable firm on earth, with revenues of $22.3 billion, and the company continues its success, in terms of top-line and bottom-line growth, to this day.

So how did Cisco retain its outside-in orientation through two decades of phenomenal growth and expansion? It kept its focus on internal coordination as business units proliferated and as it integrated new companies into its organization through its well-known acquisition strategy. Just as important, it found ways to maintain and enhance both the cooperation and the underlying resilience based on an enduring outside-in perspective that Lerner and Bosack instinctively understood and put into practice.

The Synergy of Cooperation and Coordination

The coordination mechanisms discussed in chapter 2 are about the *structures* that reorganize the divisions and resources of the company. A company cannot survive a shifting business environment without being able to shift its own architecture in response. But such restructuring invariably results in people from disparate—and sometimes competing—units being thrown together. To make this shift, the company needs to foster a collaborative environment—the cooperation—to create the synergies intended. *Cooperation*, as used here, refers not to collaboration on all fronts but rather a focused effort to stimulate alignment of behavior around ways of addressing customer needs.

As noted in chapter 2, coordination and cooperation, though related, are distinct phenomena: coordination is about the organization's *architecture*; cooperation is about its people's *behavior*. Coordination entails alignment of activities and information; cooperation concerns the alignment of goals and human behavior. Thus, coordination is what leaders do; cooperation is what workers do. Coordination is about mechanics. Cooperation is about motivations.[2]

Of course, without coordination of activities, even the most cooperative of colleagues and groups will not have the means to respond quickly to shifting customer needs. Similarly, without cooperation, even the most well-conceived coordination efforts will be unlikely to really take off. When people are afforded the opportunity to work together but lack motivation, their collaboration will be stilted, half-hearted, and inauthentic. But when members of disparate or competing silos are both willing and able to cooperate around common goals, they are likely to reorient nimbly and at lower cost than in organizations where the needs of the silo and its inside-out perspective dominate.

Creating a cooperative environment around common customer-focused goals, then, is just as important as improving cross-unit or cross-functional coordination. People must be encouraged to bust through silos when necessary and should receive rewards for collaborations that produce successful customer solutions. The company must put the customer front and center, and reinforce that value by designing metrics and incentives that reward cooperative, solutions-oriented behavior.

The Cooperation Lever

Cooperation can be vertical, horizontal, or diagonal. It can take place within borders or transcend them. But to build the resilient enterprise, cooperation requires disparate individuals and units to collaborate around the common goals emanating from their customers' objectives. Figure 3-1 provides an overview of how cooperation can be a key link in the movement from inside-out to outside-in, and shows the enablers and barriers that come along the way.

Product-centric or inside-out cooperation is typically fostered to ensure production and distribution efficiencies; individual silos typically seek to transcend select functional and geographic

FIGURE 3-1

The second lever in your resilience tool kit: Cooperation

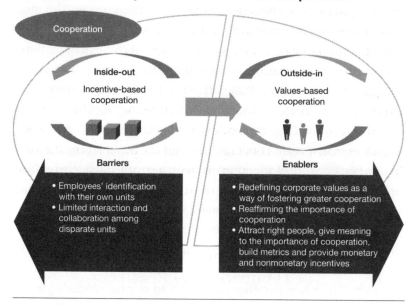

boundaries. Incentive-based rewards schemes that reward cross-silo cooperation are one among many schemes used in such companies. Pliant, outside-in companies, on the other hand, seek a more ubiquitous form of cooperation motivated by serving customers' needs most effectively rather than achieving narrow efficiencies.

While incentives remain a powerful vehicle for promoting targeted cooperation between select units, incentives alone will not do the trick. Culture and values must also be shaped to create a more all-encompassing form of cooperation because employees of resilient organizations can't identify only with their own narrow units; instead, they must expand their identity to include the enterprise as a whole. Customer-centric corporate culture and values can't be bought, but must be inculcated in the company DNA.

Even within a narrowly defined activity such as product innovation, cross-unit cooperation is essential if a company is to achieve true outside-in flexibility. Deborah Dougherty, a researcher of organizational innovation, writes that the departments within a product-focused firm are essentially different "thought worlds." This mental separation makes cross-department cooperation, even around products, a challenge. Not only do departments in such enterprises tend to hoard ideas; they also often speak what in effect are different languages, so that even when departments do come together, communication is minimal. The antidote, Dougherty suggests, is to develop collaborative mechanisms, including a collaborative corporate culture, that will bring together unique insights from each department in the product-innovation process.[3] In fact, culture-driven cooperation—and the other levers discussed in this book—work bidirectionally, with a strong outside-in culture promoting the other tactics for overcoming the barriers of organizational architecture, and vice versa.

Cooperation and Culture at Cisco: The Foundations of Resiliency

Cisco provides a powerful example of the effectiveness of an organic, customer-centric, cooperative culture. Customer centricity is a part of Cisco's corporate fabric, from the front office to the backroom engineers.

Cisco makes a concerted effort to hire, educate, recognize, and reward employees who can work together to deliver products and services that not only meet, but anticipate, customer needs. A rigorous interview process identifies job candidates who have a penchant for cooperation and collaboration. Once hired, employees are expected to embrace the Cisco "no-technology-religion" approach: Cisco is "agnostic" about platforms and standards rather than clinging rigidly to a unit or system mind-set. In Cisco's culture, the customer is of primary importance. This shared belief ensures that employees can set aside their local loyalties and work across disparate parts of the organization.

Cisco's culture is characterized by empowerment, teamwork, open communication, trust, and, most important, egalitarianism. This egalitarianism is manifested in many ways. CEO John Chambers makes himself available and encourages direct e-mail communication. Managers' offices are relatively spartan and of similar size. They are clustered in the middle of the room. There are no reserved spaces in the parking lot. Everyone flies coach. Knowledge sharing across organizational boundaries is encouraged.

Cisco believes that egalitarian culture and cooperation are synergistic. The overall effect of this "silo busting" is more ability, productivity, and innovation. When built on a foundation of customer listening and customer centricity, this can translate into better products that meet customer needs more effectively, on a faster timeline. "Customer satisfaction at Cisco is bigger than marketing," former longtime Cisco executive James Richardson (chief marketing officer), explained. "It is everyone's objective."

The Customer Advocacy Group: "Relentless Listening"

Hiring practices, values, and incentives are important inducements to cooperation, but customer centricity is also built into Cisco's organizational architecture through such units as the customer advocacy (CA) organization, which Sandy Lerner herself founded and once headed. The CA unit not only fields customer complaints and targets potential customers (those functions were once part of this unit but eventually were moved out), but represents customers to the rest of Cisco, provides technical support and strategic guidance for them, and lobbies for internal cooperation within and across silos in the pursuit of customer-centric behavior. Doug Allred who headed CA in the 1990s described its function as "relentless listening." CA collates and shares customer information within the firm and ensures that most internal activities are aligned around those customers. These activities, as well as the corporate culture that emphasizes the importance of customers, serve as catalysts for greater cooperation across disparate units within the firm.

Allred admits that when he first came to Cisco, he was not fully convinced of the company's commitment to customer centricity and cross-unit cooperation—or even the value of such commitment. In fact, he initially balked at his new title, vice president of customer advocacy. CEO John Morgridge encouraged him to live with the title for six months and then decide. Allred's first big meeting went a long way to convincing him to change his mind. "We were halfway through, and we hadn't even gotten to the first agenda item. Everyone was talking about their customer visits that week and what they were learning. I finally realized that *was* the agenda."

Allred kept the title. He did not, however, leave the organization unchanged.

Corporate IT

To move the systems closer to the customer and generate internal efficiencies, Allred brought several groups, including corporate IT, under the CA umbrella. His first battle was to increase the IT budget, no small feat. The IT budget at that time was 0.75 percent of revenue, and the board was unlikely to budge as long as IT was viewed as a cost center. But Allred believed that those who managed particular business functions were the best judge of their IT needs, and he set out to transform the entire process. The resulting "client-funded" model shifted much of the accountability for IT spending from a corporate budgeting process to individual business functions, allowing those functions to prioritize their own IT needs and determine how much they would spend on IT versus other solutions. As a result, IT would be more closely aligned with business priorities.

The immediate effect was that IT spending grew fast, as much as 100 percent annually for the first few years of Allred's tenure. As he phrased it, "IT went from being the poor cousin fighting for budget to a delivery machine." An important enabling element was the reduction in turf wars between IT and the units using its services, as well as within IT, as the increased emphasis on customer centricity enhanced cooperation and broke down the silos that otherwise might have impeded this initiative. Success, in effect, bred success and embedded resiliency ever deeper into the organization.

The success had external benefits as well. Effective IT applications had spillovers for Cisco's outside customers, many of whom looked at Cisco's own operations as a model of how to leverage IT. Hence, the real value of increasing cooperation between IT and other units was to improve the focus on external customers.

Although IT eventually moved out of customer advocacy, the reorganization had served its purpose. According to Joe Pinto, a senior vice president within CA, "Having the IT function within the Customer Advocacy Group for so many years has given Cisco an incredibly natural way of looking at IT and technology . . . to use technology to drive customer satisfaction and loyalty."

Technical Assistance Center

The technical assistance center (TAC), also within the customer advocacy unit, is another example of how Cisco engenders cooperation. In Cisco's early days, customers could speak directly to Cisco engineers about their concerns, but as Cisco grew larger, this came to be unwieldy. To solve this problem, Cisco formed TAC as the most efficient way for Cisco to provide customer support, staffing it with experienced engineers who could speak to customers needing help with complex issues, as well as less experienced employees who could efficiently handle simpler problems. A key element has been to ensure that there is information sharing both within TAC and between TAC and other units, such as product development and marketing, which enhances all these units' direct interaction with customers. Cisco also found that customers readily adopted online self-help, with a growing proportion of all problems and questions being resolved without live interaction. Between 1996 and 2002, monthly TAC logins increased from fewer than 250,000 to 4 million. As a result, the TAC doubled its caseload while growing staff by just 10 percent.

In addition to the call centers, the TAC Web site provided an online connection to customers to address frequently asked questions, offer resources to help customers help themselves, and allow the engineers time to deal with more difficult issues. If stymied, customers could always connect to live communications with a TAC engineer by clicking on a "Cisco Live" icon, which brought an engineer's face up on-screen to assist the customer through the session. However, 80 percent of all problems and questions were resolved without live interaction. Customers readily adopted online self-help: between 1996 and 2002, monthly TAC logins increased from fewer than 250,000 to 4 million. As a result, the TAC doubled its caseload while growing staff by just 10 percent.

Shape-Shifting to Ensure Customer Satisfaction

One of Cisco's primary objectives is to continuously "listen" to its customers. To that end, it administers a Web-based survey, just before a sale and just after, of customers who buy directly from Cisco or through resellers. Dissatisfied customers are contacted immediately and asked what Cisco can do to improve the relationship. The information is shared broadly, and Cisco engages specific groups that can help address those concerns. All the information gathered, especially about dissatisfaction, serves as a catalyst for more effective cooperation because disparate groups must work together to address these issues.

Taking to heart academic research that inextricably linked a company's future success to current levels of customer satisfaction, Cisco applies a five-point scale that measures customer satisfaction to all customer-facing operations across the company. Employee compensation is directly linked to the resulting overall scores. Annual bonuses are based on the level of customer satisfaction revealed in answers to one question: "What is your overall satisfaction with Cisco?" Each year a specific goal is set, and the size of the bonus for all employees is dependent on meeting it. Each individual's bonus is computed using the customer satisfaction multiplier along with a corporate revenue multiplier and a salary multiplier. Allred specified the logic of the metric: "Managers find it inconceivable to risk losing customer intimacy in order to increase operational effectiveness, because you get paid on the basis of customer intimacy. So suddenly you have to think out of the box."

As highlighted before, Cisco administers the corporate Customer Satisfaction Survey on pre- and postsales to customers who buy both directly from Cisco and indirectly through resellers. The survey includes business-focused questions, such as overall satisfaction with Cisco, and product-specific questions. Questions come from all corners of the company. Engineering, for example, uses customer responses to its questions to drive specific product improvements. Cisco also can link survey responses to any of its sixty thousand channel partners, enabling it to attribute individual customer responses to a specific partner.

Cisco works very hard to ensure a high response rate, which is typically over 50 percent. Customers access and complete the surveys online. Cisco receives the results online in real time and uses the information to locate obviously dissatisfied customers and to detect trends or potential challenges.

Maintaining Resiliency amid Reorganization

Hard times are what truly test a culture, and it was in the technology bust of 2001 that Cisco's focus on cooperation and customer advocacy proved itself a long-term winner.

Reduced sales and seemingly unending pressure on margins created an urgent need to improve the company's efficiency. To that end, Cisco decided to rethink its corporate architecture. The organization comprised three autonomous units, each serving one distinct customer segment: small and medium-size businesses, service providers (i.e., telecommunications firms), and large enterprises (see figure 3-2). Each unit housed its own sales, marketing, and engineering divisions. There was a high level of cooperation within each customer-based segment, since the employees there had a common focus, reporting structure, and history. But this

FIGURE 3-2

Cisco before reorganization

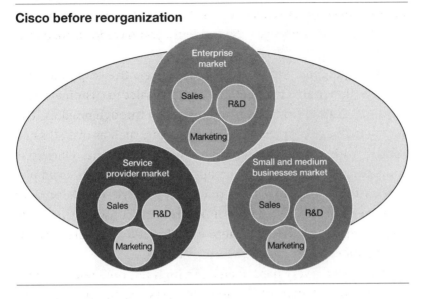

architecture created problems with coordination—in particular, extensive duplication of activities that prevented the company from achieving optimum economies of scale. What's more, the units had created their own product variations, which created duplication and confusion in the marketplace.

By 2001, duplication was a luxury Cisco could no longer afford, so the company decided to reorganize (see figure 3-3). The three customer units were retained with regard to sales responsibilities, but engineering and marketing were both centralized. The central engineering group was broken into eleven clusters organized around technology or products. But although the reorganization immediately improved cooperation and efficiency between the technology activities, it weakened their connections to customers. The newly centralized marketing function faced similar challenges on how it would integrate itself tightly with the sales organization on the one hand and engineering on the other. By organizing around its functions, Cisco had essentially taken a step closer to becoming a company focused more on technology solutions than

FIGURE 3-3

Cisco after reorganization

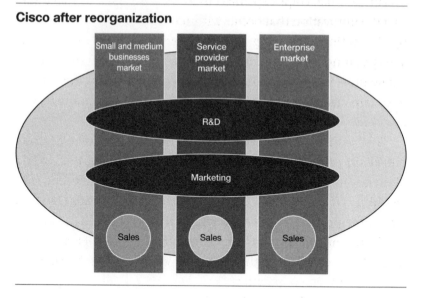

customer solutions, and risked losing the closeness with its distinct customer segments. However, management was not only aware of this at the time of the reorganization, but also made this point explicitly clear to all senior leadership and has taken a series of concerted steps over the years to ensure that its outside-in approach to its business doesn't get lost.

Financial market analysts took note. "In a time when everyone seems to be so focused on the customer," one analyst wrote, "reorganizing around product lines seems a bit strange."[4] Another analyst put it more simply: "Cisco's plan is either brilliant or disastrous."[5]

Cisco executives were well aware that the reorganization could jeopardize the company's responsiveness to customers, cause coordination problems, and get in the way of cooperation across units. Cross-functional cooperation is not something that happens naturally in most organizations; unless it was restored, both innovation and responsiveness could be significantly impeded. "Whenever you reorganize, you don't fix all your problems," former Cisco senior executive Mike Volpi explained in 2001. "We have to make sure that the innovation that occurs within the product groups is driven by the notion of solving the customer's problem." Beyond the ability to innovate waited another serious concern: whether the disparate units would cooperate on a day-to-day basis in the interest of certain customers when the connection to those customers was less clear.

Many managers believed that the company had such a strong outside-in orientation that no amount of reorganization would obliterate it, and that the firm's long-standing customer centricity would drive cooperation even if the customer segment was no longer the primary organizational mechanism Even so, as part of the 2001 reorganization, Cisco created the Customer Focus Initiative (CFI) to ensure that the company retained and reaffirmed its customer-driven cooperation.

An initial analysis was done of 150 of the company's key global accounts—100 enterprise and 50 service-provider customers—to gain a 360-degree view of the customer. (The number of tracked customers had grown to approximately 250 by 2007.) The goal was to understand intimately the issues that arose as well as identifying trends for what came to be known as the CFI 150, and use this information to fuel customer solutions, not only for the CFI program, but ultimately for all of Cisco's customers. The CFI's credo was "Listen-Share-Deliver": *listen* to customer input; *share* information gained from the customer sample; *deliver* Cisco technology and expertise to solve business issues. These three objectives were reflected in the four components of the CFI:

- *Customer information.* In moving forward with the 2001 reorganization, senior management recognized that the first step to enabling effective cooperation was to let people see all information about a customer in one place. Cisco created a central view that included broad information from internal and external sources about customers' behavior and background. This management tool enabled executives to understand what was needed and to rally greater within- and cross-silo cooperation around these customers.

- *Customer Response Program.* In early 2002 the CFI team rolled out the Customer Response Program (CRP). CRP would pass customers' concerns to colleagues in other units and then communicate back to the customers any actions Cisco had taken on their behalf.

- *Customer value summaries* (CVS). These reports summarized the information gathered through the CRP in a form that could be shared with customers. For any major issue that the customer faced, the account team would report on what the company was doing to enhance the relationship. This report was shared internally to ground future decisions that needed to be made cooperatively.

- *Executive Sponsorship Program.* This program paired a senior executive at Cisco with a number of key Cisco customers. The executive sponsors, often drawn from the top ranks, were matched with a company based on their fit with the account and acted as customer advocates and champions. Customers were encouraged to contact them at any time. The program cut two ways: by ensuring Cisco's cooperation around the customer's needs, executive sponsors not only served key elements of the marketplace, but were also forced to look at their own company through external eyes.

In 2004, as an enhancement of its policy of customer-centricity, Cisco introduced two key customer focus initiatives as a response to Cisco's Customer Satisfaction Surveys (CSS).[6] One way in which Cisco demonstrated its commitment to customers was through the Customer Experience Dashboard—a tool that uses CSS data to provide a clear view of how positive or negative a relationship Cisco is having with a particular customer. A second

CSS initiative was the Low-Score Follow-Up Program. Under this program, which uses a cross-sectional survey, goals must be met in order for account team members to receive a bonus. Furthermore, if a low score is recorded in any survey, a notice is triggered and sent to the respective account team.

Establishing Cross-Functional Councils and Boards

Another important initiative that helped Cisco remain resilient and outside-in following the 2001 reorganization was the evolution of Cisco business councils, which began organically that same year with the formation of the enterprise business council, service provider business council, and commercial business council. These were, in essence, a formal coordination mechanism—senior-level cross-functional leadership teams drawn from across the organization—for promoting cooperation by aligning values, behaviors, and resources; facilitating coordination; further enhancing cross-technology integration; and ensuring continued customer centricity.[7] Each council focused on a particular customer segment: commercial (or small and midmarket businesses), enterprise, and service provider. "The goal of the councils is to align the organization and drive productivity gains through better cross-functional collaboration, while ensuring that a customer mind-set remains the company's focus every step of the way," in the words of John Chambers.

Each business council had members, at the vice president level or above, from all the major functions and a mandate to make sure that Cisco was doing everything it could to serve its particular segment. The membership of the enterprise council, for example, included representatives from customer advocacy, manufacturing, sales, and marketing. The cross-functional membership was designed not just to ensure greater coordination among the functions, but also to generate a cooperative mind-set across the functions, allowing them to break down internal barriers that might come in the way of serving that customer segment.

While the three original councils addressed key customer segments, more needed to be done to further reduce redundancies and inefficiencies in the company's operations. So, in 2003, Cisco established the business process operations council (BPOC) to get collaboration from the multiple functions on the large operating issues that were inhibiting growth. Additionally, in 2006, Cisco added two new councils around growing customer segments: consumer and emerging markets. The emerging markets council was geographically structured around Eastern Europe, Latin America, the Middle East and Africa, and Russia and the Commonwealth of Independent States.

The councils met regularly to discuss customer issues that cut across disparate functions and technologies at Cisco. Each business council reported to the operating committee (OC), Cisco's most senior decision-making entity. The OC comprises the CEO and his direct reports, including the entire team of executive vice presidents. Thus, a cross-functional group oversaw the cross-functional councils to ensure the highest levels of cross-unit perspective on customer needs, and the cooperation required to meet these.

Council members were required to be at the director level or higher—although the vast majority of members were actually vice president level or higher—because each member had to have decision-making authority within their functions and the ability to quickly commit resources to customer initiatives deemed high priority by the council. The members needed to be able to control and, if necessary, reprioritize the resources within the function. As Dan Smoot, a vice president of customer service and a BPOC member, said, "This is not a delegate-based council where you go back to your organization and negotiate. You have to be able to have that type of say inside your organization." This made cooperation much more efficient by reducing the number of layers required for approval to one. It was also a powerful enabler of coordination among the disparate entities that would not happen otherwise. The result was a "democratization" of strategic decision making, which allowed Cisco to do more, faster.

The business councils had their desired effect. Leaders established priorities that were important for the company as a whole, rather than just their respective functions. They then set the tone for others in their respective organizations. For instance, in 2006, the commercial council sought resources to conduct surveys and profile the buying and other characteristics of small and medium business customers. Commercial marketing, which had a vested interest in this area, allocated the necessary funds and resources to gather this information, which was eventually shared with engineering and business development. It was a customer-focused effort driven by the council. Such willingness to contribute resources toward initiatives that serve the common good engendered a foundation for cooperation and reciprocity—crucial since each function will find itself on the contributing end more than others from time to time.

One of the councils' most important activities was to develop a *common vocabulary* that could be understood across units. Precision and consistency of language are essential elements in cooperation (as well as coordination). When colleagues have difficulty understanding each other, misunderstandings, frustrations, and inefficiencies arise.[8] Vocabulary even became an important part of the reorganization itself. Senior executives took pains to define the role and responsibility of a *council*—in contrast to a board, or task force, or other type of unit—so that people understood that the councils were part of a new governance system rather than an ad hoc team or temporary project group.

The guiding light for this enhanced cooperation, top to bottom, has been the unyielding pursuit of greater outside-in thinking that permeates the firm as a whole and is the result of a number of reinforcing initiatives (summarized in figure 3-4). The reward has been to see Cisco not just as a collection of internal mechanisms but also from the outside, through the eyes of the customers. Through cooperation and through the suppleness—intellectual, personal, and cultural—that cooperation bred, Cisco more than survived the challenge of the tech bust; it grew even stronger.

The Cisco story: Key initiatives

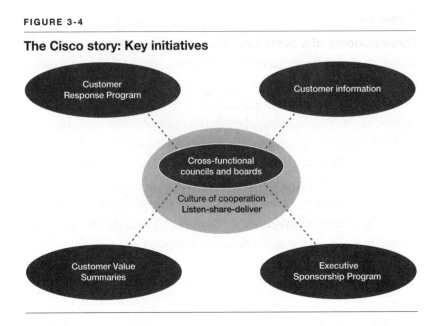

How to Create a Culture That Fosters Cooperation

How can organizations create and sustain a customer-focused culture of cooperation, even under pressure? By using people, stories, and symbols. Managers often "wonder" how they can influence, change, or transform something as amorphous as culture.[9] These *three wonders* of customer-driven culture provide an answer (summarized in figure 3-5).

People as Local Levers of Cooperation

People are the strongest representation of culture in an organization and its most powerful ambassadors. So inculcating your people with customer centricity and the value of cooperation requires careful recruiting, socialization of new employees, and education.

Recruiting for Cooperation

Recruiting high-level employees who embrace the values of customer centricity and cooperation can catalyze a major shift in

FIGURE 3-5

Three wonders of a customer-driven culture

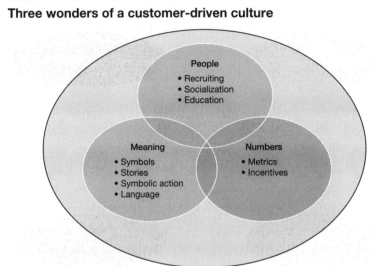

People
- Recruiting
- Socialization
- Education

Meaning
- Symbols
- Stories
- Symbolic action
- Language

Numbers
- Metrics
- Incentives

culture or can nurture and sustain an existing customer-centric culture. This was the case when John Chambers was recruited into a senior management position at Cisco. A fervent believer in the values of customer centricity that were Cisco's legacy, he brought a strong background in technology sales and management, excellent interpersonal skills, and an ability to bring together internal groups and functions to cooperate on solving customer problems.

Recruiting for "cooperators" is important at all levels of the organization, not just the top ranks. To identify such people, focus on two main qualifications. First, potential hires must be strongly anchored around the importance of the customer axis in shaping market success and be strongly committed to it. Second, and equally important, they must have a naturally cooperative nature rather than a combative or confrontational one. Cisco uses its extensive interview process to ensure that potential employees fit with the company's culture and will cooperate.

Socialization of the Cooperative Mind-set

How a company assimilates its new employees, and the message it communicates to them about values, norms, and expected behaviors in general, will determine how new hires ultimately behave. A number of researchers have observed how new hires first begin to learn about culture through the socialization programs, then continue to deepen their understanding throughout their tenure as part of the process of becoming accepted (or not) by the inner circle and coming to know its rites and secrets.[10]

Companies where a culture of cooperation is driven by the themes of customer centricity and organizational resilience can foster these values through new-employee orientation, rotational programs, and other training and development initiatives. Employees should be explicitly told that they are expected to seek out and respond positively to feedback on operations, customer service, and other issues. Equally important is an emphasis on internal cooperation across silos. Such practices serve as socialization mechanisms for all employees, reminding them that "this is how we do it here" while also reinforcing the message that no one internal group is more important than any other.

Education Necessary for Cooperation

Although education is a central component of socialization, I consider it separately because when done right, it is a particularly strong vehicle for effecting cultural shifts. Educational programs can be formalized, regularized, and quickly rolled out through an organization to deliver consistent messages. Customer-focused education programs provide employees with the information they need and the principles they should follow to solve customer problems quickly and cooperatively. At JetBlue, for example, employee orientation includes a module that covers nothing but the importance of cooperation across silos to guarantee customer-focused outcomes such as on-time push-offs from the gate.

Education may also provide information about the customers themselves. A shared understanding of customers is likely to reduce confusion and cross talk and enable cooperation around customer needs. Many of the successful companies I've studied view their education programs as central to their missions and work overtime to make them invigorating and engaging, often involving the CEO or other senior managers as classroom leaders, so that messages about cooperation are communicated from the top down.

Employees at all levels, including senior managers, must educate themselves and each other about how to enhance their organization's efforts at cooperation in the interest of customer centricity. All JetBlue managers must attend the Principles of Leadership program, which reinforces the airline's values and customer centricity. Best Buy went so far as to create a Customer Centricity University. Both companies approach education as an ongoing activity, rather than as a one-time event, and offer a variety of follow-up workshops, training sessions, and evaluations. This is much more than lip service. Only carefully crafted, comprehensive programs are likely to result in higher-order cooperation and foster the deep willingness to go to extra lengths for the customer—and in turn keep the company in front of the market.

Stories and Symbols: Creating Meaning

Stories and symbols can be memorable shorthand devices for transmitting a company's values (see "Making Values Meaningful"). Stories are not mere entertainment—though they can be very entertaining. Stories and symbols—including anecdotes, mantras, and company language generally—are key elements of the often invisible web of customer-based cooperation that is crucial to develop within and among units and entrenched silos.

Stories as a Tool

At Cisco, the story is widely told throughout the company—indeed, has become part of the company mythology—about how CEO John Chambers will keep anyone waiting for an internal meeting, even the board, if he is working with a customer to resolve an issue. Such meaning-rich stories transmit organizational values much more deeply than mere descriptions. Behavior

Making Values Meaningful

A firm's core values are the foundation of its business approach. They may be transmitted quite directly and obviously—through discussion in interviews, inclusion in printed materials, and employee pledges—or indirectly through training and education, symbols and stories, metrics and incentives.[a]

Values help define what is acceptable and unacceptable within an organization and what constitutes exemplary employee behavior.[b] But a simple articulation of values is never enough to produce a culture of cooperation. Companies must live the values at every level. They can do so in three ways.[c]

- *Make values stand for something clear and explicit.* Just as Cisco's no-technology-religion philosophy has very specific meaning to the company's employees, so does JetBlue ascribe very specific behaviors to its values and use even the most mundane reminders to emphasize the company's customers-first values. Thus, *safety* at JetBlue does not simply mean security. It involves "ensuring a sense of security for coworkers and customers." Likewise, *fun* means "adding value to customers' experience through humor."

- *Ensure that management helps shape values to the business environment and transmits them to employees.* JetBlue's management emphasizes the airline's core values multiple times in employee orientations and meetings, explaining how these values help differentiate the airline in an unforgiving industry. Senior managers model the values by serving on the front lines regularly. Likewise, John Chambers and his entire leadership team present their customer-centric vision and strategy to Cisco employees repeatedly throughout the year. In both cases, frequent repetition of values from top management serves to imprint them not just in individual employees but in the corporate DNA.

- *Make sure the values are known and shared by employees at all levels.* Cisco prints its values right on employee ID badges. JetBlue includes its values in the *Blue Book*, the employee handbook. JetBlue's employees are especially aware of the firm's values because their performance reviews—and ultimately their compensation—are based on them.

It may be easy to dismiss the importance of reinforcing customer-focused values to employee groups that do not deal directly with the customer. But many firms have found that using and reinforcing customer-focused values—rather than values based on efficiency or other performance-related principles—to reengineer business processes is highly valuable, especially as it embraces customer centricity as a centerpiece of its strategic agenda.

a. Harvey Thompson, *The Customer-Centered Enterprise: How IBM and Other World-Class Companies Achieve Extraordinary Results by Putting Customers First* (New York: McGraw-Hill, 2000), discusses the need for firms to first obtain valuable customer input by asking the right questions about the right issues (chap. 2) and then using that as the basis to articulate goals and values.

b. Michael Basch, *Customer Culture* (Upper Saddle River, NJ: Prentice Hall, 2002), a founding officer of FedEx, suggests that values are the "noncompromisables" that define the organization and the behavior of its employees, especially as related to customers (p. 54).

c. Terrance Deal and Allen Kennedy, *Corporate Cultures* (Reading, MA: Addison-Wesley, 1982), present a similar list for general organizational values (p. 22).

is exemplified but not directed ("Here's how you should act"); stories embody an organization's essence and portray valued behaviors as natural actions.

The best firm lore usually involves frontline employees. Take the story of JetBlue flight attendant Theresa Hintze. On one of her flights, a passenger snagged his pant leg and ripped it from thigh to shin. He was on his way to an important meeting and had brought no extra clothing with him.[11] The passenger asked Hintze if there was a sewing kit. There wasn't, but she had an inspiration. Working with her fellow flight attendants, she found adhesive tape in the first-aid kit and sent the passenger into the restroom to remove his pants. She turned them inside out and neatly applied tape to the tear. The rip was almost invisible, and the passenger went off happily to his meeting. At another airline, such behavior might be considered extraordinary. At JetBlue, Hintze was merely doing her job, cooperating with both customer and colleagues to solve a customer problem on the fly, as it were. To a JetBlue employee, the takeaway is the benefit of flexibility and cooperation. Should a potential customer hear the story, that's a standout in a competitive industry.

Some companies rely on serendipity and informal networks to generate and circulate such stories about cooperation. Others have a more deliberate process. It never works to manufacture stories or heroes, but companies can actively solicit firm lore from employees via surveys and discussions, then document and share these accounts widely.

Symbols, Symbolic Actions, and Language

A cross, a serpent, a star, a flag—these small symbols can embody entire systems of cultural values and behaviors.[12] In the customer-based business, symbols are just as important.

Symbolic cooperative *action* is particularly important because managers have day-to-day control over it. Actions that exemplify company values can come to represent a culture. Some researchers label managers who take a lead role in reinforcing and shaping culture "symbolic managers" who are particularly attuned to culture and its role in the firm's success and use culture to define what's truly important within the company.[13]

Language is another core symbolic—and actionable—element of culture. Simply attaching a label to the company's culture is a powerful way to encourage employees to acknowledge it. Intel's managers boast of the firm's culture of "constructive confrontation," and those words appear on the ID badges. Cisco's mandate of customer advocacy is another powerful use of language to communicate culture. Labeling yours as a "culture of cooperation" or perhaps "relentless resilience"—in many ways the same thing—could be a good way to start. But it has to be more than just a label. If this value is upheld at the highest levels, values-reinforcing cooperation among employees becomes all the more likely.

The labels companies use for their employees are another way of signaling cooperative behavior. JetBlue's employees are known as "crew members" and "coaches," rather than employees and managers. Vanguard Group founder John C. Bogle similarly insists that his employees are crew members, both to foster cooperation and as a reminder that the company's name was inspired by the HMS *Vanguard*, Lord Nelson's flagship in his great victory over Napoleon's forces at the 1798 Battle of the Nile. Labels for employees illuminate the firm's hierarchy (or lack thereof). Labels used to describe customers signal what the company thinks of its customer relationships. To many firms, the word *customer* has a transaction-related connotation that does not fully reflect the deeper and more holistic connection they would like to build with those who consume their offerings. That's why Target and Disney refer to customers as "guests." People are much more likely to cooperate to meet the needs of a "guest" than those of a "customer."

The "Numbers"

One of the strongest indicators of culture is the metrics that companies use to gauge performance and reward employees—the "numbers" (in quotation marks because some of the most powerful motivators of employee behavior, including cooperation, are hard to quantify and don't usually involve financial rewards). So companies wishing to encourage the deepest and most diffuse form of cooperation will have to use "numbers"—because not all metrics are so easy to specify—carefully, ensuring that their metrics and incentives, whether quantitative or qualitative, emphasize truly cooperative behavior.

Metrics

Most firms have historically relied on product-focused analytics or metrics—revenues, growth, and margin—and based their incentives largely on these, sometimes with internal ratings thrown. But these metrics, especially the volume/growth measures, are lagging indicators, and by the time they reveal a problem, it may be too late.[14] What's more, typical metrics are often misaligned with customer centricity. For instance, sales employees are often motivated to focus on bringing in new customers rather than nurturing existing ones, because compensation for new business is higher. Furthermore, salespeople are rarely given incentives to cross-sell or cooperate in some way with people in other silos— and there are almost no metrics to measure or reward the extent of cross-silo cooperation or coordination.[15]

To enhance cooperation, metrics should address performance in terms that are relevant and meaningful to customers while also providing an indirect reference point on the underlying drivers of performance. This might include measuring customers' time and cost (both expense and lost opportunity) to acquire a product or solution from the focal firm and get it to work, along with the number of people a customer must contact or the time it takes a customer to solve a problem.[16]

But while some metrics should be aimed externally at making customers feel valued, others should also have an internal objective: reinforcing cooperation to create greater company–customer synergies. (In many companies Balanced Scorecards provides one such impetus.)

If customer centricity is hard to measure, the enabling element of cooperation is even harder to measure. Although a few firms try to capture information about internal silo-busting cooperation directly, most infer it by looking at customers' experience with the firm, and some do it very well. Harrah's, the casino company, has mastered the cooperation-stimulating power of customer-related data and metrics.[17] In 1999, new COO Gary Loveman introduced a gain-sharing program that linked employee bonuses to improvements in customer service levels. "If the marketing works but the service doesn't deliver against expectations," one Harrah's executive told me, "you're throwing your money away."

The new program was intended to focus employees more directly on customer satisfaction. As an employee circular explained, "Payouts for reaching customer satisfaction goals stand alone. Operating income results do not affect customer satisfaction goals."[18] Loveman reinforced this principle when he introduced the plan. "If you improve service, irrespective of financial performance," he said, "you will still get rewarded."[19] Up to that point, managers' bonuses had been based on operating income improvements. In the new structure, 50 percent of the bonus was tied to operating income, 25 percent to market share, and 25 percent to customer satisfaction. Employees were implicitly expected to cooperate with one another to satisfy customers.

To understand what pleased its customers, Harrah's created the Targeted Player Satisfaction Survey. Customers use letter grades (A through F) to rate several dimensions of the casino's service, including how "friendly, helpful, and nice" employees are and the amount of time customers had to wait for service. The satisfaction scores are made very visible across the organization. A department qualifies for a bonus if it can convert just 4 percent of the non-A grades into As. These metrics motivated Harrah's employees throughout the organization to ensure that customers had a positive experience and to work hard to make sure that their internal silos didn't inhibit serving the customer. This is a perfect example of how the right metric can create greater cross-silo cooperation by aligning everyone around a common goal.

Incentives for Greater Cooperation

Incentives should be a central part of any effort to stimulate the deeper, more spontaneous cooperation required to deliver on true customer centricity, but developing incentives that will measure and stimulate cooperation across organizational barriers is not easy.[20] Disparate units make varying contributions to customer solutions. There can be a significant lag between the time a solution is first offered and when it generates value. Even defining the customer can be difficult, given the existence of intermediary sellers, multiple decision makers in business-to-business enterprises, and the like. Some organizations tie their rewards to metrics of customer centricity, while others link them to indicators of cooperative behavior.

When considering which incentives will best promote cooperation, managers must take into account the more general dimensions of incentives. Fortunately, companies can leverage both monetary and nonmonetary incentives to promote cooperation through three key strategies: monetary incentives tied to customer outcomes that are easily comprehensible and available to most employees, incentives based on cooperative behavior, and nonmonetary reinforcement.

> *Comprehensible and available monetary incentives tied to customer outcomes.* At Cisco, bonuses are based on three criteria: company performance, customer satisfaction, and an individual's performance rating. Thus, employees know the importance of customer centricity and are motivated to greater individual efforts as well as cooperation across groups and units to achieve it. Harrah's incentives, too, are designed to motivate cooperation. For most properties, if quarterly customer satisfaction goals are met, employees receive a payout based on the specific level of customer-related performance.[21] Because all employees are eligible for the bonus, there is less potential for productivity-damaging competitiveness or jealousy among employees, and greater motivation for cooperation across silos. So the customer centricity that keeps Harrah's ahead of its field is both a goal and an effect of cooperation.

Collective incentives, when used in conjunction with participatory management, can be highly effective in motivating cooperation as well. For example, FedEx used metrics, incentives, and cross-silo participatory management to raise its on-time delivery rate from 95 percent to 99.7 percent.[22] First, the company developed a service quality index (SQI), listing internal errors that could result in late delivery or loss of a package. Each item was assigned a point value, and a system was set up to track the errors. Employees' bonuses were partially based on their unit's SQI performance, prompting employees and mangers to collaborate across groups to identify ways they could reduce the number of missteps and then implement them. The process eventually led to improvements in the SQI performance and on-time delivery rate.

In general, the combination of collective incentives and participatory management increases employees' sense of ownership of the company and their willingness to cooperate. It's important to note, however, that managers must strike a balance between collective and individual incentives, to avoid demotivating individual performance.[23]

Incentives based on cooperative behavior. In companies where cooperation is paramount to the customer experience, individuals receive direct financial rewards for cooperative behavior.[24] At Jones Lang LaSalle, the legacy compensation structure was getting in the way of efforts to promote cooperation across business units. Even after the company reorganization and the creation of the corporate solutions group in 2002, the individual services units with larger margins were not interested in sharing either resources or incentives with less profitable units. To complicate matters, there were no dedicated account managers within corporate solutions; they had to be pulled from one of the business units, yet they remained housed there. As a result, account managers who served as the integrators wore two hats: (1) customer-facing intermediary working for corporate solutions and (2) member of one of the product business units. These managers' "home" units argued that they should not bear the managers' entire expense and that the firm should either hire dedicated account managers or charge the units only a portion of the cost of the managers who were working across product units. Not surprisingly, tension sprang up among the units in which account managers worked, and often made cooperation difficult.

So JLL decided to allocate the costs of an account manager across the units in which they had activity and to take incentive compensation for the manager from the compensation pools of the businesses he touched. This incentive splitting didn't completely solve the problem (the financial performance of the entire unit became the main determinant of the account manager's incentive compensation, rather than that of just his client relationships), but it did essentially force the units to cooperate more and emphasized the authority of the customer-facing account managers. To be sure, measuring and rewarding cooperation can be a vexing task, but sometimes this is necessary both to ensure that cooperation occurs and, just as important, to isolate where it is absent.

Nonmonetary reinforcement. In addition to collective and individual customer-focused and cooperation-focused financial incentives, companies with true resiliency also rely heavily on nonmonetary rewards to directly and indirectly foster cooperative behavior.

One indirect way that winning companies reward cooperation is by creating a "destination workplace."[25] JetBlue and Cisco both foster, through a variety of practices, a culture where all employees feel equally valued, no group has dominance over any other, and cooperative behavior is celebrated and valued. Best Buy diminished competition and increased cooperation among in-store employees by formally recognizing floor associates who cooperated in handing off their customers to the newly created personal shopping assistants. At Cisco, employees who gather with John Chambers at his bimonthly "birthday breakfasts" no doubt feel more valued by their leadership than do employees in companies who have no contact with senior managers. Such programs are generally inexpensive but can make a difference to promoting a culture of cross-group cooperation.

Apart from these explicit nonmonetary incentives, more implicit incentives, such as peer pressure and the guilt that arises from nonconformity, can be equally powerful. Nordstrom, the upscale American retailer, is particularly well known for its peer pressure, as evidenced in this internally famous bit of firm lore.[26] A sales associate in one Nordstrom shoe department was working with a customer. The customer finally chose a pair of shoes, only to find that her size was not in stock. The sales associate apologized, and the customer sighed and got ready to leave. At that point another associate stepped in and offered to call other Nordstrom stores to see whether the shoe might be available. The customer agreed, the associate went off to make the calls and, after a few moments, returned with the news that, while no Nordstrom had the shoe, he had found it in a Macy's store and arranged for a pair to be sent to the customer overnight—with Nordstrom footing the bill for shipping. As the customer moved on, she overheard the second associate reprimanding the first, saying that by not trying hard enough to please the customer, he had let both of them—and Nordstrom—down.

How do we:
1 get this behappen
2 create love

Good example
of service +
service
recovery

Clearly, in customer-driven companies like Nordstrom, front liners often become the best ambassadors of customer centricity and cooperation. This represents a growing recognition that serving customers is not a "lone star" effort and entails the support of numerous others within the firm, some of whom may not even directly interact with customers. Individuals who work cooperatively in support of customers are a keystone of level 4 resiliency.

Maintaining Momentum: The Co-op Mojo

Crafting a culture-related change as a means of reinforcing cooperation within or across units is always a major challenge—requiring what Edgar Schein calls a cultural "unfreezing" and "refreezing."[27] And managers confronted with effecting deep cultural change may feel that they're trying to melt a glacier with a match. Barriers to cultural change are many, including today's emphasis on short-term results, the increasingly technology-based nature of communication between companies and customers, and, most intractably, the legacy cultures of product-centric firms.[28]

Cross-silo cooperation through cultural change is rarely, if ever, achieved by a single task alone. Managers at all levels must attend to the three wonders of customer-driven culture: people, values, and numbers. They may use substantive and symbolic techniques ranging from the very simple (e.g., disseminating stories of superior customer service) to the dauntingly complex (e.g., realigning incentive structures around customer centricity) to stimulate greater customer-focused cooperation.

Because the three wonders are so interrelated and mutually reinforcing, most managers will need to pursue some combination of these elements. That calls for a juggling act, but the effort is worthwhile and the need has never been greater: effecting greater customer-focused cooperation will lead to enhanced company–customer synergies, which should have direct impact on both the top and the bottom lines. What's more, culture is a cost-effective way to embed suppleness into organizational architecture and bring about deep and long-lasting enterprisewide change.

Yet even when companies put effective coordination mechanisms in place and achieve improved cooperation among their people, they may still have difficulty getting to the highest levels of company–customer synergy if they don't attend to issues of who has power and who does not. Turning an inside-out focus outside in and driving change and resilience into the very heart of the enterprise requires attention to clout as well, the subject of the next chapter.

4

Lever 3: Clout

Empowering Customer Champions

A BIG FACTOR IN CREATING a collaborative, resilient environment is the allocation of *clout* and its distribution across organizations. Greater interunit collaboration through enhanced coordination and cooperation is one of the keys to an outside-in orientation and resultant resilience. Yet these alone are not sufficient to achieve such lofty goals. Whereas coordination enables organizations to align tasks and information around a customer axis, and cooperation fosters a more collaborative, customer-focused environment, clout—or the ability to influence decisions that traverse a firm's power structures—enables individuals and divisions to take on meaningful silo-busting roles and ultimately enhance the resilience and outside-in responsiveness needed in a shifting market.

Clout usually resides in the key decision-making units. Thoughtfully distributed, clout equips firms to achieve an outside-in orientation leading to greater resilience with greater ease and speed. Level 4 firms empower those who can drive actions around the customer axis in particular, perform roles that cut across traditional organizational units, and draw on the power-related resources they need, including authority, information, and

101

influence. It is especially important to invest the boundary spanners who oversee reorganizations with the clout needed to get the job done.

What exactly is clout, or power, and what does it mean in organizations? My Harvard colleague Linda Hill defines power as "the potential of an individual or group to influence another individual or group."[1] Jeffrey Pfeffer expands on the theme, describing power as "the potential ability to influence behavior, to change the course of events, to overcome resistance, and to get people to do things they would not otherwise do."[2]

Because power is a key source of influence, preserving and enhancing personal and group power is essential. While degree of power and influence is commonly identified with formal roles within organizations, some scholars suggest that power ultimately resides within individuals and emanates from their informal (as opposed to formal) positions.[3] So power—or *clout*—is multifaceted, and shaped by access to information, formal authority, and control over scarce resources, among other forces.

Effective cross-silo collaboration almost invariably involves modifying the power structure by assigning formal authority, bottom-line accountability, and valuable resources to existing business units and newly formed silo-busting or -bridging divisions or roles. Here, an inevitable impediment arises. Some people or units will lose clout as more power is apportioned to others, often new units or people in newly created roles. Reassigning power isn't necessarily a zero-sum game—giving one person or unit more power doesn't necessarily imply taking power away from another—but empowering one person often means that the relative balance of power between two or more individuals is upset.[4]

Empowering silo-bridging and -leveling individuals and units with sufficient clout to get the job done is a key to aligning a firm around a customer axis and redirecting its gaze from inside out to outside in. But this creates an ironic second impediment: such empowerment necessarily reduces individuals' and units' relative position vis-à-vis the silo spanners and busters. So assigning a bridge builder is likely—at first—to *increase* envy and power struggles as people and groups strive to hold tight to their own. These issues make the distribution of clout one of the thorniest issues a corporation will face on the road to resiliency.

Clout, Silos, and Power Dynamics

Figure 4-1 summarizes the possibilities related to clout when organizations move from inside-out to outside-in along with some of the enablers and impediments that will be discussed here.

When companies are organized around a product axis, product leaders have considerable clout. Because they focus on optimizing the sales and profitability of their own products, these leaders may hinder any efforts to synchronize their work with that of other product units, even at the expense of the customer, a dangerous oversight in times of heightened competition. Customer-centered

FIGURE 4-1

The third lever in your resilience tool kit: Clout

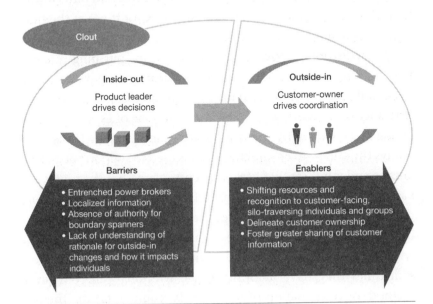

organizations make a concerted effort to redistribute clout, especially to those that are closest to their customers and those with a mandate to foster collaboration across product or geography silos. This can be done by giving boundary-spanning individuals and units more clout, or by leveling the field so that silos have to find ways to work things out rather than relying on a few dominant units to carry the day.

The potential pitfall in any corporate reorganization is that the people or units charged with overseeing the reform may be given a broad mandate without comparably broad powers to execute it. Avoiding that requires the delicate art of systematically redistributing clout so that it flows *to* those charged with building bridges from silo to silo and *away from* those most likely, by nature or position, to defend the autonomy of their own power center.

In most organizations, groups, and often individuals, have disparate agendas and typically compete for attention and resources. Who has power? Who has access to information? Who owns which customers? Who gets what resources? The balance of power constantly shifts. The ability to wield sufficient power, or at least connect with those who do, is essential for people and units in the front lines of systemic integration, especially for those at the new organizational intersections, such as translators.

To redistribute power, an organization pursuing greater resiliency through an outside-in orientation may have to make structural changes, such as giving some units or individuals formal authority over others, as well as more symbolic ones, such as providing greater visibility to certain roles or individuals. The goal is always the same—to ensure that clout is used to support the mechanisms and mind-set that best serve customers—but the routes are variable. Generally, given the negative repercussions when overt directives are used, clout is better wielded through influence than by formal authority. Sometimes firms find more formal ways to encourage such a shift in behavior within their organizations. And sometimes they have to bring in the wrecking ball. Whatever method, or combination of methods, is required, (a) the themes of silo busting and bridge building, power dynamics, outside-in orientation, and resilience are inextricably linked, and (b) managing all four simultaneously is vital to success.

One might think that companies would recognize the need to empower people who will act as silo bridge builders—or silo busters when necessary—and provide them with the necessary clout. But it can be very difficult to shift or wrest power from individuals and groups that are pursuing internally focused goals, such as product development, manufacturing, or sales. Indeed, reorganization efforts undertaken during systemic integration efforts may be doomed before they begin if those tasked with fostering integration have insufficient clout to effect coordination or to push people towards cooperation.

For organizations that already have new entities to foster cross-unit coordination and cooperation, the question of clout is primarily a matter of giving these units enough power to do their job and ensuring a balance of clout with the existing units. If no new bridges across silos have been built, reworking the power structure is a critical tool for fostering cross-silo coordination and cooperation. But if you engage in silo swapping, then you need to be aware of the fundamental changes you are making to the power structure in the organization.

Power to the Right People: Redistributing Clout

Empowering key individuals and groups to take actions—including encouraging disparate silos to make mutual customer-focused internal adjustments even at their own or others' expense—creates the company–customer synergies that characterize truly outside-in organizations. Wisely redistributing clout is thus both an everyday concern for a company's units and an acute concern for boundary spanners in times of reorganization.

The best way to effect shifts toward customer-focused cooperation is to reinforce them by a reallocation of clout—for example, by empowering customer-facing units and employees who may need to work across silos to fulfill customer promises—while retaining an adequate level of influence for units and employees who are less customer facing.

The people and units most likely to collaborate around customer needs, usually at the intersections of the organization, are the ones that need to be empowered. These are the people and groups that are in a prime position to effect systemic integration. Increasing their power involves both substantive measures, such as endowing them with formal authority, and more symbolic ones, such as promoting greater visibility for a given role or employee. Careful moves will result in a mutually reinforcing set of cultural elements, incentives, and power distribution that stimulate maximum cross-silo cooperation and company–customer synergies.

In product-centric firms, the ability to influence key internal and external decisions will reside with the profit-and-loss (P&L) units, which are structured around products, technologies, services, or geography—not surprising, since revenue-generating units are regarded as the mission-critical components of the firm. At Jones Lang LaSalle (JLL), as discussed in chapter 2, clout resided almost completely in the business units (service-based) before the cross-unit account management function was formalized, so newly appointed account managers required significant power to develop cross-silo solutions for large customers.[5]

And that's why the new structures and processes that promote greater internal coordination of systemic, customer-focused processes lead to stiff resistance from clout-rich incumbents in multiple powerful units. Specifically, making changes to bridge or bust silos often shifts influence and authority from those product-centric units to those that are closest to the customer. Silo-busting efforts around clout must focus on creating a distributed but flexible web of power that systematically and fully address unpredictable customer needs. *Resilience* can never be more than a pretty phrase as long as companies lack the structural elasticity to envelop and service customer needs.

An example: by serving as Jones Lang LaSalle's most direct link to global customers, the corporate solutions unit took the place of individual business units' connections to these customers. New units, such as JLL's account management, acquired greater prominence in the organization's power landscape because of their important role in assessing customer needs, assembling firm offerings into customer solutions, and negotiating pricing and other terms with customers. Early negotiations between the account managers and the old product-based silos to develop, price, and deliver outside-in solutions are likely to resemble face-offs like those of gunslingers in the Old West. Even when no third party is involved to oversee cross-silo collaboration—as when, for instance, systemic integration occurs by promoting greater collaboration among existing silos—issues of clout will be considerable as each entity tries to pursue its own interests.

Even when a unit's power isn't reduced, another unit's increased clout can lead to more sensitive interactions. To address these power struggles, firms must pay careful attention to who makes high-impact decisions within the new organization and whether other groups have influence or oversight regarding decisions. Rules of engagement must also be specified between collaborating entities that have greater parity, to avoid deadlock.

Finally, management must embrace and broadcast the notion that clout isn't always a zero-sum resource. In fact, as customer-centric resiliency becomes a more prominent goal, there will inevitably be more roles and responsibilities to go around, and thus a larger pool of power and influence to share, at least in some dimensions. Distributing this power thoughtfully and with built-in flexibility is especially important in the context of systemic integration, where units, groups, and individuals must act quickly and often with little warning or previously established guidelines to develop higher-value solutions for customers while markets or technologies shift. Management must also ensure that clout-related struggles don't impede the quest for systemic integration: internal entities locked in power battles can't be expected to focus fully on customer needs. This perspective may alleviate some of the tensions that arise around clout, but only if firm leaders spell it out specifically and make the new distribution of clout as clear as possible—whether related to information, authority, or influence. Ultimately, the goal is not just to mitigate the amount of conflict that occurs with the shift in priorities, but also to leverage the shifting power structure to engender a nimbler, more creative firm.

The rest of this chapter examines in detail typical strategies firms use to reconfigure clout within organizations to build a truly outside-in, responsive perspective (see figure 4-2). (See "How to Redistribute Clout Quickly and Effectively" for a quick summary.)

- Maximize access to information.

- Stipulate ownership of the customer.

- Redistribute formal authority.

- Raise silo busters' visibility and recognition.

- Emphasize the use of influence by silo-busting individuals and units, especially where they lack formal authority.

FIGURE 4-2

Key tactics for redistributing clout

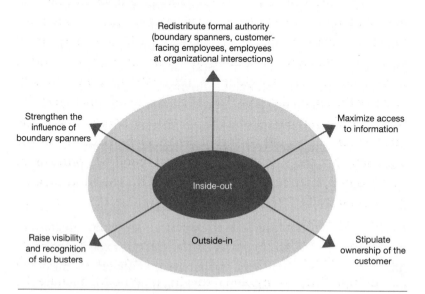

Maximize Access to Information

As discussed in chapters 2 and 3, developing a centralized information source is a key step in fostering both coordination and
cooperation. This requires a substantial investment of time and
energy, and usually entails significant improvements or changes
to the company's information systems.[6] It also requires that those
charged with overseeing the operation have the clout to force
information-hoarding units to share their information freely.

Take Harrah's Entertainment. In the late 1980s and early
1990s, competition among casinos was almost entirely within
regional markets. One casino would add an amenity—a new
game, a spa, or a gift—and its competitors would respond in kind.
However, Harrah's research into the customer perspective showed
that customers were relatively oblivious to the minor differences
between competing casinos in an area. What they really wanted
was to feel special; they wanted an improved and personalized
experience when they visited the casino. Harrah's decided that the
solution was to create a truly national brand that customers could
count on, no matter which Harrah's property they visited.

One of the first steps was to create a centralized customer
information warehouse. Harrah's had to integrate its existing customer information management systems, which were scattered
across its numerous properties, and this meant redistributing
clout from the regional groups to the centralized organization.
Many of the regional units balked at giving up information exclusivity. But the national office had the clout it needed to gain the
information that could be shared across silos. Gradually, as the
units saw that the strength of a national brand was bringing in
new business, they embraced the new system. The effort took six
years, but it paid off; Harrah's saw greater volume, more repeat visits, and higher profits.[7]

Efforts to centralize customer information raise logistical
questions: Who will own what customer information? Who will
pay for inputting, storing, and retrieving it? Who will manage the

How to Redistribute Clout Quickly and Effectively

Maximize Access to Information

1. Allow silos to opt in on customer information sharing, which will make them more likely to draw on information in addressing complex customer needs.

2. Develop a centralized communal customer information source to promote access to customer data and to encourage strategically collaborative sharing and use of that data.

Stipulate Ownership of the Customer

1. Assign cross-silo shared accountability for key customers.

2. Designate gatekeeper silos or functions for specific customers, allowing one entity to pull together internal resources to systemically address higher-order customer needs.

Redistribute Formal Authority

1. Increase the power of new silo-busting functions or figures.

2. In instances where there are no designated silo busters, establish clear rules of engagement between disparate silos.

data warehouse? How will centralization of this information affect everyone's jobs? Who will have access to what kind of information? Yet all those questions beg the most important one of all: how will the information be used to generate new forms of value for customers and the firm? Identifying and collating customer data is just the first step in centralization. Companies must then

Who will mine the data to determine areas of opportunity?

3. Designate local boundary spanners to ensure systemic integration on a micro level.

4. Use the owner-operator model to empower your front line to solve customer problems in a deeper, more integrated way.

Raise Silo Busters' Visibility and Recognition

1. Use symbolic placement of an established figure in a silo-busting role or new unit.

2. Make firmwide presentations to spread the message of silo busting and the push for systemic integration.

3. Roll out employee recognition programs to signal that clout for silo busters or promoters of systemic integration is paramount.

Emphasize Silo Busters' Influence

1. Deemphasize formal control in favor of creative and logic-driven influence, especially as needed to systemically address customer needs.

2. Encourage silos and individuals to use constructive negotiations and build reciprocity to bust silos.

ensure that access to the information is sufficiently supple so that people from different parts of the organization use the data to create new value.[8]

GE Healthcare (GEH) provides a good example.[9] A division of GE based in Waukesha, Wisconsin, GEH is a global leader in medical information and technology, specializing in diagnostic imaging equipment as well as such services as networking and productivity tools, clinical information systems, and patient-monitoring systems. As the firm's service offerings mushroomed in the 1990s, managers split the service function into three new organizations to handle its wider array of offerings: (1) performance solutions, focused on consolidating consulting offerings and integrating these better with equipment sales; (2) enterprise clients group, focused on large and long-term customers; and (3) healthcare services, focused on GEH's expanded service offerings.

Managers of the enterprise clients group soon realized that they needed to refine the criteria for selecting potential enterprise customers. Why? Some clients initially classified as enterprise viewed their relationship with GEH as merely an opportunity to secure more favorable pricing.

In response, the group needed to gather and analyze customer information from the units to refine its target-client profile. A strong mandate from senior management and the informal influence wielded by the executives within this group ensured the cooperation of the disparate units where it resided. The group used this information to redefine its ideal client: a large, multihospital system that (1) had at least $500 million in annual revenue, (2) was likely to value GE's total offering more than transactional discounts, (3) would provide GEH with regular access to its C-level executives, and (4) represented a significant growth opportunity for GE in terms of additional market share, penetration of new product categories, involvement in new hospital projects, or referral business. This new segmentation enabled GEH to reorient itself to focus on the fraction of the roughly four hundred multihospital systems in the U.S. healthcare market that offered the most potential for mutually profitable relationships.

Once the new mind-set was in place, the enterprise clients group worked closely with the disparate units that would ultimately sell and serve these customers. Being at the intersection in a customer-facing role meant that this unit had to quickly discover how to wield clout that exceeded its formal authority.

Stipulate Ownership of the Customer

People from different organizational units can sometimes trip over each other if a company hasn't stipulated who "owns" which customers, especially when customers' purchasing habits overlap across units. Salespeople from different divisions selling distinct products or services might contact the same customer on the same day, creating confusion (at best) and annoyance (at worst) on the client's part. This is not just an issue of coordination, but also directly relates to clout, as customer ownership is an important basis for power in many organizations.

Before the new healthcare services function was formed at GEH, the service group had operated as an aftermarket organization that performed only warranty and maintenance work for the equipment side of the business. Management expected that the new service unit would collaborate smoothly with equipment sales to deliver solutions to customers, but instead power struggles emerged, especially around customer ownership. The equipment salespeople would bundle services with equipment to customers, but when the service salespeople sought to approach these customers directly, the equipment salespeople would use all their clout to prevent them from doing so. "We own this customer," they would say and, because of the company's legacy as a product-focused organization, they often prevailed. But the market was changing, and GEH had to find a way to give clout to the unit providing the services that customers were now demanding.

In the meantime, these skirmishes became all-out battles between silos. The consolidation of service offerings into healthcare services sparked an internal debate about the growing significance of services and what it implied for people's value, status, and clout within the organization. Equipment representatives worried their product offerings would become commoditized and that service would become the new king. A sales executive remembers how this issue played out in the number of GEH reps calling on customers: "The customer buys diagnostic imaging and doesn't

Currently running at this export the level

break it down into 'equipment' versus 'service'; they are often confused by two reps." Another manager told me about a customer's
accounts-payable employee who had *seven* GEH people calling her
about billing issues. And GE's overall culture played a role, as well:
the company's goal-oriented culture made customer centricity
difficult. Not surprisingly, some hospitals requested fewer points
of contact or some method of coordinating solutions. And of
course, the customer-ownership conflicts had ramifications beyond
inconvenience to clients. The power struggles played out in front
of customers were unproductive, putting GEH's reputation and
financial performance at risk.

Luckily, GEH is a nimble and adaptive organization, and management moved aggressively to settle its emerging clout issues by
fostering greater cooperation among its sparring units and clarifying roles, responsibilities, and customer ownership among the
disparate silos. One strategy was to create shared accountability
for key customers while designating gatekeeper units or roles for
specific customers. In GEH's enterprise clients group, management dealt with the challenges sparked by newly ambiguous roles
by spelling out specifically who within the company owned what
relationships with managers at different levels of the customer
organization: enterprise executives dealt with more senior-level
customer managers, while local reps maintained contact with end
users of GEH's equipment or services.

The natural tension that can arise from shared ownership and
accountability doesn't always have to be negative; instead it can
create what some have described as "creative abrasion."[10] One
GEH executive told me that sharing customers created a "positive
tension between an enterprise approach and a P&L approach. We
are mutually dependent." Another explained how the shared-
accountability approach worked with regard to pricing: "We in the
enterprise clients group don't seek the authority to price across the
P&Ls, because our strategy is not to reduce the price of the products and services from our P&Ls. That wouldn't be good business.
What we do is collect the prices from the P&L." This executive

added that the group occasionally had to pressure a P&L unit to offer a more attractive price to preserve the customer relationship. But over time, such tensions dissipated as managers became more practiced at sharing clout.

Redistribute Formal Authority

Sometimes power struggles arise not so much from questions about customer ownership as from groups inadvertently treading on each other's toes as they try to develop high-value offerings for customers. Companies can combat such situations by redrawing lines of formal authority.

Clout-related tensions can arise when specific groups or individuals, especially those with boundary-spanning responsibilities, need others' cooperation but lack the formal authority to get it. This is especially the case when a middleman entity (such as JLL) is tasked with pulling together cross-unit offerings to address customers' increasingly complex needs. Overly rigid or poorly configured lines of authority often prevent people in different parts of an organization from sharing the resources needed, or encourage people to put their own interests before those of customers and the organization.

To encourage cross-unit collaboration, companies can increase boundary spanners' authority, push authority down to customer-facing employees, and use overlapping authority lines to spark the creative tension that keeps a company moving forward.

Increasing Authority of Boundary Spanners

Even after the creation of the customer-facing corporate solutions unit in 2002, final pricing authority at JLL still rested with each of the company's business units—corporate property services, project and development services, and the tenant representation group—rather than with the account managers tasked with coordinating across these units. Not surprisingly, managers of the separate businesses resisted lowering their unit's prices to meet customers' or account managers' expectations. Furthermore, each unit refused to subsidize the others' sales. Sometimes a unit would offer a valuable customer a low price on another division's offering without arranging the deal with that division in advance. The unit whose services had been cross-sold usually took the margin hit for the company, and was understandably unhappy about it.

Such tensions threatened JLL's position in the market. They hampered the development of integrated service offerings; they also resulted in higher prices because each business unit assigned a value to its contribution to a customer agreement on a stand-alone basis to maximize the unit's return. In the broadest sense, the price tensions also leached resilience out of the organization. Companies are no more supple when they're tense than, say, ballet dancers are. But because account managers had no formal authority over the business units, price negotiations often stalled or ended in a stalemate that could be resolved only by time-consuming internal negotiations.

In 2003, JLL took action. It began allowing account managers to provide input on the performance evaluations of business unit employees who had any contact with their clients. As one executive told me, "We had to empower our account managers with something other than their innate negotiating skills to get their colleagues to do things for them." By giving account managers back some of the clout they had lost, JLL partially ameliorated the problem.

JLL also created client relationship management (CRM) review panels to further encourage cross–business unit cooperation. The panels, comprising senior management from each business unit, met semiannually to review the status of all multiservice client relationships. The account manager and senior business leaders from the three different businesses would review the client's relationship with the firm, profitability, and level of satisfaction. One unit CEO recalled, "It was a bit of an inspection, but it was also a very collaborative environment to say, 'Well, what can we help you with? What are the opportunities that you see?'" Another noted, "The CRM program went a long way toward really bring-ing this together such that we could deliver the services to our clients with an individual who truly had the authority to deliver those services." Thus, the shared activities allowed business units to actually share power with account managers and oversight executives by providing input into how client relationships could be taken to higher levels of profitability and client satisfaction.

Push Authority Down to Customer-Facing Employees

When companies push authority down to customer-facing employees, those employees begin to feel an ownership in the firm. They become motivated to do what it takes to keep cus-tomers happy—including cooperating with one another across units and functions.

Recall how Best Buy reinforced its customer-focused strategy by preparing retail associates for an expanded role in store decision making. Best Buy's essential tool kit in this effort—a training pro-gram to acquaint associates with the company's target customers; equipping retail employees to understand basic financial perfor-mance measures; greater freedom to experiment with product assortment, placement, and promotion strategies—strengthened a broad-based sense of ownership over, and responsibility for, the company's profitability. Given greater clout, these front liners deepened their understanding of customers and began reaching across functions and levels as needed to serve them. The actual power distributed to the retail front was relatively limited, but the *sense* of power was great enough to pay big dividends.

Use Overlapping Authority to Spark Creative Tension

In most large organizations, formal authority lines overlap—that is, people report to several bosses. These overlaps often promote creative abrasion as people negotiate with one another, often with a fair amount of intensity and even conflict, about who has authority over what, based on what's best for the customer. Sometimes what is best for the customer is itself the subject of intense debate. Overlapping authority is particularly appropriate when units are expected to share customer ownership or when a middleman has primary responsibility for a customer, but other groups also have contact with that client. In these contexts, authority isn't taken away from one party and given to another. Rather, organizations work out among themselves who will manage which activities to serve their shared customer.

GEH again offers an apt example. When it first created its enterprise clients group, the company had identified five enterprise customers and assigned an enterprise general manager (EGM) to each. The EGM's role was to boost these customers' confidence in the company's ability to handle complex needs requiring attention from multiple units. As Paul Mirabella, former head of healthcare services, explained, "The last thing these enterprise clients wanted was to think that the same guy that was selling them diagnostic imaging equipment yesterday is somehow going to take care of all their needs. They wanted to know that they were somehow being treated differently and that we were bringing a strategic focus to the relationship. So it was critical to assign some kind of dedicated resource, who was broader than just diagnostic imaging and who could represent all of GE Healthcare and, to some degree, all of GE."

It is worth noting how the position of the EGM was overlaid with that of the incumbent sales force. Rather than taking over the equipment and sales groups' relationships with customers, EGMs had the job of growing those relationships by drawing on GEH's full range of existing resources and competencies. Instead of throwing the baby out with the bathwater, EGMs cajoled and partnered with the sales force, sharing accountability and authority as they worked to identify coordinated approaches to select groups of customers. Management helped the units work through the inevitable tensions, and the shared effort sometimes produced creative ways to tackle customer issues in ways that neither the EGMs nor the sales units alone would have contemplated.

Another example of how overlapping clout can foster creative abrasion: In September 2000, GEH announced the formation of GE medical systems cardiology, a dedicated sales and marketing organization focused on cardiology customers in the United States. The new organization was to execute a solutions-oriented sales and marketing approach across the company's portfolio of cardiology products. Thus, while individual businesses retained product development, product marketing, and overall sales responsibility for their products, the new sales organization provided customers with a single point of contact—supported by teams of product specialists—that could provide customers with a more comprehensive view of the company's cardiology offerings. In effect, GE medical systems cardiology was a middleman organization expected to align the offerings of disparate units with customer needs.

During the next few years, the new sales force successfully grew the company's cardiology-related revenue, but this required tremendous creativity and flexibility on its managers' part. As one explained, "The difficulty that we faced at times with coordination arose because of the highly competitive and focused nature of our independent businesses. It is a balancing act that we all do day to day by focusing on a particular business and working as one cardiology team." Moreover, while the different device groups were focused on the success of their respective businesses, "they also probe their own plans to achieve teamwork across the businesses and spend a great deal of time focused on the success of cardiology as a whole. We continually look at how we can complement GE's complete cardiology solution." Thus, GEH relied on spontaneous collaboration among units that had overlaid power structures, rather than granting the cardiology sales organization specific authority to develop these more reliable means of reacting quickly and effectively to customers' complex and shifting needs.

While leveraging overlapping authority lines can encourage cross-unit cooperation, it can also intensify internal tensions, as people from different places in the organization learn the difficult art of compromising in the customer's best interests. Yet in the resilient firms I've studied, by maintaining an outside-in focus, the company's formerly adversarial silos eventually come to act in concert to serve the customer.

Raise Silo Busters' Visibility and Recognition

Some companies redistribute clout by granting greater visibility to the people or groups most actively engaged in uniting silos. This move is not just a morale booster; it can also recalibrate the organization's power equation and enable boundary spanners to operate more effectively. Executives can raise such individuals' or teams' visibility by placing a widely respected person in a boundary-spanning role, communicating the importance of boundary spanning throughout the company, and designing recognition programs to signal the importance of customer-centric cooperation.

Installing a highly respected individual at the head of a boundary-spanning unit sends a clear message to the rest of the organization that the firm has made boundary spanning a top priority. GEH did this when it placed Paul Mirabella—the esteemed former head of equipment sales of GE Healthcare-Americas—in charge of healthcare services in 2003. A colleague recalls, "Putting Paul in charge of the services organization really placed a focus on services. And the services division's revenue did start growing a lot." Some felt that this move signaled a shift in the power balance toward services.

About a year later, Mirabella was asked to take back commercial responsibility for diagnostic imaging sales in the Americas while retaining responsibility for healthcare services. This change fueled even more cooperation between the two divisions. One executive from the services division observed, "When Paul took over both sales and service, we were much less likely to take services for granted." These personnel shifts were important signals within the organization of the shifting power structure.

Mirabella later used this same strategy himself when he named Tony Ecock as head of the enterprise clients group. A former partner at management consultancy Bain & Company, Ecock had also served as CEO of a Hewlett-Packard business unit. His appointment sent an unmistakable message about the value GEH placed on the new boundary-spanning group. Mirabella told me, "Tony's mission at the enterprise level is to encompass all businesses within healthcare and to be the integrator into the other businesses outside of healthcare." To bolster Ecock's visibility even further, management had him report directly to GE Healthcare's CEO.

Strengthen the Informal Influence of Boundary Spanners

Sometimes the most effective approach to managing organizational intersections is not to obliterate or recast them but rather to strategically place individuals who understand how to traverse silos using their clout. These people serve as the wiring that connects silos, helping to drive more customer-focused cross-silo solutions. But connecting silos is often best achieved by informal influence—as a substitute for, or complement to, formal authority. As a GEH executive suggested, "There is no authority. The authority is purely by leadership." Influence can substitute for authority as a subtle readjustment of power, rather than an official, resource-consuming, and complicated restructuring of the organization. This is especially important when complex, unpredictable customer needs across silos heighten the value of the ability to effectively carry out on-the-spot negotiations, cooperation, and ultimately action—the time, in short, when resilience is of paramount importance.

Simply put, many boundary-spanning managers don't have direct control over their peers or over a peer's subordinates. For this reason, the best organizations work to strengthen these individuals' powers of influence to enhance their clout. As one JLL manager explained, "The increasing complexity of the changing world we do business in makes it more difficult for people anywhere to exercise real control. As a result, we're going to have to get much better at working in a world where the ability to influence is king."

Put Influence-Minded People into Boundary-Spanning Roles

Smart companies put people into boundary-spanning roles who understand how informal social networks operate and who know how to exercise influence within those networks. GEH did this when it put enterprise general managers in charge of specific enterprise accounts. In their new middleman role, they were expected to orchestrate the efforts of salespeople from all GEH divisions that served their accounts. Says one EGM, "It really needs to be a coordinated approach, with the enterprise general manager as the quarterback in that account."

How did the EGMs exercise influence? According to one:

When I was first assigned as the enterprise general manager, I met with all of the local sales representatives, regardless of what business they were in, and told them, 'I'm here as a resource to help you to have access and continuous contact with your client's executive team.' Prior to the establishment of enterprise general managers, it was very uncommon for the local sales representatives to have an opportunity to meet with clients' leadership teams. Because I do that on a regular basis, I have access that they don't have. So they use me for any number of purposes, such as when they are trying to advance an initiative, get a deal closed, or understand what the obstacles are for securing more business.

By helping the local sales reps in these ways, EGMs demonstrated their value to the reps and garnered their support for the enterprise strategy.

EGMs also fostered a sense of ownership among local reps. One recalled, "We want to give reps better empowerment, stronger opportunity to make the calls. And telling them, 'You are going to be the one coordinating the strategy for . . . selected customers,' gives them the sense of ownership and responsibility that, when we're presenting the strategy for those accounts, will remind them that they designed and worked behind that." When people have had input into a planned course of action, they're far more likely to feel committed to carrying out that course of action.

Finally, EGMs sometimes had to resort to good old-fashioned relationship building, especially when tension mounted. As one executive noted, "[A sales rep asks why] 'this huge customer who doesn't buy much from me deserves the same terms and conditions as a small one that does? . . . I don't understand how that makes any sense.' This is the kind of thing that every enterprise executive has to deal with day in and day out. It's not insurmountable, and eventually, through a process of discussion, negotiation, logic, and debate, it all gets done. But it's nontrivial."

In addition to using influence to facilitate the relationship between the enterprise group and local sales representatives, GEH used shared activities to build ties between sales organizations (including equipment and services) that often served the same customer but lacked communication. As one manager suggested, "We're driving more and more collaboration and teamwork at the local level to build those relationships. If you say to the equipment leader who has X hundred reps and the service leader who has X hundred reps, 'Get those teams to talk,' then you're talking huge meetings with thousands of people. If you say to the local managers, 'Hey, we expect you to bring your people together for breakfast,' then I think it becomes a whole lot easier." Thus, shared activities like meetings, retreats, and brainstorming sessions serve an important role with regard to influence.

One common arena where influence can be a powerful mechanism to reallocate clout in the absence of authority is in the role of staff organizations like marketing. Again, GEH offers a useful example. The company created its strategic marketing group in November 2003 to identify unmet customer needs related to particular disease areas, such as cardiology, neurology, and oncology. It would then identify opportunities to increase revenue growth by serving those needs through tight coordination of GEH's entire portfolio of offerings. But the strategic marketing team members had no direct authority over GEH businesses. Thus, they had to draw on their powers of influence, which included demonstrating their credibility. Tactics included wielding clinical evidence to identify which technologies had the most promise for generating desired clinical outcomes for particular patient-profile and treatment situations. Strategic marketing slowly became more successful in fostering a coordinated approach to product development across the entire portfolio of GEH products and services.

Influence: Use It or Lose It

Creating a fine balance between formal authority and informal influence is about recognizing the new intersections in which this balance is crucial and then allocating resources to promote it. It may mean reconfiguring the power structure if that is necessary, but sometimes the results can come from managing the intersections by empowering select individuals to wield influence, without changing the authority architecture. This will typically include hiring people who understand how to operate through influence and not control to build customer-responsive teams rather than rigid rules and mandates from the top. Deliberate efforts must also be made to "hire" within the firm. This takes work: even when people are willing to embrace the idea of influence over formal authority, they are likely to need encouragement to use creative and logic-driven influence as well as quid pro quo approaches.

But to be truly flexible, companies must also be willing to shed those who just don't get the concept of informal influence (or who can't master the art). One service-provider executive told me a story about a manager who measured everything by how much she controlled and by how many people worked for her. She balked when he told her that things had changed, now that she was in a high-profile role where her influence would be wider—even though she would have fewer direct reports. The manager "could not get her head around the idea of influence versus command and control." She ultimately left the firm.

To redistribute clout in an organization in ways that support cross-unit collaboration, managers can use one or a combination of the strategies I've described in this chapter: stipulating customer ownership, redrawing formal authority lines, raising boundary spanners' visibility, and strengthening boundary spanners' powers of influence. Thoughtfully distributed clout, wielded in an organization with good coordination and a widespread bias for cooperation, will enable a company to make great progress toward systemic integration. The prize is not just a more harmonious organization, but also a more resilient one—an organization in which creative tension engenders quicker and more creative solutions for the shifting needs of customers across a business landscape in constant upheaval.

However, if the company's employees do not possess the required knowledge and skills—the *capabilities*—needed to deliver customer-focused solutions, influence is not enough to drive this change. A person or group that wields clout without capacities may well become a bully. The person with both appropriate clout and the necessary capabilities can be a formidable agent of change. And so it is to capabilities that the next chapter turns.

5

Lever 4: Capabilities

*Developing the Skills to Cope with
Changing Customer Needs*

IN 2000, THE 150-YEAR-OLD Chicago-based Tribune Company faced a very difficult market environment. Large advertisers were increasingly putting their dollars into national media outlets. Nonprint media were gaining ground. And classified ads, long the gravy of the print media business, were fleeing to online outlets.[1]

Tribune, along with other regional media companies, was struggling to find better ways to compete. It acquired The Times Mirror Company—a smaller operation, but one with a broader portfolio of holdings, including newspapers, television and radio stations, and online media—to expand its presence and coverage. Although the acquisition did not make Tribune a real national player, it allowed it to become a multiregional company, with important media properties anchored around a newspaper in the three most important U.S. markets: *Newsday* in metropolitan New York, the *Los Angeles Times* in California, and the *Chicago Tribune* in the Midwest.[2]

Tribune also hoped that its ownership of television and radio stations in select markets would allow it to provide a legitimate cross-media offering, something that no national newspaper or other media company could match. This would enable Tribune to differentiate itself from national print media and make the case to national advertisers that it was unique in its ability to create customer-centric synergies not only across geographies but also across media. Tribune also could argue that, while it did not have the breadth of a national media company, it had much greater depth in the markets that many advertisers cared most about. It was uniquely placed to offer both cross-region and cross-media capabilities, supported by the skills and capabilities of people who understood different media types (radio, TV, and newspaper). The goal was not only to cross-sell more media, but to combine these broad offerings with deep customer insights to develop solutions for its advertisers.

To leverage its expanded media assets into national advertising dollars, the company created a new national sales organization, Tribune Media Net (TMN), to be staffed by a team of account executives. Its leader, David Murphy, was charged with overseeing national advertising sales for all Tribune newspapers as well as leading cross-media sales efforts.

Murphy and his team knew that the TMN staffers and the employees housed in Tribune's newspapers and media business would quickly need to learn a broad array of skills that spanned geographies and media types. The line managers had to start thinking in a more integrated fashion about their businesses and operate more cooperatively across units and silos to learn about the national advertisers—their new customers.

In a level 4 enterprise built on an outside-in orientation, that sort of on-the-fly shape-shifting is second nature. Suppleness is built into the genetic code; the business is already dancing with its customers, anticipating their needs. But Tribune was a long way from level 4, and it soon became clear that TMN employees needed much more than a review of the new company products and prices: they also needed to know how to educate their customers on some of the more nuanced benefits of advertising across disparate media. "It's much less important for us to know what the current rate structure is at a given radio station, for example, than it is to know strategically what radio or newspaper or television can do for customers," one Tribune executive told me. "Why does radio work and how? Where should it fit into a media mix? Ultimately, we have to present something that has all that detail in the package." And that would require a wide, deep, and speedy retooling of capabilities for almost everyone in the organization.

As we now know, everything that the Tribune Company in general and TMN in particular undertook wasn't enough. I was privileged to have a front-row seat as the company's leadership worked to create a customer axis and orient its business model around it. Tribune was a different company as a result, far better equipped for survival in the jungle of media enterprises. But the jungle finally *is* the unavoidable fact: declining readership, circulation, and viewership intersected with dissatisfied shareholders, a new owner, and a credit crunch not seen perhaps since the Great Depression to lead the company into bankruptcy. That it will emerge seems likely at this writing; that it will be the same company seems, at best, unlikely. A hard lesson: under the most extreme tests, even the most resilient companies may fail. Or, to stretch the definition to its limit, resilient companies may reemerge from crisis with wholly new identities.

The Role of Capabilities in Systemic Integration

As a company strives for an outside-in orientation through which it achieves resilience, it constantly confronts new barriers. Structures and processes (i.e., coordination) must be reconfigured, issues of culture and incentives (i.e., cooperation) addressed, and power (i.e., clout) reapportioned to serve desired outcomes. Once the boundary-spanning mechanisms and relationships have been smoothed out, the organization often finds that it must make changes at a much more basic level: while fostering cooperation can create a willingness to collaborate, individuals within the organization still need the capabilities to do so.[3] *Capabilities* are the skills and aptitudes of an organization, including domain knowledge that may span a firm's disparate products and its customers, as well as managerial qualities like a generalist mind-set and the ability to leverage the informal connections through which most tasks are accomplished in resilient firms.[4]

If the organization does not have people who can explore, comprehend, and meet its customers' needs, the pursuit of customer-centered resilience will be doomed from the start. Imagine yourself setting out on a voyage with crew members who do not know how to sail and have no ability to learn. Capabilities count. So does pushing employees to keep strengthening them. One company I studied pushed its product salespeople to talk up new consulting-based offerings, but these reps had not studied the new solutions and were not adequately trained to talk about and present them. The result? Frontline knowledge was superficial, and commitment slight. Customers could perceive this, and soon enough, the salespeople stopped mentioning the consulting services at all.

Building a powerful set of capabilities among your people is thus an absolutely critical aspect of an aligned, outside-in company model. New capabilities are not going to arise spontaneously or through a general mandate; rather, organizations must develop them systematically. Even then, real commitment and good planning don't guarantee overnight success. Determining which capabilities are lacking and which are required, who needs them and who already has them, where to put the people who already have them, and how to help others attain the skills they need takes time and requires an investment of resources as well as constant gut checks.

Figure 5-1 provides a snapshot of the role of capabilities when organizations move from inside-out to an outside-in orientation.

FIGURE 5-1

The fourth lever in your resilience tool kit: Capability

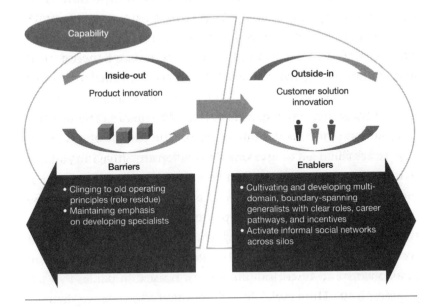

Capability building is universal in organizations. In inside-out companies, though, the focus is relatively simple—developing specialists in product innovation to create new and improved products. But what about firms with maturing product markets—ones caught up in the increasingly common vicious cycle of incremental change overwhelmed by fast followers who copy very quickly? That's when capability building has to be oriented around customer-focused generalists who can assemble flexible, customer-responsive solutions in a hurry.

Typically, few individuals or units within a company can achieve the bird's-eye vision needed to see how the company's various resources can be pulled together in such ways. The very depth of specialist knowledge that has made them so valuable in a company's product-centric days blinds them to the overall, outside-in perspective necessary in a less predictable world. Of course, firms will always need specialists to envision, develop, and deliver excellent products and services. But the people best equipped to bundle products and services in ways that customers most need are those whose integrative capabilities are most formidable. With capabilities as with so much else, finding the right balance of specialists and generalists and managing the interface between them remain the key to success.

To operate consistently, effectively, and spontaneously, people need to constantly develop new skills and be open to new ideas as the route to seamless integration twists and turns. What's more, companies will need to find ways to develop attractive career paths that reward both generalists and specialists. Developing customer-focused capabilities will usually require the introduction of new mandates, structures, and processes, including developing activities that foster cross-unit networking, bringing in external hires, and promoting generalist skills building. Resilience doesn't just happen. It takes work and, at critical junctures, money. Companies that fail to invest in building capabilities—ones that shortchange the necessary skills and networks—will likely watch their new structures, processes, and even cultures collapse. As summarized in figure 5-2, as organizations slowly rebalance their mix of talent away from product-focused specialists to customer-focused generalists, they have to undertake a number of key actions to make that transition.

Capabilities building in support of flexibility delineated in figure 5-2 involves four key actions:

- Creating new types of competencies that focus on generalist, integrative behavior

- Encouraging employees to appreciate the role of informal networks

- Shedding role residue that comes from a mind-set attached to old ways

- Setting out clear career pathways for people within the new organization

FIGURE 5-2

Lever four: Critical capabilities in resilient organizations

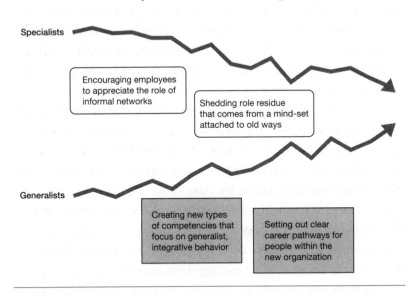

Creating New Competencies to Meet New Challenges

When Tribune Media Net was created, leadership wasted no time in developing ways to build new capabilities for its people through both formal and informal methods. First, to move the organization from a sales and fulfillment model to a solutions model, David Murphy and his team established a formal generalist-training program to teach all TMN executives how to pursue a consultative sales approach.

But training alone would not deliver the bench strength TMN needed. Murphy also found external hires from a variety of media fields, including *People* magazine, advertising agencies, cable TV outlets, and *USA Today*. By looking outside the organization for talent, Murphy increased the pool of employees who already had the skills required to manage and sell a cross-media portfolio.

Murphy also created a TMN sales development team comprising senior-level executives, mostly hired externally, who would accelerate the development of multidomain competencies.

To facilitate the transition to more integrated cross-geography/media selling, TMN formally coordinated the competencies and expertise at TMN and local Tribune resources, including newspapers and radio and TV stations. Customer accounts were assigned to the local businesses or to TMN, depending on the extent to which the customer's advertising activities were centralized nationally. For accounts that had different decision makers for local and national advertising, TMN shared ownership of the account with the local Tribune businesses. For customers who advertised locally only, account people in the local business led the sales efforts, with support from TMN on such issues as category intelligence.

To ensure the success of these efforts, TMN asked the local businesses to create three-week training modules to improve the TMN account executives' knowledge of local markets, products, and competitors. The executives were encouraged to spend more time at the local businesses because product and market knowledge spanned many different silos (e.g., geography and media type).

Murphy also took less formal steps to improve and spread the requisite capabilities companywide. For example, he leveraged the power of viral learning, training a small group of employees on a number of skills (e.g., understanding how cross-media offerings could be bundled into attractive solutions), correctly assuming that these individuals would naturally, quickly, and effectively disseminate these skills throughout the organization. Not only did this make effective use of internal resources; it also demonstrated that management valued local employees.

Thanks to these capabilities-building efforts, the TMN sales organization quickly became a much more effective, better-trained, and more knowledgeable organization, able to respond to a new and changing array of customer needs.

Understanding and Leveraging the Informal Network to Foster Capabilities

As the TMN story demonstrates, while it's crucial to develop specific multidomain capabilities in your people through formal means and activities, these new skills cannot be used effectively if people aren't also skilled at working across the informal social landscape of the organization—the network that emerges through ongoing interactions among people. As one team of researchers puts it, "If the formal organization is the skeleton of a company, the informal one is the central nervous system driving the collective thought processes, actions, and reactions of its business units."[5] Others describe informal networks as "the glue that holds together cross-functional process-improvement initiatives, alliances, and mergers."[6]

The informal network is far less easy to chart than the formal network, as the former sometimes doesn't align with the latter and indeed may be dramatically different.[7] Like vines on the walls of old buildings, informal networks usually grow organically around the formal organization's silos, and moving or reconfiguring the silos will disrupt the network. Both disruption and disparities may get in the way of coordination mechanisms, stymie cooperation, and disrupt the distribution of internal clout, until new networks can be built across various silos. The original informal networks will never completely evaporate, and these old connections can sometimes be barriers to the new mandate for collaboration— although they can also be the roots from which new connections will flourish, as we'll see. At the same time, new ties across silos that need to collaborate will not emerge right away.

As companies strive to make headway in turbulence, anticipating which parts of the organization may need to collaborate with which others is inevitably difficult, and the role of informal networks in providing the glue is critical. Most firms rely on serendipity for such networks to emerge, but resilient ones actively seek ways to foster new boundary-spanning networking capabilities among a firm's employees, because it is through the informal network that people can move around and beyond the organization's formal boundaries to create cross-unit solutions. The creation of an informal network that promotes systemic integration can be proactively managed to ensure greater collaboration among units to foster greater outside-in thinking.

Encouraging Multidomain and Boundary-Spanning Skills

Multidomain skills refer to the broad and deep understanding that your people must gain of the products, services, information, and expertise of disparate units in the organization. "Reskilling" will not only allow employees to work more effectively across units and beyond barriers; it also will enable particularly adept individuals to identify and implement new methods of integration as demands change.

Boundary-spanning skills encompass informal networking skills that allow individuals to connect across their units and groups. When people leverage informal trust and advice networks, they begin to change the firm's social landscape, working within and across it to integrate more fully around customers. An organization's informal networks are the circuits through which information is channeled and tasks completed. Interpersonal connections will be dense in some parts of the organization and sparse in others. Not everyone is equally adept at networking, especially across organizational barriers, and thus firms seeking greater integration to foster more resilience must make efforts to engender greater networking among individuals in disparate units and silos.

Shedding Role Residue

When there is a change in the formal organizational architecture or even just a change in a mandate, the shape of the legacy of individual roles usually lingers. This *role residue* always causes a lag in the ability of a firm's informal organization to support the new formal one. Individuals typically cling to their old connections and need time to feel comfortable with the new ties that may be essential for them to succeed in their emerging roles, especially when the new ties cross internal boundaries.

The challenges that the TMN sales organization faced, for example, were largely related to role residue. Because Tribune's media holdings were geographically dispersed (from the *LA Times* to the *Hartford Courant* and many points in between), executives and employees in the individual companies had been working in silos, and the concept of selling across media and geographies was foreign to them. They had not needed the capabilities to be part of a unified sales force. Furthermore, they lacked the domain skills to comprehend the disparate offerings and the connections to individuals in disparate silos that were necessary for developing coordinated multigeography, multimedia offerings.

TMN's challenge extended to nonmanagement levels of the broader organization as well. Locally based employees (e.g., those with the *Los Angeles Times*) had never worked with peers in the same type of media holding (e.g., newspaper) across geographies, or with those housed in other types of media assets (e.g., TV). Consequently, no solid links, formal or informal, had formed between these levels of the businesses. Local employees were focused on their specific media businesses within their geographic areas, rather than seeing themselves as part of a customer-focused organization seeking to integrate offerings across product types and geography.

Using Clout to Build Capability by Removing Role Residue

David Murphy approached these problems through shared activities—such as regular meetings of sales teams from disparate businesses—but they also had to be addressed through the exercise of clout.[8] Soon after the merger, Murphy told his senior salespeople, "You now work with multiple newspapers. You have a bigger toolbox. You can add greater value for advertisers. You'll make more commission. But you've got to think differently." In effect, he was telling them to shake off role residue and begin planning across media and units. Murphy did not hesitate to show his formal authority as well: "If you don't, you're out." In fact, many of the members of that audience found they could not think differently, and nearly 50 percent resigned, retired, were transferred, or were fired within a few years—even as the organization as a whole grew.

Murphy also employed *coordination tactics* to limit the amount of role residue in his organization. He appointed bridge builders, whose responsibility was to promote a cross-media point of view among local businesses.[9] The salespeople in Chicago had extensive experience with cross-media sales, so he sent some of them to Los Angeles, New York, and other cities to train local reps in cross-media sales capabilities. After the training sessions, the sales reps were sent out on calls together. Not only did they manage to sell a fair amount of new business; the joint calls also helped the reps think of themselves in a new, broader way as information brokers.[10] What's more, they developed informal relationships with people from different organizations during the calls. "By having the sales representatives of different businesses work together to engage with a customer," Murphy told me, "we were able to build teamwork. And once they captured new business, this new behavior was reinforced and solidified."

These coordination tactics and shared activities enabled the key employees to effectively shed the role residue that existed in both the formal and the informal organizations and helped people to build up new, informal networks across units.

Role Residue Isn't Always Bad

Role residue does not always frustrate change. Sometimes, it can actually help an organization form an invisible web of customer centricity that will lead to deeper cross-unit collaboration, even in an organizational architecture that is not traditionally customer centered. Cisco provides a somewhat surprising example of the positive aspects of role residue because, in this case, the roles that lingered were customer-centric ones.

In August of 2001, Cisco, as discussed in chapter 3, went through a major cost-cutting initiative and reorganized its three customer-based business units into eleven technology groups, with the hope of generating greater scale and efficiency. But even after the reorganization, engineers who had worked side by side in the old Cisco maintained their ties with one another.

Even though such collaboration was not mandated in the new organization (and could even have been viewed as counterproductive, since the new organization chart had erased all the old connecting lines), Cisco wisely recognized that such interactions utilized the expertise in networking solutions for customers that had been the engineers' formal responsibility in the old organization. This role residue enriched the organization, adding another layer of possibilities for collaboration and capability sharing. Since then, Cisco has sought to create a variety of forums through which customer-centered collaboration and connections continue within the organization. The moral: sometimes firms that reorganize through silo swapping benefit from fostering continued connections between members of their old units. Indeed, when employees have the *capability* to network among themselves, their networks endure and contribute to a more organically connected and flexible organization.

Leveraging Informal Positions to Promote Resiliency

The position of certain employees in the organization, combined with their ability to influence the informal network, can have an important effect on the overall ability of a company to achieve a more resilient perspective.[11] These individuals might be thought of as "brokers"—people who are able to connect individuals within the organization who themselves have no formal, direct connections.[12] By virtue of their position in the middle, these key figures are able to assert considerable influence and leverage, especially across formal boundaries. Their power comes from connecting others in ways that are beneficial to them—and, ultimately, can sometimes be beneficial to organizations striving for systemic integration.

When a company makes changes to its organizational architecture, as in silo swapping, it must anticipate and manage the effects that the new structure will have on the brokers in its current organization. Those being displaced from central positions will almost certainly resist, new brokers will emerge who bridge the freshly created silos. In more radical reconfigurations, few employees will initially have the breadth of knowledge, skills, and connections to immediately step into broker roles, and new brokers who can connect individuals across the new units will need to be developed over time. Either way, resilient organizations recognize the importance of brokers as powerful allies in enabling systemic integration around a customer axis. Encouraging such connections and the emergence of such informal bridges, much the way TMN did, is critical when organizations reconfigure for survival.

Supporting People as Roles Change

To avoid significant disruptions of the informal network during reorganizations, management must attend to two key activities.

First, it must actively support those people—especially those who formerly enjoyed a brokerage position—who face diminished and less central roles, helping them to maintain productivity and morale as they make the difficult shift to an outside-in perspective. To do so, management must understand the core identity issues involved. Adapting to these shifts is not just about learning new skills or gaining new capabilities; it often involves letting other skills and connections go. Identity concerns will always accompany mandated changes, especially when the networks around which key people have built their identities are no longer as valuable and prominent in the organization. Inevitably, this is an intensely personal issue. We base our identities largely on our networks, and adjusting to a new one is not unlike moving to a new city, cultivating a new set of friends, or even dealing with a divorce. As one manager at Jones Lang LaSalle put it, "The business unit represents a sense of place. It's a home. It lets you say, 'I've got a career, I've got a mentor, I've got a protector.'" Management must understand just how fundamental, and often personally disrupting, changes to informal networks can be. It may seek to ameliorate the effects of change by providing forums where individuals can sustain their old connections while at the same time fostering new ties.

Second, senior managers need to actively identify and cultivate fresh brokers to serve as the cross-unit glue in the new organization. Wise management will start by seeking people who already are important cross-unit brokers and provide them with opportunities to build new connections across the new silos. Effective brokers are adept at seeking out connections that are beneficial to the organization as well as to their own careers. As firms seek ways to assist brokers to recast their personal networks, they also need to look for other individuals within their organization who have multidomain skills and the potential to be future stars in the changing informal network.

Setting Out Clear Career Pathways

When customer-driven organizations value new, more generalist skills and stronger cross-unit informal networks, the potential increases for new career paths for the generalist managers and employees. Most product-centric organizations naturally build career paths for specialists, who advance in their career as specialists—until they reach a sufficiently senior role where generalist skills become important. Organizations seeking a more resilient structure need to balance their emphasis on developing specialists with fostering legitimate generalist career paths that begin lower down in the organization.

Building a broad and deep organization that continually rises to address customer needs requires placing people with the broad skills to support this in the right roles and offering them attractive paths for advancement. But attracting people to take on such spanning roles works only when management clearly delineates these functions not as dead-end staff roles but as organizational positions with an appealing future, and when it enables employees to see how they might progress and grow professionally if they build or enhance the capabilities required. For example, account management executives who transcend product or geographic silos should have the option of growing their roles and responsibilities along with key large accounts, moving to progressively more valuable accounts or eventually taking on a more functionally focused role (e.g., marketing director) in which they will increase their capabilities to address shifting customer needs and the complex organizational shifts that go along with them.

Further, management may loosen the strictures on traditional career trajectories by encouraging managers to rotate across specialist roles. For example, when Jones Lang LaSalle first instituted the corporate solutions group, a major question arose: what future would account managers—who seemed to have lost some of the glory traditionally associated with the P&L-bearing business units—have in the new organization? One of JLL's solutions was to create a career path that would allow executives in this group to progress to larger accounts as they gained seniority. In this way, account managers could grow with their customers, continuing to develop better solutions and advising them in deeper ways that could generate even more value for both parties. People who stayed within their units and silos were encouraged to rotate across other functional areas to broaden their multidomain skills and enhance their ability to broker information and relationships. This, too, increased the firm's overall ability to meet customers' complex needs by giving individuals more hands-on experience across units.

The Role of Specialists

Not all employees will have a chance or a need to work across units. As I have stressed repeatedly, single-silo or single-discipline specialists are still required in the systemically integrated organization. But even for those specialists who remain in established roles, management needs to clarify how improved generalist skills and cross-unit perspectives will be critical to success and career development. For example, the marketing team for a specific product line must become more knowledgeable about and communicative with marketing groups responsible for other products.

Note that establishing clearer generalist career paths doesn't mean that specialists can't keep refining their own career paths. In fact, some firms like Jones Lang LaSalle often include coexisting and even complementary career paths for specialists and generalists. It's a tricky balance, requiring the consideration of incentives and multiple other issues, but an important one to maintain on the path to the systemic integration at the heart of a resilient company.

A Change in Range of Roles and Responsibilities

Another issue to consider when thinking about career paths is the *range* of roles and responsibilities that people need to embrace. Some employees at JLL perceived that they would have less responsibility than they had had before if they took on more client-focused roles in place of service-focused ones. As one manager said, "It's not that they feel their career path is narrowing; it's just that the mix of their activities narrows." Other JLL employees expressed concern about taking more account-focused roles because they feared that the bonds they formed with customers would be much weaker than the relationships they had shared with specialist colleagues. Management worked hard to demonstrate to employees that, while the mix of their activities had shifted, the range was likely to become much broader rather than narrower. In their new roles, employees would require a more comprehensive understanding of potential customer issues, along with the ability to marshal a broad range of cross-unit resources simultaneously. Over time the new roles were embraced. As one JLL executive explained, "They all started to see each other differently and see their role as different because they were no longer just in their functional business silo—instead they were now working in roles that crossed many service lines."

The Need for Foresight

As they pursue greater capabilities, companies tend to focus on the immediate requirements for new skills and short-term advancement opportunities for people with the right skills at the moment. That's understandable, but it's also dangerous because this strategy draws organizational attention away from future talent needs. In fact, almost half of business leaders and HR managers interviewed in a McKinsey study expressed concern that their senior leadership had failed to align talent-management strategies with broader business strategies.[13] The study also revealed that management's rigid thinking frequently prevents individuals from taking on different—often more generalist—roles. Why? Because they're afraid that if they move out of their units, even to more customer-focused roles, managers will think they're not sufficiently committed to the company's strategy. Ironically, this fear only furthers silo-bound thinking and behavior even as it impedes organizational resilience.

Consider JLL's difficulty in attracting candidates for its account manager positions, primarily because the company had historically measured success by the level of management responsibilities that an executive had achieved within a business unit. Because promotions had been tied primarily to internal success, many employees were not accustomed—and certainly not trained—to serve in more integrative, client-facing roles; and advancement opportunities for those willing to walk this path were unclear and uncertain. Job security was a particular concern for potential account managers. One of the early executives in this job told me, "One of the big fears was that these accounts don't last forever," he said. "So if a person left his or her specialized area of expertise to run an account, and after three years there was a change and the firm was no longer providing services for that account, employees feared they'd be out of a job."

When it comes to structuring career paths, organizations that develop attractive roles and career ladders for generalists can trigger widespread change. High-level executives will feel new motivation to step out of familiar roles and take ownership of company-wide efforts, especially if the new positions have a high profile and significant responsibility for cross-unit efforts, as well as the potential for generous compensation. As one of the account executives in such a generalist role said, new and attractive career paths for generalists "will give people more of a comfort that they're in a core service of the firm, and that even if the account they're managing goes away, we're an account-oriented firm, so they'll just move to a different account."

To further develop career paths, firms can require rotation of key employees across units or silos. Most large companies aren't organized to do this easily, but JLL mandated that account managers spend time within each of the firm's major units to gain greater knowledge of the units, optimize their multidomain skills, and ultimately serve customers better. Customer surveys, in turn, clearly showed the benefits of rotation. As one manager recalled, "We heard about the need to keep the relationship fresh and positive by bringing in new ideas and information regularly. That implies that you're going to have to rotate these account managers." In other words, the career paths of resilient organizations must reflect that resiliency.

Possibly - Stop the assigning of clients to individual CSR.

Influencers Can Lead the Way

Some companies encourage their people to take on new roles by placing key influential individuals on the new career paths. This signals how important the firm considers these roles to be and, by implication, how committed it is to the mission of systemic integration. JLL took this approach with its international directors, a new generalist position it created in 2002. The company placed some of its most skilled, highest-level executives in the job, which made it more attractive to others. As one executive noted, "People have watched as senior, credible, and successful individuals have moved around the organization and taken on new roles that move away from the traditional business-unit hierarchical chain . . . Twelve people have come to me and said, 'If you are starting a list of potential account managers to consider, add me to it.'" Part of the attraction of the international director role was that it represented another, potentially faster way to ascend to senior management. "It means we have many more career opportunities for people . . . instead of being able to get to the top only through a business unit."

Talent Marketplaces and Other Mechanisms Promote New Career Paths

Finally, it's important to create mechanisms for identifying and developing people willing to follow the generalist career path. Some companies have created "talent marketplaces."[14] These are usually modeled after the informal marketplaces most commonly found in professional service organizations such as law firms, universities, and R&D operations. Formal talent markets are increasingly used by large companies such as American Express and IBM as the best way to match employees to available positions in a dynamic and changing marketplace.[15] Such markets provide a flexible way for firms to develop parallel career tracks for generalists and specialists, along with opportunities to move across those tracks. They also can identify people with the capabilities to develop long-term relationships with particular customers.

Some global corporations, including JLL and several high-profile management consulting firms, post all opportunities on their internal Web sites and allow employees to apply for them online. Such marketplaces ultimately strengthen the firm's capabilities by encouraging cross-unit movement and offering generalist career paths, by identifying the people who will strengthen your firm's ability to respond to a shifting industry landscape.

Capabilities and Networking: A Self-Perpetuating Cycle

Restructuring around the customer for resiliency inevitably brings about shifts in capabilities, informal networks, and career paths, but the shifts need not cause cracks in the organization. Promoting shared activities, offering new training programs, encouraging value-creating role residue while tackling debilitating role residue, and developing attractive career paths for generalists all help build a self-reinforcing, pliant platform for systemic integration.

Management Must Support Capabilities Building

No shift in an organization's capabilities can take place without the support of management at the highest levels. Top managers need to be at the forefront, specifying and emphasizing the importance of the new capabilities and career paths, both for individual success within the firm and for the overarching goal of resilience. Even so, executives may still find that the initial steps aren't enough to break through or transcend organizational barriers to growth. Sweeping solutions, often in the context of major structural shifts, may be needed to accelerate the development of customer-focused capabilities and networks.

That was the case for Jones Lang LaSalle at the turn of this century. With the creation of its corporate solutions organization in

2001, JLL was able to position itself as a global provider of integrated real estate services and enjoyed significant top-line growth from 2001 to 2005. But customers also wanted to work with experts in local markets—a capability that some of JLL's resource-rich competitors, such as CB Richard Ellis, could provide.

JLL wanted to follow suit, but lingering rigidities within the company architecture stood in the way. Because roles within the firm were seen as too narrowly focused around select clients, primarily because of the company's service-based structure, JLL had trouble recruiting local employees, especially from its competitors. As one manager said, "Some brokers don't want to come to our organization because they want to do tenant rep or leasing work around a single client," rather than the broader services across multiple clients or broad-based account-focused work they aspire to have.

Peter Roberts, JLL's chief executive officer of the Americas region, realized that he needed to take a completely new approach if he were to make career options within JLL more attractive to both inside candidates and outsiders as well. So in 2005, as discussed in chapter 2, Roberts and his team replaced the corporate solutions organization and the three service-based entities within it with two new units, clients and markets.

An important benefit of the new organization was that it would enable JLL to optimize the division of labor between its account management and local market resources. Account managers in the clients organization would generate much of the transaction activity, and people in the markets organization would execute as needed. Though this seems on the surface like a rigid division of responsibilities, the new strategy actually encouraged greater resilience. Henceforth, both sides would have to understand customer needs at a deeper level than before and combine their capabilities effectively to meet these needs in a truly integrated fashion. At the same time, the markets organization could focus on developing more business in the local markets.

Clearly, this was a reorganization that served many masters, but its greatest lasting achievement might have been accelerating

JLL's development of the requisite capability mix of generalists and specialists. The creation of the clients and markets organizations allowed each unit to focus on developing talent around those key facets. At the same time, colocating staff around clients or markets engendered greater connections among those individuals that furthered outside-in thinking.

To preserve its long-standing expertise in products and services within an organization built around clients and markets, JLL took two major steps. First, some service specialists were embedded in account teams of the new clients organization, while others were assigned to markets organization teams. The expectation was that along with embedding expertise in these organizations, the specialists would stay connected to each other—and this community, while virtual, would keep those capabilities alive. Second, the firm developed and disseminated product expertise through a dedicated Product Management Team within the clients organization. This ensured that product-related capabilities weren't overlooked in the new JLL and that they were used to improve customer relationships through tight linkage with the clients organization. By leveraging the more powerful regional resources of the markets organization, the firm hoped to increase penetration of key geographic markets often dominated by competitors with richer local resources. The new single-service client relationships generated could then be leveraged to sell multiple services, with growing clients assigned account managers from the clients organization as a single point of contact.

This structural overhaul addressed many of the capabilities issues discussed in this chapter. For one thing, by taking an account-focused approach, the clients organization could foster a strong set of customer-focused, multidomain skills that spanned the service silos of the legacy organization. The focus of JLL's previous corporate solutions structure, therefore, shifted dramatically in the clients unit, with customer needs moving to the fore and service expertise becoming the backdrop. In practice, the strong service knowledge of the people in the old organization served the current firm in the form of positive role residue, with newly customer-focused employees falling back on product-centric knowledge and functions in the service of solving customer problems.

The new structure also set up defined career path opportunities that gave people a much greater range of positions and trajectories. As Peter Roberts put it, "Now there are multiple chains of opportunities, and the key is exposing folks to opportunities beyond what they formerly were able to think about. So, for example, we create the ability for people who have been markets people to manage transaction-only accounts and strategic alliances. Now they can think about managing across a geography or a portion of a geography or be a generalist in that geography."

How well JLL's people embrace the new roles and use these to develop deeper and more mutually profitable customer relationships will determine the company's success going forward. As one executive told me, "A wholesale change like this forces everybody to get out of their comfort zone in some way. The question will be, how long can they stay outside of their comfort zone or will they go somewhere else? If they find a new comfort zone, we will be able to adapt and flex more quickly than we ever were able to before."

Change Capabilities as Your Organization Changes

The rule of unintended consequences is hard to ignore. Try as we might to anticipate them, every answer comes with its own unexplored cache of problems. That's why capabilities solutions have to be viewed not in isolation but as part of a perpetual cycle of changes to an organization's architecture. Each new tactic solves a problem or set of problems and also creates new issues that must be addressed. Managers must maintain a clear but flexible perspective on their organizations, especially as a firm nears systemic integration; indeed, by definition, this form of integration is about continuous improvement and an ability to shape-shift in response to turmoil.

A company that is well coordinated, works cooperatively, distributes clout intelligently, and has the right people with the necessary capabilities in the right places to respond quickly to a demanding marketplace has moved very far down the road to resilience. For some companies, in fact, this is a perfectly acceptable end state—at least until customers' needs change.

For most companies, however, these internal efforts at creating a profitable customer centricity will have to be complemented with similar efforts related to people, organizations, and partners *outside* the walls of the company. That, after all, is where you finally want your perspective to lie. "O would some power the giftie gie us," the poet Robert Burns once famously wrote, "to see ourselves as others see us." It's as important in business as it is in each of our lives. Chapter 6 addresses this issue.

6

Lever 5: Connections

Forging External Links to Stay Focused and Agile

THE FOUR CS we've explored so far all will help move a company closer to alignment along a customer axis—a position of resiliency. Using these levers individually and collectively, you can begin to see your enterprise from outside in, rather than through the narrow inside-out perspective of existing silos and other internal power centers. Rather than marching in lockstep with your own products and services, you'll start all discussions with your customers' vantage point—moving to their time, not yours. However, companies hoping to unlock top- and bottom-line growth, and the deepest outside-in perspective, must consider the extraordinary potential value to be created through *connections*—the fifth and final lever for achieving sustainable customer centricity.

What do I mean by *connections*? External relationships, or partnerships, that can provide better cost structures, more advanced capabilities, and a wider range of solution components than a single company could offer on its own. The more effective partners a company has, the better it will be able to handle unpredictable

[handwritten marginalia: focus it seems hard to get funds to bring in new tech, hard to get stuff for exper]

customer needs. In today's credit-restricted context, any one firm finds it increasingly difficult to retain a broad footprint over its own value chain. Nimble firms increasingly focus on a few key activities and partner for the rest. Partnering allows firms to leverage the assets that their partners bring to the table, vastly increasing their potential activities. Their customer solutions can be assembled across a much broader array of offerings—for instance, Apple alone offers a small number of applications for its iPhone, but because of its partners, it can offer *thousands* of applications! At the same time, this model of cross-leveraging assets gives Apple flexibility to move into and out of activities much faster than if the firm owned those itself—a significant advantage in a shifting economy. It is no surprise that well over a billion applications have been downloaded since Apple launched its applications store.

But broadening systemic integration to include external relationships requires that both the firm and its partners act as one to meet customer needs, a far more complex proposition than achieving such integration within a single firm. Happily, many of the tools that apply to internal integration can be applied to external partnerships.

Figure 6-1 shows the barriers and enablers that impact companies that try to embrace connections as part of their outside-in perspective that will be discussed in this chapter.

In the connections arena, the contrast between the less nimble inside-out and more flexible outside-in agendas is starkest. The bunker mentality that surrounds internal business units is magnified exponentially if the bunker is the whole business, and busting through may be exponentially more difficult. But the reorganizations that make firms outside-in through systemic integration *internally* can yield ever greater results when undertaken *externally* across enterprises, given the right partners. A truly resilient, level 4 firm embraces the notion that its raison d'être is not simply to push out as much of its product or service as possible, but rather to begin with a defined customer problem space. Its self-definition

FIGURE 6-1

The fifth lever in your resilience tool kit: Connection

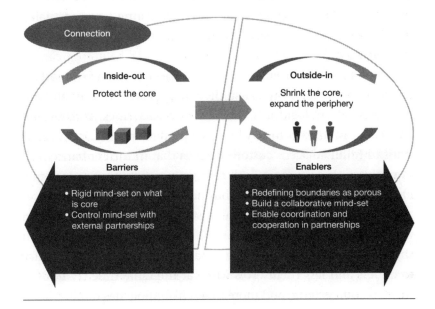

is founded on the problems it wants to tackle, rather than its products. Such agnosticism liberates it to reshape its borders to include
partners who can provide key inputs for completing the customer-
problems puzzle. Building an ecosystem of partners not only gives
a resilient firm access to the best-of-breed for each modular component that goes to the customer, but also gives it the flexibility
to reconfigure partner relationships as customers' needs change or
the mix of customers shifts.

But to effect this sea change, a company must let go of a rigid
mind-set that emphasizes sharp boundary maintenance and
instead embrace a partnering mind-set where interdependence on
a set of external partners is acceptable. In doing so, the firm
becomes adept at identifying, contracting, and managing its
external relationships.

Busting through silos that are *external* to the organization
often enables the company to create a resilient machine that is

Partners could include both in hospital but also vendors

orders of magnitude more powerful than a company that exists in a siloed, partner-free state. In turn, the more good partners a company has and the better its systemic integration with each of them, the better its chances of developing long-term profitable relationships with its customers, which, in their turn, further bolster resilience.[1]

Companies can leverage external connections in two important and complementary ways. First, they can *shrink the core* of the company through strategic outsourcing of select activities. And, second, they can *expand the periphery* by using product and service partnerships to fulfill adjacent customer needs that in turn enhance relationships with customers. Both changes necessitate a fundamental identity shift from defining the business around what one produces to defining oneself around the customer problem space within which one operates.[2] As figure 6-2 illustrates, working on both shrinking and expanding is somewhat paradoxical in that firms try to do less and less themselves while at the same time try to offer their customers more and more much like Apple has done.

already doing billing (suite)

outside computer vendors

FIGURE 6-2

Shrink the core, expand the periphery

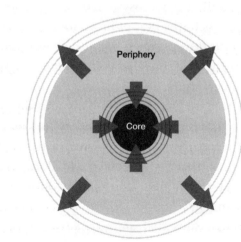

This chapter will examine how each of these approaches can be instrumental in shaping a firm's success, especially in difficult economic times. The shrinkage of the core through strategic outsourcing provides firms with an avenue to cut costs and deliver higher margins without jeopardizing quality and price in any way. At the same time, the expansion of the periphery through value-adding complementary offerings enables firms to stabilize price pressures driven by commoditization while growing volume as well. While the core shrinkage allows firms to drive the bottom line (margin), the expansion of the periphery enables it to tackle top-line (revenue) and bottom-line growth.

Condensing the Core: Do (Most of) What You Do Best, Outsource the Rest

The practice of partnering with suppliers who provide key inputs has exploded in the past several years. By some estimates, global outsourcing is worth over half a trillion dollars annually. *Fortune* 500 companies routinely make billion-dollar deals with major partners like IBM or newer players such as India's Genpact.[3] Such outsourcing not only allows firms to reduce their costs; it also gives them greater flexibility to scale up or reconfigure their inputs from a broad array of specialist suppliers as customer needs evolve. Resiliency can be taken to a new level as firms can quickly and at minimal cost adapt to changing market needs by adjusting their supplier portfolio or by having their incumbent suppliers make those adjustments.

Many companies have redefined their cores and handed over once "sacred" activities—manufacturing, back-office activities, internal business processes, even critical services such as R&D. Every major internal function is now subject to the prospect of outsourcing, and it's a rare one that's performed completely in-house anymore—from logistics and procurement (an estimated $179 billion global outsourcing business), to information technology ($90 billion), customer care ($41 billion), and human resources ($13 billion).[4] With potential partners proliferating everywhere, it's becoming possible to buy almost any comprehensive service offering off the shelf.

Increasingly, companies see outsourcing as a way to reduce their costs without compromising quality. Indeed, in some cases outsourcing may *enhance* product quality, allowing firms to differentiate their offerings further and actually raise prices. This works only when firms work closely with their suppliers and become tightly integrated with them. The same systemic integration that has relevance across a firm's internal silos becomes relevant for firms' partnerships with their suppliers.

The benefits of evolving supplier ties into strategic supplier partnerships are numerous and well documented.[5] In an *Industry Week* survey of manufacturers, 87 percent of the companies that say they have made significant progress toward "world-class operations" employ strategies that involve working more closely with suppliers as partners rather than merely as vendors.[6] As one financial services executive suggested, if you don't outsource, "you won't survive."[7] I would add, "And if you don't integrate with your outsourcing partners, you won't survive long."

Intimate supplier relationships have been especially important to survival in consumer electronics, where successful companies must get their products to market faster than ever. Dell, for instance, has cut the development time for its notebook computers in half over the last decade, and Apple has more than doubled the number of iPod models available annually in the last five years.[8] These firms have leveraged their tightly integrated supplier relationships to achieve impressive results.

Apple's ultrathin iPod Nano is a good example of great results achieved through tightly integrated partnerships for key inputs. Working with Cypress Semiconductor (click-wheel control chip), PortalPlayer (audio chips), and Samsung (flash memory), Apple created a high-quality, best-selling product that achieves an estimated gross margin of about 50 percent.[9] While no outsider can make a precise cost analysis, we can reasonably assume that

Apple's suppliers provide the firm with key inputs more cost-effectively than Apple itself could. And the extensive body of commentary on Apple and its outsourcing practices shows convincingly that the company is aggressively proactive at integrating key suppliers into genuine partnerships, rather than treating them as interchangeable vendors.

Services firms have also entered into the game, successfully working with customers on some of their back-office activities and other services. Today, a whole range of professional services firms—from legal to advertising to real estate management—are aggressively getting customers to outsource key internal tasks to them. Once again, the benefits come from both reduced costs and enhanced efficacy in fulfilling customer needs.

Tightly integrated supplier networks can be a powerful catalyst for resiliency. These networks take some firms far beyond what they could ever achieve alone, allowing them to focus on key customer needs while outsourcing much of the design and development to their key suppliers, as Apple has done. At the same time, by leveraging suppliers that may themselves bring in new innovations, they can develop new products faster, be more responsive to market shifts, and do it all in a cost-effective manner.

Yet despite the overwhelming benefits of tightly integrated supplier networks, developing strong, value-creating supplier relationships is a major challenge, requiring the reshaping of internal and external silos to harness the strengths of both the company and its partners. This is where attention to connections becomes critical.

Redefining What's Core

To build strategic, well-integrated outsourcing relationships, companies need to first recognize which activities they must retain in-house. As *core competence* becomes more popular as an orienting theme, firms have become more willing to outsource noncore activities.[10] Until relatively recently, though, many companies placed rigid boundaries around what they considered core, never yielding these "sacred" activities to suppliers or other partners. Now, those boundaries are shifting and shrinking as companies redefine core competencies as those things they do so well that they become their basis for differentiation. Examples include 7-Eleven's in-store merchandising, Pfizer's drug marketing, and American Express's segment-based offerings.[11]

Today, there is virtually nothing—even core-of-the-core activities—that is not a candidate for outsourcing. Partnerships at this level require significant trust, with the originator of the deal usually retaining some degree of control. Sometimes a company will actually create a network of trusted suppliers by spinning off one or more of its own divisions. The spun-off entity is often able to generate even more value for the parent company by virtue of its external status. Working with a range of customers (some of them competitors of the parent company), the new firm can deepen its expertise via exposure to best-in-class practices while leveraging greater scale. Thus, spin-offs are able to sharpen their focus, developing specialized expertise along with economies of scale that allow them to be more effective sellers, even as they continue to work closely with their parent companies to develop products and perform activities core to the parent.[12]

As a firm condenses its cores, it must become more sophisticated at identifying and creating ties with suppliers so that they can be integrated into its organizational architecture. For years, the pharmaceutical industry resisted outsourcing previously core activities, such as product development. Then, driven largely by the staggering number of molecular compounds they wished to explore and the escalation of the associated R&D costs, big pharmaceutical companies formed partnerships for manufacturing and marketing of their products with biotech firms around the world. The biotech firms are likely to have strong core skills in product development but lack the capital and marketing and distribution expertise of the major pharmaceutical firms.[13] Large pharmaceutical companies also have discovered the benefits of outsourcing development to contract research organizations (CROs) and smaller pharmaceutical firms, many of which are based in emerging economies. Drug giant Merck paid $30 million up front and will pay up to an additional $240 million for rights to a diabetes drug developed by Glenmark, an Indian pharmaceutical player.[14]

Integration Challenges at Bharti Airtel

Bharti Airtel, India's leading wireless phone company, turned the notion of outsourcing on its head.[15] In the process, it discovered just how difficult it can be to systemically integrate a partner that takes over a core-of-the-core activity.

In 2003 Bharti had 6 million mobile subscribers, about 25 percent of the Indian market, and demand for wireless service was growing incredibly fast. That same year, India became the eighth-largest telecom network in the world, with 1.5 million people signing up for cell phone service every month. Sunil Mittal, Bharti's CEO and founder, saw how challenging it would be to build out Bharti's network rapidly enough to meet demand (an estimated one hundred new communities added to the network each month) and to compete with capital-rich rivals such as Reliance and Tata. So Mittal made a difficult and dramatic decision: he signed away the firm's telecommunications network to Ericsson, Siemens, and Nokia—network suppliers with which Bharti already had relationships—and focused his organization primarily on customer-facing activities.

In the mobile phone industry, outsourcing the network is viewed as akin to cutting out the heart of the company. "People gasped in horror," Mittal said.[16] "This is the lifeline of your business, it's something you can't afford to lose," outsiders told him.[17] Colleagues, too, were shocked. "They reacted as if I had suggested giving the family jewels to outsiders."[18] Some of Bharti's high-level managers had significant reservations. But Mittal and his management team stood firm. After all, they already relied on partners for the functioning of much of the network operations. "If something goes wrong with my switch, there's no way anyone from Bharti can do anything about it," said Mittal. "An Ericsson guy is going to have to come and fix it."[19] This highlights the essential nature of systemic integration: if your customer has a problem, it can be a problem for all of the partners in the relationship. Together, you must work to anticipate, solve, and prevent such customer issues.

So Bharti went ahead, signing contracts worth $400 million to outsource the network. Mittal also made a ten-year, $750 million deal with IBM to take responsibility for Bharti's IT services, including its intranet, billing, and customer account management, excluding only telecom-network-specific structures and networks. The contracts also stipulated that Bharti personnel who had been responsible for the outsourced tasks would be transferred to the new partner, reducing the pain of layoffs and ensuring that the transition was smooth.

The new organizational architecture enabled Bharti not only to better predict and control its costs, but also to focus its energies on marketing, new business development, and service innovation. At the same time, by forging long-term connections with suppliers and giving them some "skin in the game," the arrangements ensured that suppliers would remain committed to delivering superior customer outcomes for Bharti. As Akhil Gupta, joint managing director of Bharti Airtel, said, "For the first time in telecom history, perhaps anywhere in the world, the network equipment vendor and the operator would be on the same side of the table."[20]

Although the "reverse outsourcing" has paid off for Bharti, it was a rocky process. Both coordination of activities and cooperation across barriers were required, including clarifying the limits of the relationship with IBM. Some Bharti employees did not wish to transfer to the vendors, so additional motivations and incentives had to be offered. But by staying focused on its key activities while relying on its suppliers for the rest, Bharti was able to keep up with demand and retain its position as India's leading wireless provider, with over 30 million subscribers.

In fiscal year 2006, the company's revenues were up about eightfold from its $509 million in sales in 2003, and its stock was priced at five times its 2003 value. This makes Bharti, with a market cap of $26 billion, the country's fourth most valuable firm. Gupta said that, by pushing the limit of outsourcing, "not only did we sign a terrific set of deals; we have redefined the complex vendor-operator relationship in this industry."[21]

In 2007 Bharti spun off all its cellular towers into a separate entity, Indus Towers, a joint venture co-owned with two other mobile operators that are also spinning off all their cellular towers to this venture. Henceforth, another important part of Bharti's infrastructure will be procured from this external supplier. Building tight systemic integration with its suppliers has allowed Bharti to stay focused on its key tasks and rely upon its suppliers for the rest, leading to a powerful position in a fiercely competitive industry.

Supplier Partnerships on a Ladder of Integration

When companies like Bharti create partnerships that condense the core, they must work to maximize the value of their relationships by climbing a *ladder of systemic integration* with suppliers. That involves establishing and managing a variety of social and contractual mechanisms to progress through four relationship stages: *transaction, enhancement, investment,* and *ownership* (see "The Ladder of Relationship Integration").[22]

Let me emphasize a key point: because the role of suppliers today is much more closely linked to your firm's core, they have much greater influence not only on the nature and value of your offerings but also on your ability to meet customers' complex demands in a timely and effective manner.[23] From being reactive sources that develop inputs based on your specifications, they become proactive partners who codevelop new products and services with you. In this context, suppliers' behavior can have a much greater ripple effect on

The Ladder of Relationship Integration

My research shows that climbing the ladder that is visualized in figure 6-3 often involves using a high degree of *relational creativity* to develop ways that partners can work together—ways that neither side might have imagined before. Not every supplier relationship must reach the highest rung of the supplier-relationship ladder. Rather, you must take into account the context and goal of your partnership and then determine the best level of integration for it.

- The *transaction* rung. On the lowest rung, the supplier is selected for a specific task based on its bid. The main selection criterion is usually price. The required work is well specified, and outputs are easily monitored. There is minimal need for interaction between the partners. Transaction-level relationships are common for the delivery of noncritical commodities whose quality is easily monitored. Long-term relationships aren't common here since firms often play suppliers off each other to constantly drive down costs.

We do NOT want to be this level to our customers

FIGURE 6-3

Steps to systemic integration

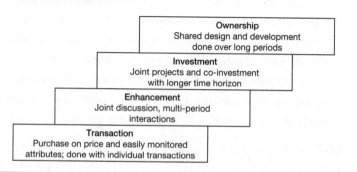

[handwritten margin notes: "Per Se" / "s to our clients"]

- The *enhancement* rung. To climb to the second rung, suppliers and buyers discuss the procurer's objectives for the products and services to be supplied, explore alternatives together, and usually sign a contract that extends the relationship beyond a single transaction. This rung represents the beginning of collaborative problem solving that may have little or nothing to do with the work specified in the contract.

[handwritten margin note: "Medspeed"]

- The *investment* rung. On the third rung, operational and role-specific boundaries begin to blur as the originating partner and its supplying partners seek deeper ways of collaborating to their joint benefit. In some instances, employees from the supplying partner become integrated into the company's operations, or vice versa. This could be a temporary, project-based arrangement (e.g., product development) or part of ongoing operations. As the name implies, this stage can involve increased investment of assets, including physical and human capital.

[handwritten margin notes: "Jues" / "Wellspring"]

- The *ownership* rung. At the highest level, the procuring partner turns over key, often core-of-the-core, activities—such as product development, manufacturing, or marketing—to its partner, which takes full responsibility for their execution. While the ceded work may be taken over in its entirety, managers still need to ensure a smooth and appropriate interface between the supplying and originating partners. In these relationships, the supplying partner has the greatest amount of latitude with regard to how the activities are conducted. Sometimes the supplying partner becomes a true solution provider, coming to "own" a problem area and handling issues however it deems most effective. At this level, systemic integration is imperative.

As firms develop more integrated partnerships, the need for both coordination and cooperation increases. The synchronization of tasks and information, hallmarks of coordination, is absolutely critical in alliances. Firms need to create administrative systems and processes to ensure that they and their suppliers are just as well coordinated as their internal units are. They also need to ensure cooperation among the partnering entities so that the behavior and goals of the two firms are aligned—a thornier issue that companies fail to address at their own peril.[a] At the same time, they have to ensure that issues of clout don't cloud the partnership. Power dynamics can be salient and can sink many partnerships if those issues are not contained and managed.

a. For a comprehensive account of building collaborative partnerships, see Yves L. Doz and Gary Hamel, *Alliance Advantage,* (Boston: Harvard Business School Press, 1998).

a firm's ability to drive customer-centric resilience. Advancing a firm's relationships with its suppliers up the ladder of systemic integration is akin to internal silo busting but requires even deeper and more careful cooperation and coordination.

Starbucks Steams Up Supplier Relationships

When people buy their morning—or afternoon and nighttime—coffee at Starbucks, they enjoy a seamless retail experience.[24] They order their gourmet mochaccino latte and don't think twice about how much behind-the-scenes systemic integration went into satisfying their highly specialized, microniche desire. Starbucks is not just integrated internally around a customer axis; it is an exemplary case of cross-enterprise connections designed to satisfy demanding customers. Inside every cup of coffee sold at Starbucks is the evidence of an architecture of many companies working as one.

The first Starbucks store, opened by three friends in Seattle's Pike Place Market in 1971, sold specialty coffee by the pound, not the cup. At the time, coffee was a commodity. A 25-cent cup was served in thick china cups in diners and family restaurants, and brewed in bubbling percolators at home. Then, in 1982, Howard Schultz came along with a new idea: sell espresso drinks and replicate the environment and sensory experience of an Italian coffeehouse. He and his partners succeeded beyond their wildest dreams. Starbucks created an extraordinary bond with its customers and became much more than just a purveyor of coffee: "We are not in the coffee business serving people," says Schultz, "we are in the people business, serving coffee."[25] By 2006, Starbucks was an international institution, an icon, and a fixture in the lives of its clientele—an empire comprising thirteen thousand stores in over thirty-five countries, with sales of $7.8 billion and net income of almost $600 million.[26]

But by the end of the 1990s, Starbucks saw that its business was in danger of becoming commoditized once again. No longer could a cup of coffee—even with all the variations that Starbucks served in its distinctive environment—provide the company with the growth it sought. What's more, many competitors, including Dunkin' Donuts and even convenience stores, were offering lattes and mistos, usually at lower prices than Starbucks.

So Starbucks sought new paths to growth by reestablishing and redefining its relationship with its customers. It began to offer its coffee products in non-Starbucks locations, including kiosks and cafés, grocery stores, bookshops, and airplane meal carts. Then it sought to enlarge the meaning of the Starbucks brand by branching out into a variety of complementary, but noncoffee, lifestyle offerings, including merchandise, music, and books. A senior manager confirmed, "We recognize that it is not about a store that houses or holds a lot of things. It is about a place that allows a customer experience to happen, and there are things in our stores that are sort of props in the experience."

To maintain its mission of serving people, Starbucks has shapeshifted, becoming a master of making and leveraging connections with external partners. Indeed the "Starbucks experience" that customers enjoy has been built on enduring, multifaceted, well-integrated relationships that allow the overwhelming success of what is essentially a high-priced commodity in a competitive space.

Because Starbucks is so dependent on external relationships, it has developed a rigorous process for finding, selecting, and managing high-quality partners. Representatives from several functional areas, such as purchasing operations, technical product development, and even business unit operations, help the procurement operation understand how a specific supply relationship will affect operations. A major criterion in choosing suppliers is that the potential relationship be mutually beneficial. According to John Yamin, vice president of food, "We want both Starbucks and the vendor to make money. If the vendor is successful as well, they are more likely to stay. We won't go into partnerships where the vendor won't make money or grow with us." Thus, the best supplier isn't necessarily the lowest-cost one. Starbucks's approach to identifying supplier partners ensures that it finds not only the highest-quality ones but also those that are most wired for seamless integration with Starbucks on multiple levels, such as strategy, culture, and operations. Without a pliant architecture *and* mind-set on both sides of the equation, the partnership's resiliency will always be compromised.

Once Starbucks selects a supplier partner, the company forges a strong working relationship. During the first year of a partnership, senior management from both companies meets three or four times, with subsequent annual or semiannual reviews to ensure ongoing commitment, alignment of key objectives, and operational focus in this crucial early stage. This clearly pays off: in many cases, as one manager said, "The suppliers have made recommendations that resulted in reduced supply-chain complexity and significantly reduced costs without having to 'skinny down' their margins." Vendors are coached to ensure consistency and quality of Starbucks products: "We will train their staff on how our products should look, taste, and feel. They will use our proprietary recipes, so we want to make sure they have the skill level to make the product on a consistent basis."

Starbucks also works hard to ensure that its own employees see the value in cultivating positive ties. Internal training programs coach employees on leadership and negotiation skills to enhance the collaboration—for example, by showing how to create dialogue between the partners. One major goal of such practices is to make the partnership work even as positions change and people enter or leave their organizations. As one executive explained, Starbucks seeks "to institutionalize the concepts of partnering such that it doesn't matter who sits in what leadership position in either company." This aligns suppliers with Starbucks's customer centricity, to the point that it becomes second nature: what the supplier does naturally is what Starbucks would want it to do in contributing to end-customer satisfaction and the bottom lines of all parties. As Michelle Gass, vice president of beverage, told me, "The culture is very relationship oriented. It's built on trust."

Starbucks also builds trust with its partners by using a two-way, open-book costing model. The partners can see the company's margins, and Starbucks can review its suppliers' costs. The rewards for the supplier are volume and the boost to reputation that the association with Starbucks brings. And Starbucks gets preferred customer status in terms of pricing, profit percentage, and resources committed.

Starbucks's relationship with its cup and lid manufacturer, Solo, shows how a relationship can climb the ladder from the transaction rung to the ownership rung. According to Buck Hendrix, vice president of purchasing, Solo is "investing in our business in a way that is consistent with our global supply strategies. Solo is right there with us at a strategic level." For example, in 2000, Solo purchased a European manufacturing company, Insulpak, and in 2001 acquired Sanyo Pax, a Japanese disposable container supplier, largely to better supply Starbucks in those regions.[27] In return, Starbucks committed to a long-term global supply agreement with Solo. Thus, Solo and Starbucks are moving into a more systemically integrated relationship, one in which each party makes significant investments in the other while both align their objectives and operations to meet customers' needs as fully as possible.

Perhaps most important to the Starbucks brand is its deep relationship with its coffee growers, the central pillar in its reputation for improving the economic, environmental, and social conditions of the developing countries that supply its coffee beans. Starbucks works with Conservation International to develop sourcing guidelines that promote sustainable coffee farms, and gives preference to suppliers that meet those guidelines. It also works with Fair Trade to help growers form cooperatives and negotiate directly with coffee importers, which are also encouraged to develop long-term relationships with growers and to furnish credit. Starbucks pays Fair Trade prices for its arabica beans regardless of market price—which can fall below subsistence level.

Again, these practices are mutually beneficial. The quality of coffee and the economic benefits have made the cooperatives more stable organizations as the farmers have become more committed to them. This partnership is also a powerful outside-in move. Customers' demand for environmental/social accountability has been increasing steadily, and "going green" is one area in which businesses are not only surviving, but thriving.

By maintaining high-value relationships with multiple suppliers, Starbucks has condensed its way to value creation for itself, its partners, and its customers. In moving up the ladder of supplier integration, Starbucks reveals an important dimension of redefining the core—that through increasingly integrated supplier relationships, companies can become savvier and more mature in how they define core activities, ultimately gaining the confidence and capabilities to outsource more. Thus, redefinition of the core and the use of strategic supplier partnerships works bidirectionally. Firms like Starbucks actually acquire a distinctive capability for managing external connections, allowing them to externalize more work and leverage partnerships more effectively—another way in which resilience becomes a force multiplier.[28]

At the same time that firms like Starbucks, Bharti, and Apple outsource increasing portions of their activities to systemically integrated partners, they are highly attuned to their customers' changing needs. And they are not alone: in their suppliers, they have more than one set of eyes to look at the changing marketplace, more than one set of heads with which they can brainstorm new ideas for products and services, and more than one set of hands with which to deliver those to the marketplace.

To successfully capture the potential of ties with suppliers, firms need to be able to manage the quality of those connections. Bridging the boundaries that naturally emerge when working across organizations is not an easy undertaking. Nor is overcoming suspicion, fear, and territorial behavior to build a cooperative relationship, or coordinating tasks and information between entities that have very different internal systems and processes (also see "Condensing Yourself into an Unprofitable Corner"). But the payoffs from surmounting those obstacles are significant.

Expanding the Periphery: More Hands in More Pots

As companies seek to win in turbulent times, they focus on developing solutions that promote ongoing company–customer synergies. As these solutions increasingly go beyond what is produced within a firm's boundaries, firms must *expand the periphery*, and they can do so in two main ways. First, they can *increase the depth and scope* of their in-house offerings—a strategy that tends to make an already big battleship even harder to turn. Or they can *partner with allies* that have complementary products and services, and the expertise in dealing with them.

When firms discover they don't have all the pieces they need to create effective solutions, they often look outside to expand their capabilities. Although some companies have turned to acquisitions to meet this challenge, an increasing number have started forming strategic alliances.[29] From 1996 to 2001, U.S. companies announced fifty-seven thousand alliances, a rate of over one partnership per hour.[30] The word *alliance* encompasses a broad array of interfirm relationships. Many such ties are between

Condensing Yourself into an Unprofitable Corner and Other Pitfalls of Partnerships

Not every company has mastered the art of condensing the core as well as Starbucks. In some cases, companies have gone too far and have given up something they should not have; in others, they have chosen the wrong partner in the wrong location. But most poor outcomes result from a firm's lack of deep knowledge of what to outsource, to whom, and how to manage it.

One partnership domain where mixed—or worse—results are common is outsourcing across geographies. Geographical constraints and cultural differences often add a layer of complexity to the challenges of integrating a firm with those of its suppliers. Both coordination and cooperation are harder. Several studies reveal that as many as half the organizations that shifted processes overseas failed to generate hoped-for financial returns.[a]

The many pitfalls of condensing the core include:

- *Backing yourself into an unprofitable corner.* Some firms yield high-value core activities to partners and keep the low-growth or less profitable products and processes for themselves. For example, IBM inadvertently lowered the margins it enjoyed in the PC industry's early days by outsourcing high-value components to Microsoft (operating systems and applications software) and Intel (microprocessors). Brand-name companies may become captive to their key suppliers and lose motivation to make ongoing investments in new technology, allowing innovation to reside disproportionately in their suppliers.[b]

- *Enabling a supplier to become a rival.* Partnerships may help suppliers amass the expertise, funds, and scale to compete directly with their partners. Motorola, for example, contracted with Taiwan's BenQ Corporation to design and manufacture millions of low-end wireless phones. Soon enough, BenQ released a similar handset under its own brand name and became the number-two seller of wireless phones in the high-growth markets of China and Taiwan.[c] It then acquired Siemens's mobile phone business, making it the fourth-largest manufacturer of wireless phones in the world.[d]

- *Enabling customers to become rivals.* Customers can also become competitors. Wal-Mart's brand of laundry detergent, introduced in 2001, outsold P&G's Tide in stores soon after its release. The discount retailer's dog food also grosses more worldwide than the brands of Purina, one of its primary suppliers in this category.[e]

- *Misreading the levels of trust.* As partnerships move up the relationship ladder, suppliers earn more trust and are given wider latitude. However, the trust has to work in both directions. A study of a major auto-parts manufacturer and hundreds of its retailers found that the manufacturer trusted most of the retailers, but over half of the retailers distrusted the manufacturer. As a result, many of them were actually "unfaithful" to their big partner and developed alternate sources of supply without informing the manufacturer.[f]

- *Playing (and losing) the power game.* The downside of supplier relationships involves power dynamics—either side with power may exploit it. For example, power in consumer products has shifted from vendors, including P&G and Rubbermaid, to the major retail chains, especially Wal-Mart, which can dictate pricing and other terms with most suppliers.

- *Misallocating value among partners.* In successful partnerships, existing value is not simply reapportioned among the partners; greater value is created and shared. But sharing can be complicated, requiring successful measurement and division

of value such that both parties see a return.[9] Some companies end up focusing more on their share of the pie and in
the process shrink the size of the entire pie for all.

a. Ravi Aron and Jitendra V. Singh, "Getting Offshoring Right," *Harvard Business Review*, December 2005, 135–143.

b. Pete Engardio et al., "Outsourcing Innovation," *BusinessWeek*, March 21, 2005, 84–94, discuss multiple hazards of outsourcing innovation.

c. Adam Pick, "The Rise and Rise of ODM Handset Manufacturing," *Electronics Manufacturing Asia Online*, November 16, 2006, http://www.emasiamag.com/article.asp?id=76; and Pete Engardio, Michael Arndt, and Dean Foust, "The Future of Outsourcing," *BusinessWeek*, January 30, 2006, 50–58.

d. *Mobile Europe Online*, "Siemens Lets Handset Business Go to BenQ," June 26, 2005. http://www.mobileeurope.co.uk/news_analysis/111236/Siemens_lets_.

e. Wayne Goodwyn, "Risk and Reward in Vendorville," National Public Radio, June 3, 2003.

f. Nirmalya Kumar, "The Power of Trust in Manufacturer-Retailer Relationships," *Harvard Business Review*, June 1996, 92–106.

g. Ranjay Gulati and David Kletter, "Shrinking Core, Expanding Periphery," *California Management Review* 47, no. 3 (2005): 77–104.

firms that have complementary products, services, or assets that
they can commingle to offer targeted customers. While some
alliances are for joint creation of a single, higher-value product
(e.g., Sanyo and Taiwan-based Quanta Computer Inc. formed a
joint venture in 2006 to produce flat panel TVs), a growing number focus on collaborating to create complementary offerings.[31]
Take Apple, which partners not only with its suppliers, but also
with a large number of firms that produce accessories for its popular iPods and iPhones, sharing information with these firms to
allow them to get an early start in product development, and selling their products in Apple stores.

The trend toward periphery-expanding alliances has made for
some surprising bedfellows. For instance, 7-Eleven's collaboration
with Anheuser-Busch to develop in-store displays and product

assortments gave the low-end retailer first-look rights to several of the brewer's new products.[32] In return, Anheuser-Busch got access to 7-Eleven's proprietary customer information, which has helped both businesses to cobrand NASCAR and Major League Baseball promotions. 7-Eleven also collaborated with Hershey to create an edible straw based on Hershey's Twizzlers candy, receiving exclusive rights to offer the straw for its first ninety days on the market. To further promote the new product, 7-Eleven partnered with Coca-Cola, its syrup supplier, on a Twizzlers-flavored Slurpee drink.[33]

Teradata, a global provider of business intelligence and data warehousing solutions, has over the years evolved its information technology collaboration with customers to more deeply consultative engagements involving complementary vendors. This evolution has been driven by rapidly increasing business complexity and rising volumes of detailed data companies must capture and manage. A solution was once typically comprising one-third Teradata hardware, one-third Teradata software, and one-third Teradata professional services. In the past decade, Teradata has significantly expanded its role and value in customer engagements by orchestrating more collaboration to include technology and business partners who provide valuable complementary offerings. Such customer-centered periphery expansion has been described as a "two-sided platform strategy." On one side were the collaborative partnerships that Teradata formed with its customers.[34] On the other side are vendor-partners with complementary business software that enhances the utility and thus value of Teradata's offering. As a result, these complementors enable Teradata to expand its periphery by offering up a larger number of adjacent products and services to serve customers with Teradata's core offerings. To succeed, Teradata had to analyze and evaluate customers' underlying business challenges and then inject themselves into those critical areas with offerings that transcended what they themselves produced. At the same time that Teradata is delineating its outside-in solutions, it now also orchestrates an ecosystem of partners to collectively tackle the market with a unique constellation of dynamic solutions.

By forging joint selling and codevelopment alliances, companies not only get their hands in more revenue and profit pots; they
also can become more visible to customers, thus deepening their
customer relationships and further stimulating revenues and profits. Expanding the periphery is not merely about cobranding, providing Web links to partners, or sharing proprietary information
on a one-time basis. Winning firms expand their peripheries by
ascending the ladder of integration with allies. At the highest
rungs, these alliances generate the highest-value solutions for customers and the highest returns for firms involved.[35]

Starbucks Expands Its Periphery

As much as it validates the value of shrinking the core, Starbucks
also models successful periphery expansion and shows how
closely related these two activities can be. Shrinking is a matter of
outsourcing key inputs; expanding is about adding goods or services that complement what you are already selling. A single partner can sometimes serve both ends, another reason why the care
and feeding of connections is so important. As we've seen, Starbucks does not choose partners lightly.

As with its suppliers, once an alliance is formed, Starbucks
insists on tight coordination and cooperation to ensure that the
joint offering provides a seamless customer experience. The systemic integration also enables the partners to conceive of new
joint products. Thus, Starbucks expands its footprint, and these
creative offerings enhance the customer centricity that drives its
success.

Starbucks-allied partners fall into three categories: licensees,
"complementers," and international partners.

Licensing Alliances

Starbucks's most common alliances are *licensing* deals in which
licensees operate what are essentially Starbucks stores within their
own businesses but do not actually own the stores, as a franchiser

would. Starbucks's initial license arrangement—with HMSHost, which operates the largest airport concession in the United States—illustrates how the core is often contracted and the periphery expanded at the same time. Although airports are an attractive target for high-end refreshment retailers, Starbucks had found the market extremely difficult to penetrate. The license arrangement solved that problem—since HMSHost was already there, Starbucks could excise airport penetration from its core concerns. But the arrangement also expanded Starbucks's periphery by allowing it to reach existing and new customers in a retail arena previously closed. So successful was the experiment that Starbucks went on to create licensing arrangements with grocery and retail chains, such as Target and Safeway; hotels, including Marriott; and United Airlines.

One of the company's most successful alliances has been with Barnes & Noble (B&N) bookstores. In some cases, Starbucks owns and operates a retail store in space leased from Barnes & Noble. Other B&N stores operate their own cafés where they sell Starbucks products. Thanks to this partnership, Barnes & Noble is the second-largest coffeehouse chain in the United States, and Starbucks is the bookseller's exclusive provider of coffee, another periphery it would have had trouble expanding on its own.

Such alliances have to be carefully worked out. For instance, Starbucks's relationship with B&N, as successful as it has been, has not always been smooth sailing. Conflict arose when Starbucks began to establish retail stores in the Midwest. Until then, the brand had been available in the region only in Barnes & Noble cafés. After some negotiation, the partners agreed to a set of boundaries, and Barnes & Noble became the primary developer of the Starbucks concept within its stores. Sometimes conflicts like these, if resolved to the satisfaction of both partners, deepen and improve the relationship. But the Starbucks–B&N friction also shows that partnerships are fraught with risk. To make them work you have to be prepared to referee the conflict that is ubiquitous in alliances.

Complementers

Starbucks has also partnered with food companies to expand and
distribute the brand through *complementary* relationships. Starbucks's ice cream is made and distributed by Dreyer's; its Frap-
puccino beverage is manufactured, distributed, and marketed
through a fifty-fifty joint venture with PepsiCo; its packaged coffee in supermarkets is marketed and distributed by Kraft, one of
the company's main competitors in the at-home coffee consumption market.

As hard as it was to make, the decision to work with rival Kraft
has paid off handsomely. Kraft, a strong and experienced con-
sumer-packaged goods company with one of the largest direct-
selling teams in the food industry (thirty-five hundred
salespeople), was chosen by Starbucks specifically for its strength
with grocery chains. "We were looking for someone who had a
presence in the coffee aisle," one executive said. "If you are not a
player there, you can get pushed around"—meaning that Starbucks might ultimately have lost out when it came to how its
product was merchandized.

Another benefit of the partnership is that Kraft uses marketing
tactics unlike those Starbucks has typically employed. One Starbucks operations executive cites Kraft's "barista mobile," to distribute samples of Starbucks coffee, as a prime example of why the firm
chooses to "partner with companies who have an appreciation for
our brand and are both flexible and creative." Indeed, Starbucks
increasingly looks to periphery-expanding partners for innovation.
Barnes & Noble challenged Starbucks to develop an automated
espresso machine that would allow B&N to train its employees
faster and provide more consistency and faster service. The
machine has since been rolled out into all Starbucks retail stores.

Another alliance propelled Starbucks into a whole new drink
category: alcohol. In 2005, Starbucks and Jim Beam Brands Company, a unit of Fortune Brands, announced the launch of Starbucks
Cream Liqueur.[36] The liqueur is sold in liquor stores, restaurants,

and bars, but not in Starbucks coffeehouses, and has drawn a new group of customers who are Starbucks fans but not necessarily typical purchasers of spirits.[37] Within months of release, Starbucks Cream Liqueur ranked number three in the superpremium cordials category, with a market share of 11 percent.[38]

By expanding the periphery, Starbucks has been able to position itself not just as a high-end coffeehouse but as a "purveyor of premium-blend culture."[39] The company has branched out into entertainment products and services, without, as one executive put it, "straying too far" from the original coffeehouse experience. Offering customers CDs of the music they hear in the store has led to many successful promotions. *Genius Loves Company*, for example, a Ray Charles CD produced through a joint venture with Concord Records, won several Grammy awards and sold 800,000 copies at Starbucks stores alone. ITunes, Apple's digital music store, has an entire section of Starbucks cuts.[40] The company has also successfully promoted movies, sold DVDs, and sponsored discussion groups (with free coffee, of course) about best-selling books. The Starbucks creative team has even considered publishing new authors and producing films. Starbucks plans to increase promotions of artists who are not yet household names—"stars in the making," as Timothy Jones, manager of the chain's music programming, says.[41]

These moves have motivated changes to the store design, largely to accommodate new nonfood products. The space devoted to drink preparation has been reduced and reimagined to promote efficiency.[42] Starbucks sees the entertainment-related promotions as adding "to the emotional connection with the customer."[43] Not only do products appeal to customer preferences, but their presentation satisfies another deep lifestyle need: the company simplifies the process of making choices about music— and, increasingly, books and movies—amid an overwhelming glut of options. Ultimately, these changes deflect the pressures of commoditization on Starbucks's core product, and it can continue to sell premium-priced coffee.

Expanding the Periphery, Avoiding the Pitfalls

Expanding the periphery does not always work. Research shows that a majority of alliances end prematurely, almost always damaging partners financially.[a] The failures are due to a number of common pitfalls, many of which are associated with the inability to fully leverage the customer-centricity levers, including:

- *Coordination.* Coordination problems often center around governance, operating procedures, decision making, and resource management. As boundaries between firms blur, defining the rules of engagement becomes paramount. Controls, operating protocols, information exchange, and IT standards must be carefully worked out and embedded in partners' processes. If leadership and accountability are not clearly defined, multiple points of contact can overwhelm the alliance's functioning. Finally, the partnering firms must consider what kind of resources—and whose—should be used in the alliance and whether they should be used separately or in combination.[b]

- *Cooperation.* When cooperation breaks down, issues related to incentives, accountability, conflicts of interest, and competitive dynamics crop up. An important subset of

---

Expanding the periphery can become addictive (and there are other pitfalls; see "Expanding the Periphery, Avoiding the Pitfalls"). "Should we be looking for growth by buying other lifestyle-oriented retailers or specialty food concepts?" one Starbucks executive pondered. "Should we become the 'Starbucks of rice noodles' and leverage our core competencies in operating and real estate development? Or should we be taking the Starbucks brand and

cooperation issues relates to ensuring the confidentiality of any proprietary knowledge that may be shared in a partnership. For example, in some partnerships, previously guarded business processes may be shared with outside partners, and thus firms must take pains to protect intellectual property, especially when collaborating with direct competitors.

Thoughtful conflict resolution efforts go a long way toward strengthening partnerships to avoid turf battles and preserve customer centricity. Contract terms provide some protection but are rarely enough to engender cooperation. Ultimately, cooperation between partners requires trust.[c] This requires a concerted effort by both partners to build mutual confidence and work through relationship issues as they come up.

- *Identity diffusion.* Some companies offer too many products and services, and end up with alliances that are too broad and hard to manage. In trying to be all things to all customers—"customer-compelled," as George Day calls them—they are less able to focus their resources effectively.[d] For example, Sears for a time offered real estate, insurance, and financial management services in addition to its broad range of retail goods.[e] Most ultimately foundered. Such alliances can be seen as "partnerships for partnerships' sake." Companies shouldn't form alliances just because they can.

finding new and different things that coffee can do?" Tempting as it is to expand, you have to control those centrifugal forces that pull you further from the center. Even a resilient organization can be stretched to the breaking point.

International Partners

Finally, Starbucks has expanded its periphery internationally by leveraging the capacities of regional partners, rather than their

- *Myopic expansion.* Some companies neglect to take a customer-based view in the first place, seeking alliances based only on product or service synergies rather than selecting companies that have not only a complementary set of offerings but also a philosophy, strategy, and operational approach conducive to eventual systemic integration. By failing to take a big-picture, outside-in view of their alliance partnerships, they ultimately fail to build a customer-focused portfolio.

a. Gulati and Kletter, "Shrinking Core, Expanding Periphery."

b. Ranjay Gulati, Tarun Khanna, and Nitin Nohria, "Unilateral Commitments and the Importance of Process in Alliances," *MIT Sloan Management Review* (Spring 1994): 61–69; and Yves L. Doz and Gary Hamel, *Alliance Advantage: The Art of Creating Value Through Partnering* (Boston: Harvard Business School Press, 1998).

c. See Tarun Khanna, Ranjay Gulati, and Nitin Nohria, "The Dynamics of Learning Alliances: Competition, Cooperation, and Relative Scope," *Strategic Management Journal* 19, no. 3 (1998): 193–210; and Tarun Khanna, Ranjay Gulati, and Nitin Nohria, "The Economic Modeling of Strategy Process: 'Clean Models' and 'Dirty Hands,'" *Strategic Management Journal* 20, no. 7 (2000): 781–790, for more information on cooperation challenges in alliances. Additional information on the antecedents of trust can be found in Ranjay Gulati and Maxim Sytch, "Dependence Asymmetry and Joint Dependence in Interorganizational Relationships," *Administrative Science Quarterly*, 52 (2007): 32–69; and Ranjay Gulati and Maxim Sytch, "Does Familiarity Breed Trust? Revisiting the Antecedents of Trust," *Managerial and Decision Economics* 29, no. 2–3 (2008): 165–190.

d. George S. Day, *The Market-Driven Organization* (New York: Free Press, 1999).

e. Ibid.

products or services. Unlike with most of its domestic retail stores, which are company owned, the company allows foreign firms to open Starbucks stores in markets in which the foreign players are already well established, providing Starbucks with a larger geographic footprint than it could quickly or easily establish on its own. One of the earliest alliances was with Japanese specialty retailer Sazaby, which opened a Starbucks store in Tokyo in 1995. Starbucks continues to refine this method of international expansion. Foreign allies provide financing and advice on issues pertaining to real estate, regulations, suppliers, labor, and culture. Starbucks provides operating expertise and control.

Developing such long-term, mutually beneficial, customer-focused relationships with suppliers and allies has allowed Starbucks to climb the ladder of systemic integration. Its relationship-building capacity has enabled the company to grow far beyond what it could have achieved otherwise. Skillful use of connections has allowed it to differentiate itself from new competitors entering the premium coffee segment, such as McDonald's and Dunkin' Donuts, and to keep itself in a strong position despite the economic pressures around it.

EDS Saves the Day with an Expanded Periphery

Starbucks has used connections and periphery expansion to add value to an already robust enterprise. Other firms have used connections as lifelines. Consider the case of a well-known tech company that has been using partnerships in an attempt to grow: Electronic Data Systems (EDS).[44] In late 2002, EDS's market position had been declining. This wasn't surprising, given that the firm's competition included IBM and the growing number of low-cost Indian business process outsourcing (BPO) companies. In 2005, as EDS prepared to renegotiate its contract with its largest customer, General Motors—almost 10 percent of the firm's revenues—things looked grim.

CEO Michael H. Jordan, who had joined EDS in 2003, turned to partnerships. He budgeted a $1 billion investment in connections aimed at turning EDS into the leader of a federation of companies known as the Agility Alliance. The group featured ten primary partners, including Cisco, Dell, and Microsoft. Most of these allies already had solid relationships with EDS or had worked with the firm as vendors.[45] By expanding its periphery dramatically, EDS planned to engage in joint product and service development and leverage access to early previews of partners' offerings, ultimately using higher-value solutions to land more contracts. For example, EDS worked with storage stalwart EMC Corporation to develop better ways of managing customers' overgrown IT networks. It also agreed to a $420 million joint venture with HR consulting firm Towers Perrin to take a stronger run at the $3 billion human resources outsourcing market.

These partnerships inevitably involved deep collaboration at higher rungs of the ladder of systemic integration. As Jordan put it, "Our past alliances were meeting for a drink at a bar. This is settling down, sharing an apartment." And the results from its new approach are already evident. EDS is encouraging clients to use, or even switch to, partners' products, creating potential major revenues for allies like Sun and EMC. Similarly, EDS maintains the largest external contingent at Microsoft's partner-development lab, with fifty people on-site. "They are treating us like their own software house," says Simon Witts, vice president of Microsoft's enterprise and partner group. EDS also operates two Agility Alliance Development Centers, where its own and partner-firm engineers collaborate on IT solutions. The firms' sales teams also work together in-house and in the field before submitting joint proposals.[46]

The Agility Alliance didn't need long to show signs of success. In 2000, Weyerhaeuser Company, a major player in the paper industry, pointed to EDS's connections when it outsourced software integration, storage consolidation, and Internet phone deployment to the firm. And the Austrian government granted its first outsourcing contract to EDS on the same basis.[47] In 2007 Coca-Cola FEMSA, Latin America's largest bottler, signed a three-and-a-half-year contract extension with EDS.[48] The periphery expansion strategy has also paid off in the form of favors from powerful friends. In 2004, Scott McNealy, then CEO of Sun, helped bring EDS to the table in negotiations for substantial contracts involving DaimlerChrysler—a major Sun customer. EDS won the contracts, displacing IBM, a rival of both EDS and Sun.

The clearest indicator of EDS's success with connections has been the firm's revived revenues. By late 2006, two years after the Agility Alliance was announced, the partnership network had directly influenced almost $15 billion in sales, including major deals with Kraft and Cardinal Health, provided more than $3 billion of new business, and been a factor in over three hundred contract wins.

Expanding and Condensing at Once—A High-Value Dynamic for Creating Resiliency

Firms that effectively expand their peripheries and condense their cores can generate higher-value offerings (through allies) and potentially enjoy the most efficient cost structures without sacrificing quality (through supplier partnerships). Synergies are likely to arise between the two activities that allow partners to benefit from each other in ways not available if they undertook just one of them.

For example, when a company condenses its core, its suppliers may have to expand their peripheries—by increasing the range of their offerings or finding partners through which to do this—to better serve the firm. This is what real estate company Jones Lang LaSalle did.[49] As its customers shrank their cores and outsourced real estate management activities, JLL expanded its periphery to meet those growing sets of customer demands.

Similarly, when powerful companies condense their cores, they may share expertise with their suppliers and partners to help the partners/suppliers improve performance, which ultimately helps the powerful company improve its own performance. For instance, by improving interpartner distribution logistics (i.e., sending jeans directly from the factory to the retailer), Wal-Mart and Levi's both benefited.

When alliances involve both actions—condensing cores and expanding peripheries—they often need to operate at the highest rung of the integration ladder. IBM, for example, condensed its core by establishing a contract manufacturing relationship with Solectron. To provide better service to IBM, Solectron purchased an IBM repair facility in the Netherlands, thus expanding its periphery. By selling off the center, IBM condensed its core still further and essentially created a stronger supplier. All 102 IBM employees of the Netherlands facility continued on as Solectron employees, including the repair center's manager.[50] Today, Solectron employees are able to move easily between the two companies, sometimes becoming employees of IBM. By condensing its core, IBM has more ability to expand its periphery by offering even more highly integrated solutions to its enterprise customers.

Connections and the Silo-Shaping Levers

As a company moves up the ladder of integration with its suppliers and allies, the relationships tend to become more complex and require much more attention—especially since shifting customer needs will have more complex repercussions. Fortunately, the challenges involved in creating systemic integration with external partners are quite similar to those in overcoming internal barriers and reshaping organizational silos, and the same levers—coordination, cooperation, clout, capability—can be used.

Two of the levers are particularly relevant to the partnerships that result when firms condense their cores and expand their peripheries: *coordination* of work and *cooperation* through cultural elements and incentives as illustrated in figure 6-4.

Coordination

Coordination is about effective information exchange and task management. Thus, for both alliances and supplier partnerships, creating a dynamic and continuously improving interface is crucial for systemic integration. Partners that coproduce or codeliver a joint offering must share information about customer needs. For supplier partnerships, coordination is about ensuring that tasks, whether related directly to customer needs or not, are completed effectively. As suppliers take on more core tasks for their partners, firms must share more customer-related information and practices

FIGURE 6-4

Managing connections

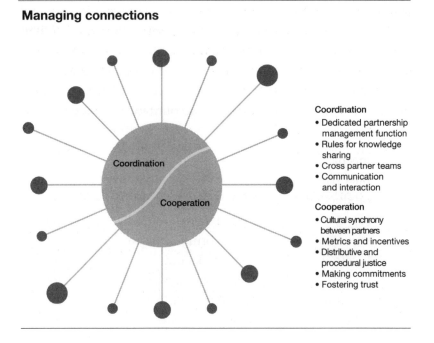

Coordination
- Dedicated partnership management function
- Rules for knowledge sharing
- Cross partner teams
- Communication and interaction

Cooperation
- Cultural synchrony between partners
- Metrics and incentives
- Distributive and procedural justice
- Making commitments
- Fostering trust

with suppliers, helping them to generate inputs that will be part of higher-value customer solutions.

As we saw in chapter 2, synchronizing the efforts of internal units happens largely through formal and informal coordination mechanisms. Coordination among companies also demands a range of mechanisms that vary in formality. Some may be contractually specified, others based upon less formal mutual agreement. Choices include:

- *A partnership management function.* Some winning companies dedicate specific resources to the management of their external partnerships. Designated alliance-management structures have allowed HP, Oracle, Eli Lilly, and Cisco to generate more value through their alliances than their competitors. Cisco, for example, has a senior vice president in charge of corporate development who is responsible for mergers and acquisitions, management of strategic alliances, and technology incubation.[51] Such firms are likely to have a 25 percent higher long-term success rate and generate almost four times as much market wealth as companies without such a function.[52] Alliance managers typically perform a variety of other roles, including knowledge management, internal coordination, and dealing with partnership-related accountability issues.[53]

- *Rules for knowledge sharing.* Specified knowledge-sharing mechanisms and rules are particularly important in supplier partnerships, especially those that involve complex production. Toyota, for example, established a supplier association to promote information exchange and held a variety of social events to bring its network of suppliers together. Toyota also created a unit whose sole responsibility is to gather production knowledge from the suppliers and diffuse it throughout the company. It established other groups to facilitate knowledge sharing between the suppliers and enable transfers of employees between Toyota and supplier organizations.[54] These and other measures have helped Toyota enjoy long-term supplier relationships that contribute to its reputation as a preferred partner.

- *Cross-partner teams.* Cross-partner teams may have a broad charter (e.g., to deal with coordination issues as they arise) or a more targeted one (e.g., to serve a large customer account). Either way, they are the beating heart of systemic integration because they are usually able to develop stronger customer centricity than other ad hoc groups can.[55] Genpact, a service provider based in India, organizes project teams with two leaders: one from Genpact and one from the client company. Together, the leaders rank priorities, define quality standards, monitor the team, and designate levels of compensation.[56]

- *Communication and interaction.* Successful partnerships follow a communications plan that involves regular meetings, feedback methods, education programs, advisory
  councils, and a dispute resolution methodology.[57]

The Importance of Cooperation in Making and Keeping Connections

Within organizations, even the most elegant coordination mechanisms, the strongest emphasis on capacities building, or the most
careful distribution of power won't foster true customer centricity
without cooperation-promoting mechanisms. Cooperation issues
are perhaps even more central to the success of external partnerships—because they affect the apportionment of value among
partners. Winning alliances use cultural elements and incentives
to enhance their collaborations, including:

- *Cultural synchrony before the partnership begins.* Potential
  partners must find ways to become familiar with one
  another—especially regarding cultural norms and values.
  Not only will early familiarity lay the groundwork for systemic integration, but it will surface issues that have the
  potential to doom the partnership. Starbucks conducts a
  careful assessment of the synergies that might exist
  among partners and also evaluates cultural fit, hosting
  Discovery Days, where prospective partners are invited to
  talk about a wide range of issues, including cultural com-
  monalities and differences.

- *Cultural synchrony during the partnership.* Symbols and messages are easily shared, subtly powerful promoters of culture. One Indian outsourcing partner matched the decor of
  its facilities with those of its largest client and posted the
  client's vision statements on its own walls.[58] Rubbermaid

has taken "culture matching" to an even higher level. The company's corporate headquarters includes an exact replica of a section of a Wal-Mart store (Rubbermaid's largest customer), right down to the bar codes on the products. This "layout" room helps Wal-Mart managers visualize product placement and demonstrates Rubbermaid's commitment to making things easy for its customers. Rubbermaid employees on the Wal-Mart account work in an area that is also a replica of Wal-Mart's corporate offices in Bentonville, Arkansas, including walls plastered with Sam Walton wisdom.[59]

- *Metrics and incentives.* Just as incentives within an organization reflect and reinforce the firm's culture and foster cooperation, incentives between organizations can play the same role, but to be effective, they must be based on well-defined metrics and performance measures. One successful practice is to use customer satisfaction figures—or even customer performance measures—to evaluate alliance partnership success, rather than revenues or profits alone. Another route is to define a set of metrics that reflect the goals and objectives of both partners in the alliance: Honda provides top management at its suppliers with a monthly report card that details the supplier's performance based on Honda's metric targets.[60] If there are problems, Honda expects the supplier to develop a plan for remedying them.

- *Distributive justice.* Partners must create a set of metrics to ensure that each receives a fair share of the value a partnership creates. With suppliers, this often takes the form of fair pricing for goods or services provided. As we've seen, distributive justice is built into Starbucks's relationships with its coffee growers.

- *Procedural justice.* While distributive justice pertains to the perception of fair treatment in a partnership from an economic standpoint, procedural justice is about the perception of fair treatment in day-to-day interactions. Research on procedural justice in supplier relationships suggests this form of justice often has stronger effects on relationships than even distributive justice does.[61]

Measures that can help ensure high levels of procedural justice include:

- Communication between members of the partner organizations, at all levels of power and authority, with particular emphasis on decisions and policies, especially those that may seem unfair.

- Impartiality in dealing with multiple partners. For example, a large and powerful party could treat channel partners fairly by ensuring that they all, even the smaller ones, receive an equitable share of the business.

- Providing a mechanism, such as an advisory council, through which small or vulnerable partners can appeal policies and decisions.

- Treating partners with respect and courtesy. This form of justice is particularly important for the creation of trust. Operating protocols and feedback mechanisms—such as visits, interviews, and surveys—go a long way toward promoting the perception of procedural justice.

- *Relationship-specific investments and commitments.* By aligning incentives, partners are more likely to make sticky investments (those that cannot be put to use elsewhere easily) that benefit the alliance.[62] Recall that Solo, Starbucks's cup and lid supplier, purchased a company in Japan and a U.K. manufacturing facility to better supply Starbucks's operations in those countries. In return, Starbucks committed to a longer-term global supply agreement with Solo.

- *Interfirm trust.* Trust is the cornerstone of healthy partnerships. With mutual trust, all parties can shift resources from the monitoring and management of the relationship to enhancing the collaboration.[63] Most important, trust allows partners to make leaps of faith based on their belief that each is interested in the other's welfare and thus unlikely to act opportunistically.[64]

  Trust can be built through distributive and procedural justice, and interpersonal and interorganizational relationships built with experience, as well as through incentives and rewards. It also can be engendered by high levels of mutual dependence between the partnering companies. P&G, for instance, rewards sales managers for enhancing the profits of *both* P&G and its retailer partners like Wal-Mart. Trust is particularly valuable in industrial buyer–supplier relationships, where transaction costs are high and information sharing is key. One researcher found that Toyota, the most highly trusted auto manufacturer, had transaction costs that were about 20 percent of those at GM, the least trusted automaker.[65] This sped up decision making, enabled mutual adjustment, and made the combination more market-responsive.

Resiliency in an Expanding Universe

Connections between firms and other groups have important implications for sustained success. External relationships are a natural extension of the systemic integration that takes place internally. Companies need not only to rethink their organizational architecture and reshape silos to develop a more responsive and resilient customer-centric mind-set, but to look beyond their own boundaries, seeing the organization as a "metasilo"—but one with permeable borders—that can be integrated with others precisely because its boundaries are not rigid. Such networks of external ties, thoughtfully created and managed, might exponentially increase the ways in which firms can respond to shifting economic imperatives.

The frontier of external relationships is still expanding in many ways. First movers can lock out others and consolidate positions of strength by forming exclusive ties. Firms can leverage their existing ties to discover opportunities for new relationships.[66]

In a relational world, advantage resides with those who not only spot relational opportunities first but are agnostic enough about their own identities to leverage those ties fully and know how to foster seamless integration across the boundaries that separate them from their partners. At the same time, they need to remember to continue to break down their internal silos, combining internal with external silo busting to ensure that, both at the core and at the periphery, the perspective belongs not to the offering but to the customer. This is the end point of the quest for level 4 resiliency. And it's what the conclusion is all about.

Conclusion

Road to Greater Customer Centricity

Mapping the Journey to
Greater Resilience

IN 2001, A SENIOR executive who had just arrived at Lafarge North America, a leading cement supplier, asked some of the salespeople about their accounts. "They told me there were just two types of customers," he said. "The ones who like to golf and the ones who like to fish."[1] In a word, aligning around the customer axis meant spending a Friday afternoon on the golf course with the customer contact.

Lafarge's relationship-based marketing (although the firm didn't call it that), was built around pushing product out.[2] And it largely worked. In 2001, the company's operations in the United States and Canada included hundreds of plants, quarries, production facilities, distribution terminals, and some sixteen thousand employees. That year, though, things began to bog down. Seeking further growth through acquisition, Lafarge S.A., the majority shareholder of Lafarge North America, bought Blue Circle Industries, a U.K.-based cement company with a significant presence in

195

FIGURE C-1

The journey across the four levels of resilience

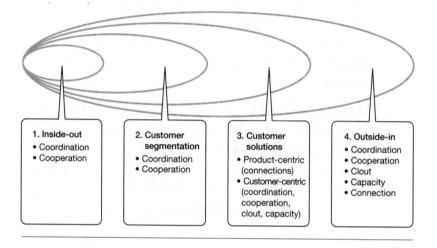

| 1. Inside-out
• Coordination
• Cooperation | 2. Customer segmentation
• Coordination
• Cooperation | 3. Customer solutions
• Product-centric (connections)
• Customer-centric (coordination, cooperation, clout, capacity) | 4. Outside-in
• Coordination
• Cooperation
• Clout
• Capacity
• Connection |

North America, and became the world's largest cement supplier. But greater size did not increase profits. From 2000 to 2001, the cement division's revenues rose just 2 percent, while operating income fell 1 percent.

That's when Philippe Rollier took the reins as president and began the journey to recovery through systemic integration. Lafarge's story is a living example of how the five levers—the five Cs—intersect with the four levels of customer centricity (figure C-1 summarizes how firms leverage each of the five levers discussed in this book as they move across the four levels). Just as important, it shows how even in a commodity industry like building products, outside-in thinking can plot a path to growth, build in resilience, and set success in, well, cement.

The Four Levels

The four levels discussed in the introduction are not only a hierarchy of attainment—that's the outcome, not the journey—but a process of shifting your perspective.[3] They represent not where you are in the marketplace, but the lens through which you view the marketplace and customers.

- *Level 1—Inside-out.* This is a simple inside-out perspective. The company focuses on products and services and their specific features, and its offerings are based largely on the company's existing capabilities and needs: "We make, you take."

- *Level 2—Customer segmentation.* The perspective has swung 60 degrees toward the outside-in view. The company now understands its customers well enough to segment them and organize itself to tailor products and delivery strategies to specific groups: "We know who and where you are, and can use that to encourage you to buy what we sell."

- *Level 3—Customer solutions.* Add another 60 degrees to the perspective swing. The company genuinely understands that the customer has complex, overlapping needs and has organized itself to create customized solutions that deliver real value: "You've got problems; we can deliver solutions."

- *Level 4—Outside-in.* The perspective has swung a full 180 degrees. The company recognizes that (a) it cannot always deliver the optimal solution with the products and services it creates internally but must work with outside entities to do so; and (b) it must be able to rapidly change its own architecture and processes in order to respond to the customer's shifting needs: "Your problems are our problems, today and tomorrow."

As I have stressed, not every company will necessarily need or want to travel the entire journey to an outside-in orientation, but in companies that already experience dynamic interdependence between units or where customer dynamism necessitates sophisticated and flexible responses, outside-in thinking is the ultimate goal—and the way to keep companies healthy.

Level 1. Product Centric: Rigid—and Vulnerable

Inside-out companies are driven by R&D and manufacturing, or service lines. Marketing and sales departments are there simply to push the product. Internal boundaries are well demarcated, and external borders are inviolable. Such companies have little or no cross-unit or cross-product coordination of activities; clout rests with the units most involved in developing the offerings. Capabilities, incentives, and corporate culture all center on products and services, and the company makes scant use of external partnerships.

There are two main types of product-centric firms.

- *Product or service maestros* produce superior products or services through a focus on quality and innovation.

- *Low-cost leaders* offer the lowest possible prices for their goods and services based on a very-low-cost structure.

Both are characterized by the simplest form of interdependence between units. Centralized corporate resources (such as shared R&D or back-office functions) capture limited operational synergies or promote production- or marketing-focused enterprise-wide programs. Performance metrics and incentives are designed around products or services, and specialist employees will move along career paths within product-based or service-based silos. Senior managers, meanwhile, strive to optimize the company's portfolio of offerings while pushing for more efficient production and delivery.

Lafarge, with its historically inside-out modus operandi, was just another competitor in a commoditized market. Its lack of differentiation or customer responsiveness in a tightening market was costing it. When it began to seek new paths to growth and got into acquisitions, it had to become more customer segmented—and "golfers versus fishermen" was not going to be a meaningful distinction.

Level 2. Customer Segmentation: Beginning to Bend for the Customer

Customer-segmented firms remain focused on product development or operational excellence. But they start asking customer-related questions such as, "Who's buying our products and services?"

Often, hard times (read, declining financial performance) will stimulate the shift from inside-out to customer segmentation. Organizations may use their deeper understanding of customers to stimulate cross-selling through coordination between product or service lines. They also often commit more resources to their marketing department or to outside marketing specialists by, for instance, using focus groups and quantitative surveys to identify customer segments.

But while a company can gain insights from these moves, it doesn't necessarily establish disciplined processes for translating insights into action. Marketing departments often have limited power and may speak a language that's foreign to most other units. Externally, the borders are holding firm—no one is talking about extensive alliances, much less seamless partnering—but internally, the boundaries are loosening up. Still, even when insights are shared, marketing's messages aren't always heard by line managers or R&D. To bridge this cross-functional divide, firm leaders must use the five Cs—as Lafarge's cement division did.

Identifying Three Customer Segments at Lafarge

In the face of declining profit, Rollier tasked Lafarge's cement division with finding creative ways to stimulate new growth. Management responded initially by reorganizing Lafarge North America into five geographies, each with responsibility for sales, manufacturing, distribution, and customer support for its *region*, not for a sole *product*.

The next step was to reorganize the five new geographies around customer segments—but to do this, Lafarge needed to know the precise groupings around which to create the new modular units. Lafarge knew everything there was to know about Portland cement and cement-related materials; it had even developed a variety of cement-related services. But except for the people who dealt directly with customers, Lafarge didn't understand its customers well enough to define segments. As one manager put it, "Our plans historically had focused on . . . 'What do we make?' 'What *can* we make?' and 'What is convenient for *us*?' And telling the customer, 'Here it is.'"

Lafarge had run into one of the first barriers to aligning its operations around the customer: its traditional product-centric organizational architecture. To begin overcoming its inside-out mind-set, the division raised its marketing department's profile. First, it persuaded some of the division's regional executives to sponsor the new plan and began sending regular memos about the new effort to the general managers of the cement division's forty-five business units. This eventually helped the business unit leaders take more collective responsibility for marketing efforts, as well.[4]

Under the direction of Jim Braselton, the division's senior vice president of marketing and sales, and his colleagues, the division used market research and marketing-strategy consultants to generate a customer segmentation. At the outset, the most basic terms had to be defined: even the definition of *segment* varied from unit to unit. Finally, four business units were chosen to serve as pilots. Eventually, the team segmented ready-mix concrete suppliers (the division's largest customer group, accounting for 70 percent of revenues) into three categories:

- *Basic buyers* (which bought 32 percent of Lafarge's ready-mix concrete) were price sensitive, and their purchases were not influenced by the product's performance characteristics or Lafarge's level of support or services.

They were typically smaller concrete suppliers serving companies doing basic construction (such as sidewalks), or higher-volume suppliers that used their size to negotiate lower prices.

- *Relationship buyers* (18 percent of the ready-mix business) were usually family-owned suppliers operating in a specific region. They typically lacked the technical resources (such as lab equipment and specialty technicians) for sophisticated concrete work and were thus willing to pay higher prices in exchange for support and services such as market intelligence (including figures for regional housing starts or GDP growth) and help with making joint sales presentations to large clients (such as municipal airports).

- *Performance buyers* (50 percent of the ready-mix business) manufactured and sold specialized concrete for large infrastructure projects, including high-rise construction. They typically maintained a large network of concrete-manufacturing plants and relied on Lafarge's sophisticated lab facilities to meet the testing requirements of their large customers, which mandated regular testing of concrete to ensure consistency in strength and curing times.

Lafarge then separated each of these three segments into "high-tech" and "low-tech" customers, according to their specific technology needs. Sales teams and marketing organizations of each regional unit were tasked with assigning current and potential customers to one of the three segments and developing segment-specific, multiyear action plans for top- and bottom-line growth, based on each assignment.

Benefits and Added Complexity of Segmentation

The segmentation initiative was the first step to melting boundaries within the organization. For starters, managers and employees began using a standard language to discuss their markets and customers. As Manuel de Miranda, the division's vice president of strategic marketing, explained, "Everyone talks about customers as . . . relationship buyers, basic buyers, and performance buyers, and there is now a lot of commonality across the marketing and sales functions and across geographic regions. They are all looking at their markets in the same way, using the same prism." Jim Braselton added that having a common language "created an entry gate to a discussion with customers that is more focused on our offer and their needs because prior to that, you wouldn't be able to narrow the scope of the discussion, so you might be all over the map."

As Lafarge began tailoring products and services to the needs of different customer groups, cross-unit cooperation emerged. Relationship buyers did not normally have their own lab testing capabilities, but many still needed the concrete to meet certain specifications for their own customers. Lafarge decided to start offering the firm's lab testing services to these buyers—and this meant that the division's product and testing units had to work together. The new relationship paid dividends, in the form of an increase in incremental revenue.

The new emphasis on segmentation also caused some organizational upheaval. Each region's sales districts developed segment-specific action plans that required tight coordination and cooperation between their sales, distribution, and manufacturing functions. To support a plan offering performance buyers a guaranteed supply of cement from a particular plant, the relevant plant manager would have to agree to manufacture enough cement to meet customer demand, and an area distribution manager would need to ensure the cement's on-time transport from the plant to appropriate distribution terminals.

To secure this coordination and cooperation, Lafarge assembled an advance team for each plant within a region. These cross-functional groups comprised a plant manager, a district sales manager, an area distribution manager, a finance person, and occasional representation from other functions such as HR. As one manager recalls, "We did this to get alignment, to get buy-in. For example, a finance manager who sits in the head office of the Montreal region is actually a leader of one team. Why? Because he needs to understand the manufacturing implications, the difficulty that distribution needs to go through, the issues that sales forces have whenever they deal with customers." The teams met at least monthly to evaluate whether plant and distribution groups could deliver on the sales district action plans; they also participated in the division's annual strategic-, operational-, and budget-planning processes.

Unfortunately, because advance team members had different functional responsibilities, they often had conflicting interests. Area distribution managers cared most about operating and freight costs, district sales managers about product pricing, sales volumes, and market share—and so on. To break down these legacy silos and align divergent interests around its new consumer axis, Lafarge inserted specific action-plan goals into each team member's individual performance plan. For example, if an action plan stipulated a certain amount of blended cement be sold to particular performance buyers at a certain price, this amount was specified in the sales targets against which the district sales manager's performance was measured. Advance team members rated each other's annual performance, including information on how these individuals interacted with their peers and the degree to which they demonstrated teamwork skills. To put additional weight behind the new process, these evaluations directly affected the size of team members' annual salary increases.

The division further stepped up efforts to improve cross-unit cooperation by reinforcing that customer orientation was a central value. Employee education programs provided hypothetical cases, and employees discussed ways to better meet customers' needs and improve sales—for example, a customer calling to say he's facing a construction delay and will be postponing his purchases from Lafarge. In the past, employees might have simply accepted the situation and lived with the financial consequences.

But a customer-focused response meant probing into the cause of the delay. If it derived from, say, soil instability caused by water saturation, a Lafarge representative could then explain to the caller how fly ash, one of the company's new products, could help reduce soil moisture and improve stability enough to initiate construction on time. Of course, to make such recommendations, employees needed to cultivate new capabilities and become generalists with broad knowledge of Lafarge's offerings—a critical shift away from the silo mentality.

Lafarge had begun to differentiate itself from the competition, and to gain customer share and loyalty by wrapping its offerings and parts of its organization around the customer. It was healthier, and realized that continuing on the path to alignment would make it more robust yet. Lafarge was ready for level 3.

Level 3. Customer Solutions: The Quantum Leap Toward Resiliency

The solutions stage represents a quantum leap on the journey of systemic integration and thus yields major competitive advantage and financial returns. But this 120-degree shift toward an outside-in perspective is also the hardest advance to make. Coordination and cooperation efforts, first launched in the customer-segmenting stage, must be stepped up, and clout and capabilities become increasingly important. Internal boundaries, of necessity, have become pliable. Some firms entering this stage also establish limited external connections, to boost the value of their customer solutions.

Mastering this stage requires both a dedicated shift from selling products or services to solving specific problems, and an often unexpressed migration of self-perception. In a subtle but important shift, a company's identity starts to be defined not just by its offerings but from the customer problem space it chooses to address, from primarily boosting customer purchasing to raising customer satisfaction to enhancing customer success.[5]

To deliver solutions, firms must first be armed with a detailed segmentation of their customer base. Unlike in level 2, however, the focus is not on positioning products and services for each segment, but rather on developing a holistic understanding of these discrete groups—finding out what keeps the customers in each segment up at night. Knowledge of key "pain points" lets companies explore how their products or services, or some adjacent offerings that they can easily develop or acquire, can address those concerns. The goal is to find not only desirable offerings but critical issues customers either can't or won't tackle themselves.

As the solutions-oriented company reassembles its assets to meet the customers' needs, level 3 firms may discover a mix of products and services from across their own units that will solve customers' problems. Or they discover opportunities to create or acquire new offerings. These combinations are sometimes customized for individual customers; in other instances, they are built as scalable platforms for large groups of customers. Either way, they are positioned as solutions that customers prize and are willing to pay handsomely for. By focusing on delivering a mix of offerings driven by specific customer needs, these firms deflect commoditization pressures and partake in a portion of the value that they create for their customers.

Barriers to Entering the Customer Solutions Level

Because moving into the solutions stage requires such broad and deep integration work, most firms stay stuck at a previous level. Ironically, many don't even realize they're stuck. They embrace the terms *customer centric* and *market-driven responses* without understanding what they really mean—the shift in identity that the company must make to place customer needs first in all strategic and tactical thinking.

Moving to the solutions stage involves deep integration work in every dimension of firm life: strategic focus, structure and processes, culture and incentives, power, capacities, and career paths. In the systemically integrated firm, these elements, aligned with the integration domains of the first four silo-busting levers, work to create a flexible and diffuse customer centricity that can adapt to today's more complicated and unpredictable market demands. The challenge is great, but the rewards are greater.

Because a solutions orientation means providing value for clients, rather than simply selling them quality products, value drivers become paramount. To discern, and even solicit, customers' needs and dreams and then reorganize one's own company around those dreams requires a major psychological shift in the organization. The company has to learn to need as the customer needs. Indeed, the two become partners in need.

Lafarge Moves to a Customer Solutions Focus

Having sharpened their focus through customer segmentation, senior managers in Lafarge's cement division set out to improve profitability. Their plan? To identify which of the firm's offerings generated the most value for each target customer segment and then to work across units to deliver those solutions to the appropriate customers. For each sales district, the marketing team developed a list of what directors called *currencies*—product attributes, services, promotional tools, delivery options, pricing techniques, and sales approaches that had potential value.

Marketing then prioritized these currencies based on the relative value they created for each customer segment. To do this, it used two external resources: a market research study listing the factors customers considered while selecting suppliers, and a report identifying which product and service attributes had the most favorable impact on customer satisfaction for a broad cross section of customers. The prioritization process whittled the original list of 114 currencies down to 40.

The marketing group then enlisted a pricing-strategy consulting firm to help conduct interviews with sample customers from each segment. The intent was to ensure that the narrowed list of value drivers correlated with the needs of the division's actual customers, as well as to discover any additional value drivers that might have been missed. The conversations were not prescribed around the list of value drivers but were open ended around the customers' needs and concerns. The interviews generated a wealth of information, including insights related to recent trends among end users. The marketing team isolated nineteen value drivers expected to resonate with customers and developed a pricing framework consistent with customer perceptions of the proposed currencies' values.

Lafarge made savvy use of clout and cooperation here. Though it hadn't endowed its marketing department with any greater formal authority, the cement division had elevated marketing's influence by mandating it to take the lead role in identifying customer value drivers. Similarly, the division's internal units and functions couldn't have contributed insights into the value drivers without extensive cross-boundary cooperation. Clearly, the division's increased resiliency was paying internal dividends, but no one could be sure that customers would value the currencies until Lafarge actually tried to sell them: "The proof will be in the pudding as to whether customers are willing to pay," acknowledged Braselton.

Rolling Out the Offerings

With a clear pricing strategy in place, Lafarge was ready to roll out an initial set of high-value offerings to customers. Senior management decided on twelve for which the capabilities already existed—albeit in scattered form—within the company. Even so, pulling the elements together would be a challenge. As one executive told me, "Many, if not all, of those currencies are cross-functional between sales, marketing, distribution, and manufacturing. And so we have to ensure a line into those functions, such that everybody works together to deliver as one." Silo busting and systemic integration were drawing these functions together. If the confederation worked, success would break Lafarge out of the commodity trap in which it was competing on price alone.

To prepare for the rollout, Lafarge rebranded the offerings under the banner "performance innovations." Since variance in the sales and delivery processes associated with these performance innovations would undermine Lafarge in the eyes of its customers and defeat the entire effort, the teams were created to develop standard operating procedures for the twelve vanguard currencies.

Achieving this kind of consistency would require strict coordination across units. SOP teams included frontline sales representatives, technical sales experts, and district sales managers. The teams also drew on support from HR and other functions, including people with P&L responsibility who, as one executive explained, "brought in a commercial sort of filter to make sure the technical guys weren't going too deep into technical stuff and delivering engineering solutions that weren't sellable." Thus, the SOP teams served as powerful cross-unit transcenders, ensuring that sales and delivery practices were optimized and standardized across geographic units.

An example: The SOP teams developed standard slide sets to be used in all presentations related to a given offering, along with stipulating the number of specific products technical representatives were required to support, when these representatives should be engaged, and even the time the reps needed to spend on an offering. The SOP teams even stipulated the specific language to be used in discussing a given currency. The teams also helped train sales reps in using these standards—a multipronged attack on the company's old silo thinking.

Additional Cross-Unit Activities

Lafarge has implemented several other cross-unit coordination mechanisms besides the SOP teams.[6] Most recently, it defined six regional networks, each comprising the marketing and sales managers from all units in the region. Six times a year, members of these networks visit a local unit's "problem" customer, touring the site and discussing the customer's concerns with them. The members then develop a solution, which is implemented by the host unit. The following year, the network conducts a joint follow-up to check on the progress at that location. Such shared activities provide participants with concrete skills and capacities to tackle emergent market issues and promote greater interaction and informal connections among these units while also creating an enduring bond with the customer.

Lafarge also reshaped its culture to further emphasize customer centricity and systemic integration. Along with top management exhortations, the company introduced metrics to monitor and incentivize behavior. In 2005, for example, the firm began using a standardized customer satisfaction survey to highlight areas requiring urgent unit attention. The survey helped the central marketing team spot issues requiring a firmwide response (e.g., customer-focused training needs) and provided a measure of annual progress.[7] The insights produced have prompted the division to create a new customer-focused measure known as OTIFIC (on time, in full, and invoiced correctly) deliveries.[8]

These efforts—and the advantages they provided—bolstered the marketing department's influence. With greater clout, the department could more easily focus the rest of the organization on creating value for customers. Marketing upped its influence by reminding the units how its own activities directly affected their bottom lines. A former marketing leader explained, "If regional heads want to cut a marketing expense, they now realize that the cut will almost certainly affect future revenues."[9] As one key indicator of marketing's raised profile and greater power within the firm, regional heads, who had rarely focused on marketing during their unit visits, now typically discussed marketing plans at length and often spent time with at least one customer when they made the corporate rounds.[10] As one executive stated, "Lafarge can now count marketing as one of its core competencies."[11]

Lafarge's enhanced customer centricity generated impressive business results. According to its own estimates, by 2007 the marketing function's accumulated contribution to the division's bottom line was $150 million, the equivalent of a 2 percent price increase. This was expected to rise in 2008 to approximately $260 million, which would translate to a 3.5 percent price increase.[12]

Level 4. Outside-in: The New Protean Organization

At the customer-centric level, the perspective has swung around 180 degrees from the inside-out, product-centric model. Outside-in companies have truly internalized the notion of *solve, not sell.* They've broken down internal rigidities and become agnostic about their own external borders. Their goal is to solve customers' problems by *any* means necessary, including those outside the firm. Thus, in addition to coordination, cooperation, clout, and capability, an outside-in firm actively cultivates the fifth level— connections with suppliers and other allies to bolster the value of its solutions by expanding its periphery while at the same time seeking out ways to cost-effectively shrink its core.

This is the highest level of systemic integration, as all the company's systems—internal and external—have been aligned around delivering the best possible solutions to customers' complex problems. Pliancy has been maximized. Level 4 companies can bend in whatever direction customer exigencies dictate. Resilience is a given. But level 4 is also an evolutionary response to the rise of the customer. As customers have become more and more accustomed to a wide range of choice, high quality, and low cost, they have learned to shop the world. Customers have become brokers-of-one in the marketplace. And as they have become increasingly sophisticated in their demands and increasingly agnostic themselves to brands, countries of origin, and virtually all the other points of distinction that once dominated the sales equation, the very definition of maximum outside-in—and the basis of business survival—has evolved with them.

A customer segmentation focus was fine for customers that mainly wanted to be recognized as unique, and it's generally still fine for companies that exist largely outside the flames of commodity hell. Its successor, a customer solution focus, was also cutting-edge when customers could still be dazzled by firms that shifted their identity to solve their unique problems; that, too, is still enough for many companies. But as borders have disappeared in the marketplace, many customers have also come to expect borders to disappear within individual marketers. The question isn't *What can you do for me with what you have?* The question is *How can you meet my needs?* Period.

Organizations that answer *that* question satisfactorily, my research has shown, are the most likely to escape the commodity trap. They maintain an outside-in perspective on their business, putting themselves in customers' shoes and forging strategic, seamless partnerships with multiple groups: suppliers that can provide key solution components or perform important functions; allies that offer complementary products and services; and even customers themselves, which get involved in developing the very offerings they buy.

This calls for a firm to integrate itself with numerous players that provide key inputs, while at the same time orchestrating the multiple outputs needed to serve the customer. Truly resilient, customer-centric firms must use the first four levers—coordination, cooperation, clout, and capabilities—to dissolve boundaries between their own internal silos even as they forge connections to external partners. A prototypical firm at this stage acts like a general contractor, coordinating the activities and offerings of internal and external organizations—business units, functional groups, suppliers, allies, consultants, customers—to develop and deliver the highest-value solutions, generating the highest level of company–customer synergy, and reaping the consequent rewards.

Such a firm will typically organize itself around customer segments, then insert product specialists into segment-based units to ensure that they can assemble the best possible offerings. Specific product organizations will probably remain, but their primary function is to support the customer-structured units. Front-facing units such as sales and marketing set the strategic direction. At this level, external connections become superactive. Firms offload noncore activities to strategic partners so they can focus on the activities that give them the sharpest competitive edge, or they partner with key allies to provide offerings that, when combined with their own products and services, deliver even more value to customers. No product, service, or function is so "sacred" that it must be kept in-house. And all key performance metrics are related to customer outcomes.

Moving into level 4 requires a major shift in the definition of what a company is. A level 4 firm operates as a many-faceted, porous entity that blends with other entities, even competitors, adding or shedding facets as needed to extend the most valuable and profitable solutions to its customers. Thus, a level 4 firm must recast its identity not so much around a set of products or services that it produces and sells, but rather as an entity whose raison d'être is defined around a set of target customers and their problems. Indifferent in its sales efforts about what it produces, the firm focuses on seeking the most effective ways to address customer issues either with its own offerings or with those of others. In some instances, it might even provide external options to a customer when its own offerings (partnered or otherwise) fail to fully solve a problem or meet a particular need.

Not surprisingly, many business leaders are reluctant to form connections with outside entities, especially rivals. Many firms are unwilling to outsource activities they already perform well and to share their most intimate secrets with customers, never mind competitors. Who can blame them, given the high failure rate of business alliances? Even in the best of times, it's not an easy thing to imagine putting your organization on shaky ground. Paradoxically, though, as the ground in the marketplace turns to quicksand, a web of connections may be the thing that holds companies up. While many studies have shown that the majority of all business alliances fail to deliver the intended results, select companies defy the odds and have a much higher success rate with their alliances.[13] Their success comes from the application of systemic integration to their external partnerships in the same way it is applied to internal silo busting. Both applications build resilience—first within the organization and then in its relationship with customer needs. And the resilience, in turn, allows the organization to bend with the episodic storms that rip through the economy.

A truly customer-centric company overcomes the unease inevitable with such a sweeping transition and focuses on building relational capabilities that allow it to discover and enter productive partnerships more frequently than others and then align those around its customer mandate. Does such an organization exist? Yes and no. No company is fully and seamlessly customer centric, but winning enterprises—like Lafarge—are approaching this paradigm, especially through their use of external connections.

Connecting Across Industries at Lafarge

As Lafarge moved into the solutions-focused stage of systemic integration, it recognized the need to take yet another step: it began to ally itself with firms offering complementary products and services.

For Lafarge, safety—its own and that of its customers—has long been a core value. The company had always strived to improve its customers' safety record, and not only in their use of Lafarge products. Lafarge first put together its own training program about reducing on-the-job injuries at, say, construction sites, but managers soon recognized that they could create an even more valuable program by partnering with a firm that specializes in this service, and identified Tennessee-based PureSafety. Lafarge now offers its customers PureSafety's online training modules as part of a packaged safety-related combination.

The second partnership involved a more complex offering. One of the high-impact currencies Lafarge had selected was a business audit for customers. The company spotted the potential for this currency as it began working more closely with customers to improve their use of Lafarge's cement products. As one executive told me, "We recognized that there was room for improvement along several aspects of the business chain, ranging from preventative maintenance to cement mix optimization to upselling to our clients' own customers." A business audit would involve "looking at customers' entire P&L and using best-practice metrics to identify potential deficiencies and generate recommendations to address these."

Pretty smart, but—as Jim Braselton explained, "We clearly did not have the internal capability to deliver that." Rather than abandoning the currency or referring customers elsewhere for it, Lafarge joined forces with Roebuck Consulting Group, which offers business audits to companies, including those from Lafarge's target segments.

Though still in its infancy, the plan is for Lafarge and Roebuck to offer customers analysis and recommendations in the area of "overall business improvement." Specific dimensions covered will include revenue enhancement, manufacturing effectiveness, and efficiency, logistics, and organizational effectiveness. As in the PureSafety alliance, everyone will win if this partnership works as expected. Lafarge will gain the capabilities it needs to develop a business audit offering. Roebuck will achieve access to the market represented by Lafarge's customers. And customers will get a service that enables them to burnish their own bottom line. Expectations are that customers will be happy to pay a premium for it, enhancing Lafarge's bottom line as well.

Outside-in and Seamless Partnering at Apple

In contrast to the cement industry, the world of high-tech consumer electronics has more energetically embraced strategic partnering.[14] As we've seen throughout this book, Apple's iPhone represents a virtual global village of suppliers and partners. Another phenomenally successful product, the iPod, shows how profitable such partnering webs can be.

The iPod has given rise to a periphery-expanding accessories industry valued at over $1 billion and boasting everything from iPod-compatible portable speakers and music-player cases to, yes, toilet paper–holder docking stations. In 2007, more than one hundred thousand airplane seats on four airlines were retrofitted to enable travelers to charge their iPods and view iPod-downloaded videos on seat-back screens. Perhaps the most integrated iPod-related partnerships have cropped up in the auto industry. Since BMW first debuted iPod connectivity (through a glove compartment connector) in its 2004 model-year cars, many automakers have followed suit, including Chrysler, Ford, and Honda. GM is even offering the iPod rotate-and-click interface on the center console of its 2008 Cadillac CTS.

Such partnerships require a high level of integration—GM and Apple will need to share more information about their next-generation products and even suppliers (e.g., of click-wheel parts) to ensure compatibility. For Apple's allies, partnerships also come with something of a dark side: the company is notorious for imposing its expectations related to design and other aspects of all deliverables on its partnering firms, and it doesn't hesitate to sever ties when these expectations aren't met. "It wasn't a malicious thing. It's almost machine-like," says Gary Johnson, former CEO of PortalPlayer, which was sold for half its peak market cap in 2006 after Apple decided to stop using its chips in later-generation iPods. Apple, in effect, practices a sort of "forced integration," a blunter version of the guiding principles that Starbucks provides to its prospective and established suppliers. But high-value partnerships have helped many of Apple's core products achieve astonishing dominance in the marketplace. By codeveloping products through tightly integrated relationships, Apple and its allies have cultivated long-term relationships with the most important partner of all: the customer.

Journeys Need Leaders

None of what I have described in this journey up the four levels can happen without leadership that appreciates maximizing resilience and understands the challenges of achieving it. Executives at the firms I researched for this book got it. They rallied their management teams around the vision of an outside-in orientation as the driver of lasting resilience. They understood the strategic value of the four levels and presented compelling visions of how best to use the five Cs to climb them. And they drove the required structural and cultural transformations throughout their company.

More important still, their own perspectives migrated from inside out to outside in. These executives began to see their offerings not in terms convenient to the firms or their existing silos, but those dictated by their customers' needs. The problems these CEOs and senior managers set out to solve were posed by their customers, not by their own products and services. Finding solutions to these problems became the guiding principle of the corporate architecture, from bridging silos to blowing them apart, from shrinking the core to expanding the periphery.

The personal pliancy of these leaders became the corporate pliancy of the companies they led. Their individual resilience morphed into a suppleness that has pervaded entire organizations. At the very extreme, these leaders were flexible enough, confident enough, and focused enough to dissolve their firms' old being almost into nothingness and, out of near nothingness, to create a new path to survival and prosperity in a marketplace roiled by declining output, prices, and profits.

True Resilience Through Boundaryless Behavior

No firm that I know of has completely attained my definition of *truly seamless*, but companies such as Jones Lang LaSalle, GE Healthcare, Best Buy, Cisco, and Lafarge (the cement division) are well on their way to a high level of *internal* seamlessness. And all use the four internal levers of silo busting—coordination, cooperation, clout, and capabilities—in concert to drive strong customer centricity and to pull perspective from inside the firm looking out to outside it, looking in. This is the heart of systemic integration: the harmonizing of silo-busting measures across multiple dimensions to create a flexible, diffuse culture that rises as needed to address customers' needs and responds quickly to unpredictable marketplace conditions.

Service provider Jones Lang LaSalle has taken the even more dramatic step of silo swapping to structure its organization fully around the customer. But for any systemically integrated company, even the word *silo* has taken on a new meaning. Any formal silos in the truly customer-centric and systemically integrated firm are porous, interdependent, and working together toward dynamic, productive connections. Coordination and cooperation mechanisms allow for regular and effective work across divisions and groups. Clout also is spread across the organization, so that even back-end units become customer facing. Capabilities in these firms also reflect a customer-driven, multidomain approach, with the development of more and more generalists. Increasingly, these generalists advance along new, attractive career tracks that offer greater customer-focused responsibilities, both internally and externally. Thus, all five silo-busting levers work together in this stage—partners in a systemically integrated way to effectively solve customer problems.

As firms like JLL and Lafarge refine their implementation of the internal silo-busting levers, they are simultaneously working the same levers to move toward greater external integration. In shrinking the core and expanding the periphery, they place alliances at the center of their strategic agenda. They buck the dismal odds of success of such ties by extending their systemic integration across the boundaries that separate them from their partners. A deliberate approach to sustained coordination, cooperation, reconfiguration of clout, and capabilities allows them to succeed with connections where others have failed.

Mastering the elements of systemic integration is not an end in itself. This is not a journey that can be plotted on MapQuest—so many hours to get there, so many miles to go. As long as markets, competition, and technologies shift, so will customer needs, and the faster they shift, the more resilience you will need to get out in front of wherever the customer is going next. True outside-in thinking—level 4 ideation—is less about invention than reinvention. It opens the door to the constant shape-shifting businesses need to remain viable, valuable, and successful even in the hardest times. My hope is that this book will be your invitation to walk through that portal.

Notes

Introduction

1. Ranjay Gulati and Nitin Nohria, "Thrive or Survive? Breakaway Strategies for Success in Turbulent Markets," Working Paper, Harvard Business School, 2009.

2. The terms *outside-in* and *customer-centric* are used interchangeably throughout the book. The terms *inside-out* and *product-centric* are also used interchangeably throughout the book.

3. See Richard Ellsworth, *Leading with Purpose* (Stanford, CA: Stanford Business Books, 2002).

4. Noel Tichy, *Control Your Destiny or Someone Else Will* (New York: HarperCollins, 1994), 7.

5. For details on this, see "The Untold Story: How the iPhone Blew Up the Wireless Industry," *Wired*, January 9, 2008.

6. *Electronic News*, "Samsung, Infineon, Big Players in iPhone," July 3, 2007.

7. The importance of integration across boundaries has been an enduring theme in prior management research. In *The Functions of the Executive* (Cambridge, MA: Harvard University Press, 1938), telecommunications veteran Chester Barnard suggests that optimally efficient and effective interactions within a firm are more likely to occur with shorter lines of internal communication and fewer barriers to collaboration. Tom Burns and G. M. Stalker, *The Management of Innovation*, 2nd ed. (London: Tavistock, 1966), distinguished between *mechanistic* and *organic* organizations, with the former focused on predictability and order through centralization and hierarchical control, while the latter are characterized by more autonomous local units that can make continuous adjustments. They suggest that the former are best suited to stable business contexts, while the latter are most appropriate in dynamic and unpredictable environments. Similarly, management guru Peter Drucker's pivotal *The Concept of the Corporation* (New York: New American

Library, 1946), based on his observations of GM, proposes that the customer is the cornerstone of success, and that all internal processes must have a customer focus. He also advocated internal integration in multiple forms in his seminal work. James G. March and Herbert A. Simon, *Organizations* (New York: John Wiley, 1958), developed the idea that integration is a key task within organizations that arises from specialization and interdependencies among subunits. They also propose that integration is challenging due to conflicting goals and lack of shared understanding among various constituents of external constraints faced by the organization. Paul R. Lawrence and Jay W. Lorsch in their seminal work address what they consider to be the core issues of *differentiation* and *integration* in *Organizations and Environment: Managing Differentiation and Integration* (Boston: Harvard Business School Press, 1967), with the former referring to the circumscription of boundaries around interdependent activities, while the latter refers to the various ways to link those to each other. The optimal level of each is dependent on the degree of uncertainty faced by an organization. More recently, Christopher A. Bartlett and Sumantra Ghoshal in their book *Managing Across Borders* (Boston: Harvard Business School Press, 1989), revisit these issues in the context of multinational organizations. Charles A. O'Reilly III and Michael L. Tushman, "The Ambidextrous Organization," *Harvard Business Review*, April 2004, described *ambidextrous* as those that can simultaneously be differentiated into some units that focus on existing businesses and others that attend to new innovations, with the common thread of integration coming through their senior executives. Morten T. Hansen and Nitin Nohria, "How to Build Collaborative Advantage," *MIT Sloan Management Review* 46, no. 1 (2004), talk about the importance of creating "collaborative advantage" within firms by fostering greater integration among disparate units within an organization. In an account of multiunit enterprises, David A. Garvin and Lynn Levesque, "The Multiunit Enterprise," *Harvard Business Review,* June 2008, talk about the key role not only of dedicated integrators but also of defined overlaps in roles and responsibilities across key units as well as information channels to disseminate information to appropriate units. For comprehensive accounts of this rich literature on organizational design, please see Jay R. Galbraith, *Organization Design* (Reading, MA: Addison-Wesley, 1977); Michael Tushman and David Nadler, "Information Processing as an Integrating Concept in Organizational Design," *Academy of Management Review* 3, no. 3 (1978): 613–624; and Henry Mintzberg, *The Structuring of Organizations* (Englewood Cliffs, NJ: Prentice Hall, 1979).

8. In this book, Harley-Davidson is mentioned only briefly and Target not at all due to space constraints.

9. It is difficult to make comparisons with direct competitors for some of the other firms because either they don't have an obvious direct competitor (e.g., Starbucks, Cisco) or they are part of a larger entity (e.g., GE Healthcare). As discussed elsewhere, Tribune is the only exception in this sample that has filed for Chapter 11 bankruptcy protection.

Chapter 1

1. Burkhard Bilger, "Salad Days," *New Yorker*, September 6, 2004, 136. For more details on this story, see http://www.freshexpress.com/FreshExpressStory.asp.

2. A rich body of work by marketing scholars has tried to comprehend and operationalize what has been described as "market orientation" that reflects an enterprise's capability for generation and dissemination of customer information and responsiveness to it. For a comprehensive account see George S. Day, *Market Driven Strategy* (New York: The Free Press, 1990); and Rohit Deshpande, ed. *Developing a Market Orientation* (Thousand Oaks, CA: Sage Publications, 1999).

3. Recently, marketers have taken to referring to this as *purpose-based marketing*. Suzanne Vranica, "Veteran Marketer Promotes a New Kind of Selling," *Wall Street Journal,* October 31, 2008.

4. At the same time that the glories of customer centricity were being sung, however, some researchers sounded a more cautionary note and suggested that companies should take a more balanced approach to what seemed like a universal business imperative. In particular, Clayton M. Christensen, *The Innovator's Dilemma* (Boston: Harvard Business School Press, 1997), provided a compelling account of how too much listening to customers can sometimes blind companies to potential disruptive innovations in their industry.

5. Information on Best Buy and all quotations of executives in this chapter are taken from author interviews and the following cases unless otherwise noted: Ranjay Gulati and Alberto Gastelum, "Best Buy Inc." (Evanston, IL: Kellogg School of Management, 2006); and Ranjay Gulati and Lisa Khan-Kapadia, "Best Buy 2006–2007" (Evanston, IL: Kellogg School of Management, 2007).

6. Unmesh Kher, "Who Will Buy It?", *Time*, April 2005.

7. EVA stands for Economic Value Added and is a measure of company, business unit, or product-line financial performance. It is calculated by deducting the cost of capital invested in a particular unit from

that unit's net operating profit after taxes. See http://www.investopedia. com/terms/e/eva.asp for more information. ROIC, or return on invested capital, is a measure of financial performance. When used to measure internal business performance, it is generally calculated as net operating profit after taxes divided by total capital. See http://www. investopedia.com/terms/r/returnoninvestmentcapital.asp for more information.

8. Ariana Eunjung Cha, "For Soccer Moms, New Best Buy Fits the Bill," *Journal Gazette,* October 3, 2005.

9. *Voxant Fair Disclosure Wire,* "Best Buy Co., Inc. at Goldman Sachs 12th Annual Global Retailing Conference—Final," September 9, 2005.

10. Looking across time, we can see how the prevalent organizational architecture in each era has evolved as customer needs have changed, albeit with a lag as organizations adjusted to shifting customer preferences. In each instance, however, firms sought an architecture that mirrored the markets and their own goals of those times. Studies of organizational architecture have typically examined the inherent trade-offs involved in building silos within organizations and tried to link the optimal level of integration among the silos to be contingent on the market context. Silos have formed in organizations for as long as organizations have existed. The kind of silo at issue here became prevalent in the early 1900s as industrial organizations formed and took on significant size. As companies grew, division of labor became necessary, and they created discrete units to carry out specific functions, typically research and development, manufacturing, sales and marketing, and distribution. The goal of the functionally integrated company was to maximize production capacities, increase knowledge, deepen expertise, achieve fiscal discipline, gain economies of scale, and improve accountability by function. Customer centricity in this context meant delivering novel products that customers desired at reasonable prices and through accessible distribution channels. The speed at which firms responded or launched new products was not that important an issue at the time. Functional organizations started to hit their limits when the speed at which new products were introduced started to increase dramatically. And so management began its earliest efforts at integration. Leaders sought to create various kinds of connections and pathways among the various groups in order to speed up decision making and improve production and distribution efficiency across the company. In the second half of the twentieth century, as the industrial

companies grew and prospered, they not only continued to increase the speed at which they were launching new products, but also diversified their portfolio of products. GE, among others, sold an array of different products, while GM made different versions of one product, with both companies selling domestically in the United States as well as overseas. The primary differentiator was still the product, and firms believed that the primary avenue for success was through developing and delivering innovative products. As this era unfolded, many companies began to restructure themselves and create product-focused groups or divisions, and as they expanded into various markets, they also created geographical units. These later became labeled *strategic business units* (SBUs). The logic here was that by placing all relevant functions within a product or geographic unit, that unit could speed up decision making, focus on rapid product launches, and in general remain focused on its product and geography as the primary market space around which it had to ensure success. As long as customer needs were met primarily by frequent launches of innovative new products, things were fine. As product-based firms grew, they increasingly sought to connect their autonomous divisions, typically by linking their product units and their geographic units in what became known as the *matrix organization*. Such organizational architectures often featured silos within silos. The complexity of organizations seemed to get ahead of what customers wanted. In their quest for global dominance and the search for mythical production, distribution, and marketing synergies, organizations created complex structures that took center stage. Skip ahead to the late 1980s and early 1990s, the beginning of the age of commoditization and the full blooming of the customer revolution that began nearly a century earlier. Management suddenly found itself face-to-face with product proliferation, low-price competition, and drastically shortened product life cycles, especially in technology-intensive industries. In such a climate, customer centricity naturally emphasized speed, rather than simply leveraging economies of scale and scope, as in previous eras. In this era, firms used cross-unit linkages to craft reduced cycle times for products and features, especially in technology-intensive industries. An SBU or a matrix organization became an anachronism for many as they discovered that the duplication of functions across units was a cost they could no longer afford, or that they were losing opportunities as their customers demanded more integrated products and services that required them to link their units. To achieve the greater speed and nimbleness demanded by customers, many firms sought to integrate the activities that took place across functional units, product units, and geographical units. *Business process reengineering*, which came increasingly into prominence, involved the streamlining of processes and the creation of new ones, all with the goal of managing predictable and repetitive activities in a more efficient—and speedier—way. These integration and reengineering efforts helped to create the horizontal organization and led to the creation of a set of processes that encompassed connecting units to accomplish predictable and repetitive activities in a more efficient manner.

11. A number of scholars have taken issue with the status of large and complex organizations as we know them. One of the endemic issues most point to includes the challenges of cross-unit integration while at the same time retaining the benefits of specialization that ensue from having specialist units. See for instance, Charles Heckscher and Anne Donnellon (editors), *The Post-Bureaucratic Organization: New Perspectives on Organizational Change* (Thousand Oaks, CA: Sage Publications, 1994); Paul DiMaggio, ed., *The Twenty-First-Century Firm: Changing Economic Organization in International Perspective* (Princeton, NJ: Princeton University Press, 2001); Frank Ostroff, *The Horizontal Organization* (Oxford: Oxford University Press, 1999); Bruce A. Pasternack and Albert J. Viscio, *The Centerless Corporation* (New York: Simon and Schuster, 1998).

12. James Thompson, *Organizations in Action: Social Science Bases of Administrative Theory* (New York: McGraw-Hill, 1967); David Nadler and Michael Tushman, *Competing by Design* (New York: Oxford University Press, 1997); and others, discuss details related to the forms of work-related interdependence, each of which requires a more complex form of integration to manage. First proposed by Thompson, work-related interdependence exists in three forms. In *pooled* interdependence, business units with different product or market focuses act independently, except for the sharing of corporate resources (e.g., HR). In *sequential* interdependence, units divide work such that each performs a particular portion of a given task and then hands it off to other units. For example, insurance companies process claims using sequentially interdependent processes. Thus sequential interdependence requires more coordination and timing than pooled interdependence for effective performance of work. *Reciprocal* interdependence, which requires the most coordination, is one in which all groups or units must simultaneously work together toward a common goal, and requires that business units and functional groups collaborate deeply and actively to address their tasks. For example, in contrast to less complex forms of

integration/interdependence, in reciprocal interdependence, some-times there is no clear-cut handoff of activities from one group to another; rather, the groups must engage in mutual adjustment of tasks and activities.

13. Paul Lawrence and Jay Lorsch, *Organizations and Environment*, was one of the earliest accounts to propose that a key challenge for orga-nizations is balancing modular units, or what they called *differentiation*, with links between those units, or what they called *integration*.

14. Jay R. Galbraith, *Designing Complex Organizations* (Boston: Addison-Wesley Longman, 1973), identifies a key challenge that orga-nizations face in dynamic environments: increasing their "information processing" capacity in changing contexts where new information must constantly be collated, processed, and acted upon.

15. It is important to note that interdependencies may be exogenous or endogenous. The exogenous ones are those that are predetermined by the nature of the tasks and the market context. The endogenous interdependencies are those that we discover as we interact and work together, and thus are harder to anticipate in advance.

16. I've borrowed the term *expeditions without maps* from Karl Weick, *Sensemaking in Organizations* (Thousand Oaks, CA: Sage, 1995), who describes an oft-cited incident—originally recounted by Nobel laureate Albert Szent-Gyorti—of a group of Hungarian army soldiers lost in the Alps. While Weick's focus was on showing how the mere possession of a map (even one of the wrong geography!) can improve collective motivation and goal-focused behavior, my emphasis here is on missions for which you may truly lack a map but still must get some-where. A more recent account and precise use of this phrase is provided by Phanish Puranam and Murali Swamy, "Expeditions Without Maps: Learning to Coordinate Under Structural Uncertainty" (Working Paper, London Business School, April 2008, available at http://ssrn.com/abstract=1153142).

17. An abbreviated and earlier account of the levers can be seen in Ranjay Gulati, "Silo Busting: How to Execute on the Promise of Cus-tomer Focus," *Harvard Business Review*, May 2007: 98–108.

Chapter 2

1. Information on Jones Lang LaSalle and all quotations of exec-utives in this chapter are taken from author interviews and the follow-ing cases unless otherwise noted: Ranjay Gulati and Lucia Marshall, "Jones Lang LaSalle: Reorganizing around the Customer," Case 410-007 (Boston: Harvard Business School, 2010); and Ranjay Gulati and Lucia

Marshall, "Corporate Solutions at Jones Lang LaSalle," Case 409-111 (Boston: Harvard Business School, 2009).

2. Note that there are other possible ways to distinguish between coordination and cooperation. In the information processing view of the firm as developed in the Carnegie School by Herbert Simon and James March, as well as in the behavioral game theory literature inspired by Thomas Schelling, coordination is viewed as being about aligning viewpoints—getting everybody to share a common understanding of a situation. Cooperation is about getting people to feel motivated about doing what is collectively good. Thus, *coordination* is getting people to agree on a common understanding of what needs to be done; *cooperation* is getting them to feel motivated to do it. While these definitions are distinct from what I use in the book, they are not incompatible in spirit. Fundamentally, coordination is about information, whereas cooperation deals with incentives.

3. Scott Snook, *Friendly Fire* (Princeton, NJ: Princeton University Press, 2000).

4. Jay R. Galbraith, *Designing Complex Organizations* (Boston: Addison-Wesley Longman, 1973), provides a comprehensive account of the wide array of coordination mechanisms and the trade-offs each may entail.

5. Peter Drucker, "There's More Than One Kind of Team," *Wall Street Journal*, February 1, 1992, for instance, discusses three types of coordination among organizational teams: (1) *baseball-type*, in which members have fixed positions from which they do not deviate, allowing individual accountability and training; (2) *football-type*, where members also retain fixed positions but must work together as a team in more situations; and (3) *tennis doubles–type*, in which members have a primary but nonfixed position and must commit to contributing to a team rather than individual performance. Drucker's categories apply to teams engaged in a variety of tasks, as opposed to my focus on silo busting toward greater synchronized integration, but it's an interesting and apt scheme.

6. For a discussion of how organizational architecture and the structure and processes within it can be reshaped to affect meaningful change, see Robert Simons, *Levers of Organizational Design* (Boston: Harvard Business School Press, 2005); and David A. Garvin, *General Management: Processes and Action* (New York: McGraw-Hill, 2002).

7. Michael L. Tushman and David A. Nadler, "Information Processing as an Integrating Concept in Organizational Design," *Academy of Management Review* 3, no. 3 (1978): 613–624.

8. For a discussion of the use of business processes to enact change see: David A. Garvin, *General Management: Processes and Action* (New York: McGraw-Hill, 2002); and Michael Hammer and James Champy, *Reengineering the Corporation* (New York: Harper Collins, 2001).

9. Alberto Gastelum (former Agilent employee), personal communication with author, December 2006.

10. Tushman and Nadler, in "Information Processing as an Integrating Concept," refer to these as "linking" mechanisms; David Garvin and Lynn Levesque, in "The Multiunit Enterprise," *Harvard Business Review*, June 2008, similarly talk about the importance of placing "integrators" in large multiunit organizations to facilitate decision making.

11. In the context of multinational organizations, Bartlett and Ghoshal referred to integration arrangements such as these as *centralization* and *formalization* (Christopher A. Bartlett and Sumantra Ghoshal, *Managing Across Borders* [Boston: Harvard Business School Press, 1989]). The former refers to instances where the corporate center takes over certain key tasks that span the organization, and the latter refers to cases where the firm formalizes certain roles and interactions within the organization.

12. For a comprehensive account of organizational processes, see David A. Garvin, "The Processes of Organization and Management," *MIT Sloan Management Review* 39, no. 4 (1998): 33–50.

13. For a discussion of how companies overcome the limited use of customer information within organizations, see Ranjay Gulati and James Oldroyd, "The Quest for Customer Focus," *Harvard Business Review*, April 2005.

14. See especially David Nadler and Michael Tushman, *Competing by Design* (New York: Oxford University Press, 1997), 71–87, for a detailed discussion of grouping options, including grouping by activity (e.g., work process), output (product/service), customer (segment/need), or any combination of these.

Chapter 3

1. The information on Cisco and all quotations of executives in this chapter are taken from author interviews and the following cases unless otherwise noted: Ranjay Gulati and Lucia Marshall, "Cisco Business Councils: Unifying a Functional Enterprise with an Internal Governance System," Case 409-062 (Boston: Harvard Business School, 2009); and Ranjay Gulati and Lucia Marshall, "Cisco Systems: Building

and Sustaining a Customer-Centric Culture," Case 409-061 (Boston: Harvard Business School, 2009).

2. Chester Barnard, in *The Functions of the Executive* (Cambridge, MA: Harvard University Press, 1938), was perhaps one of the first to note the importance of these two distinct facets of organizations. He refers to two methods for inculcating cooperation within organizations, incentives and persuasion, both of which are covered in the discussion that follows. The theme was later developed by Paul Lawrence and Jay Lorsch in *Organizations and Environment: Managing Differentiation and Integration* (Boston: Harvard Business School Press, 1967), whose notion of integration covers both facets as well.

3. Deborah Dougherty, "Interpretive Barriers to Successful Product Innovation in Large Firms," *Organization Science* 3, no. 2 (1992): 179–202.

4. George Chidi, "Analysis: Cisco's Reorganization Cannot Unpop the Bubble," *InfoWorld*, August 24, 2001, http://www.infoworld.com/articles/hn/xml/01/08/24/010824hnciscofollow.html.

5. Amy Larsen DeCarlo and Kate Gerwig, "Synergy or Stupidity? Rejiggered Cisco Targets the Telecom Market by Way of the Enterprise," *Call Center Magazine*, September 5, 2001, http://www.callcentermagazine.com/shared/article/showArticle.jhtml?articleID=8709945.

6. Ranjay Gulati and Lucia Marshall, "Cisco Business Councils: Unifying a Functional Enterprise with an Internal Governance System" Harvard Business School Case N5-409-062, p. 9.

7. Ranjay Gulati and Phanish Puranam, "Renewal Through Reorganization: The Value of Inconsistencies Between Formal and Informal Organization," *Organization Science* 20, no. 3 (2009): 422–440.

8. For research that shows the importance of language and categories on fostering greater cooperation, see Peter L. Berger and Thomas Luckmann, *The Social Construction of Reality* (New York: Doubleday, 1966); Paul M. Hirsch, "From Ambushes to Golden Parachutes: Corporate Takeovers as an Instance of Cultural Framing and Institutional Integration," *American Journal of Sociology* 91, no. 4 (1986): 800–837; Edgar H. Schein, *Organizational Culture and Leadership*, 2nd ed. (San Francisco: Jossey-Bass, 1992); Etienne Wenger, *Communities of Practice: Learning, Meaning, and Identity* (Cambridge: Cambridge University Press, 1998); Beth A. Bechky, "Sharing Meaning Across Occupational Communities: The Transformation of Understanding on a Production Floor," *Organization Science* 14, no. 3 (2003): 312–330; and Joseph F. Porac

and Howard Thomas, "Cognitive Categorization and Subjective Rivalry Among Retailers in a Small City," *Journal of Applied Psychology* 79, no. 1 (1994): 54–66.

9. For a detailed account of the performance benefits of culture, see John Kotter and James Heskett, *Corporate Culture and Performance* (New York: Free Press, 1992), chap. 1. The authors show that, over an eleven-year period, firms with strong cultures increased revenues by an average of 682 percent versus 166 percent for their peers, expanded their staffs by 282 percent versus 36 percent, and grew their valuations by 901 percent versus 74 percent; perhaps most startlingly, the strong-culture sample improved net income by 756 percent, versus a gain of only 1 percent among their peers. For a discussion of the formative elements of culture and its role in fostering companywide cooperation, see Charles A. O'Reilly III, "Cooperation, Culture, and Commitment: Motivation and Social Control in Organizations," *California Management Review* 31, no. 4 (1989): 9–25.

10. Schein, *Organizational Culture and Leadership*, 18–19; and John Van Maanen and Edgar H. Schein, "Towards a Theory of Organizational Socialization," in *Research in Organizational Behavior*, vol. 1, ed. Barry Staw (Greenwich, CT: JAI Press, 1979).

11. Edvaldo Pereira Lima, "Winning Cultures," *Air Transport World*, February 2006, 54.

12. Clifford Geertz, *The Interpretation of Cultures* (New York: Basic Books, 1973), discusses at length the role of multiple types of symbols to culture (p. 126).

13. See Deal and Kennedy, *Corporate Cultures*, (Reading, MA: Addison-Wesley, 1982) for attributes of symbolic managers and how they manage culture within a company (chap. 8).

14. Richard Whiteley, *The Customer-Driven Company: Moving from Talk to Action* (Cambridge, MA: Perseus, 1991), notes that many companies see revenues and market share as strong indicators of customer satisfaction largely because the firms receive no complaints. But he cites a *Wall Street Journal* poll in which only 5 percent of customers believed that companies listen to them in the first place, and would thus presumably be unlikely to complain (p. 152).

15. Lior Arussy, *Passionate and Profitable: Why Customer Strategies Fail and 10 Steps to Do Them Right!* (Hoboken, NJ: Wiley, 2005), chap. 2.

16. For a review of innovative ways in which companies including Royal Bank of Canada, Continental Airlines, and SBC are currently

using customer data to enhance their customer-centricity, see Ranjay Gulati and James Oldroyd, "The Quest for Customer Focus," *Harvard Business Review*, April 2005, 92–101.

17. Harrah's information from author interviews and Thomas DeLong and Vineeta Vijayaraghava, "Harrah's Entertainment, Inc.: Rewarding Our People," Case 9-403-008 (Boston: Harvard Business School, 2003).

18. Ibid, 6.

19. Ibid.

20. See Brian Hall, "Incentive Strategy Within Organizations," Course Note 9-902-131 (Boston: Harvard Business School, 2002) for a review of several dimensions of incentive strategy within organizations. Also see, John Roberts, *The Modern Firm* (New York: Oxford University Press, 2004) for an extensive discussion of the balance between individual and collective incentives. David Kreps ("Intrinsic Motivation and Extrinsic Incentives," *American Economic Review* 87, no. 2 [1997]: 360–361) provides an extensive discussion of general issues related to intrinsic motivation and extrinsic incentives. He argues that employees with high intrinsic motivation will exert effort to perform in the absence of extrinsic incentives, but only to a point: after that, extrinsic incentives must be present to encourage higher levels of effort in most cases.

21. DeLong and Vijayaraghava, "Harrah's Entertainment, Inc.," 6.

22. Michael Basch, *Customer Culture: How FedEx and Other Great Companies Put the Customer First Every Day* (Upper Saddle River, NJ: Prentice Hall, 2002) 165.

23. Roberts, *The Modern Firm*.

24. Jefferey Pfeffer, "Six Dangerous Myths About Pay," *Harvard Business Review*, May–June 1998, 109–119.

25. Corey Rosen, John Case, and Martin Staubus, "Every Employee an Owner. Really," *Harvard Business Review,* June 2005, suggest that a "destination workplace" is a company that offers "good jobs, generous rewards, and a supportive environment." They note Google as a strong recent example (p. 127).

26. Jennifer A. Chatman and Sandra Eunyoung Cha, "Leading by Leveraging Culture," *California Management Review* 45, no. 4 (2003): 22.

27. Schein, *Organizational Culture and Leadership*, chap. 16, discusses the concepts of unfreezing and refreezing culture as derived from Kurt Lewin's work. Unfreezing comprises the presence of sufficient disconfirming data to promote disequilibrium, the connection of the

disconfirming information to key objectives, and a strong enough sense of psychological safety to allow the possibility of change. Refreezing can only take place when new group behaviors produce enough confirming data for a return to equilibrium.

28. Jay R. Galbraith, *Designing the Customer-Centric Organization: A Guide to Strategy, Structure, and Process* (San Francisco: Jossey-Bass, 2005), discusses light, medium, and heavy levels of customer-centric culture, with case examples of each.

Chapter 4

1. Linda Hill, "What It Really Means to Manage: Exercising Power and Influence," Course Note 9-400-041 (Boston: Harvard Business School, 2000), 2.

2. Jeffrey Pfeffer, *Managing with Power* (Boston: Harvard Business School Press, 1992), discusses power issues extensively, especially as related to implementation: how leaders mobilize political support and other resources to get things done. Quote is from p. 30.

3. Note that the following discussion of power will blend two types of power sources: personal and positional. Personal power emanates from an individual's ascribed characteristics or experience, encompassing attractiveness, expertise, track record within and outside of the organization, and effort. Positional power is based on the individual's—or the business unit's—location within the multiple networks of the organization or the authority vested in the individual/unit by the organization; sources of positional power include formal authority, relevance, centrality, autonomy, and visibility. Clearly, each type and source of power is likely to be valued by individuals and units within an organization, and they will fight to retain or increase these in the face of changes, such as a shift to greater customer focus. See Linda Hill, "Power Dynamics in Organizations," Course Note 9-494-083 (Boston: Harvard Business School, 1995), for an extensive review of these categories of power; Pfeffer, *Managing with Power*, provides another comprehensive review of organizational power sources.

4. Ranjay Gulati and Maxim Sytch, "Dependence Asymmetry and Joint Dependence in Interorganizational Relationships: Effects of Embeddedness on a Manufacturer's Performance in Procurement Relationships," *Administrative Science Quarterly* 52, no. 3 (2007): 32–69, describe how power need not be a zero-sum game. They show how asymmetry in dependence as well as joint mutual dependence can both be important in shaping relationship outcomes.

5. Information on Jones Lang LaSalle and all quotations of executives in this chapter are taken from author interviews and the following cases unless otherwise noted: Ranjay Gulati and Lucia Marshall, "Corporate Solutions at Jones Lang LaSalle," Case 409-111 (Boston: Harvard Business School, 2009); and Ranjay Gulati and Lucia Marshall, "Jones Lang LaSalle: Reorganizing around the Customer," Case 410-007 (Boston: Harvard Business School, 2010).

6. Ranjay Gulati and James Oldroyd, "Coordinating Centralized Information and Decentralized Decision-Making" (Working Paper, Harvard Business School, 2009), discuss the benefits and challenges of developing communal information sources.

7. Gary Loveman, "Diamonds in the Data Mine," *Harvard Business Review*, May 2003, 109–113, describes Harrah's customer database in detail.

8. See Ranjay Gulati and James Oldroyd, "The Quest for Customer Focus," *Harvard Business Review*, April 2005, 92–101, for a detailed account of how to drive this process effectively within organizations, including examples from Royal Bank of Canada, Continental Airlines, and others.

9. GE Healthcare information from author interviews and Ranjay Gulati, James Oldroyd, Suzanne Carpenter, and Abbas Khan,"GE Medical Systems," (Evanston, IL: Kellogg School of Management, 2002); and Ranjay Gulati and Alberto Gastelum, "GE Healthcare," (Evanston, IL: Kellogg School of Management, 2006).

10. Dorothy Leonard-Barton and Walter Swap, *When Sparks Fly: Igniting Creativity in Groups* (Boston: Harvard Business School Press, 1999).

Chapter 5

1. By the time of this book's publication, the Tribune Company had undergone fundamental changes, including an ownership change and eventually bankruptcy that moved it away from the integrated strategy discussed here. Those ownership shifts that included divesting some of the media properties in the Tribune family are a testimony to the difficulty that firms face in trying to build a resilient organization on an outside-in orientation in a turbulent market place.

2. Information on the Tribune Company and all quotations of executives in this chapter are taken from author interviews and the following cases unless otherwise noted: Ranjay Gulati, James Oldroyd, Stephanie Pfeffer, and Abbas Khan, "The Tribune Company: Redefining

Sales" (Evanston, IL: Kellogg School of Management, 2002); and Ranjay Gulati, Alberto Gastelum, and Melissa D'Arabian, "The Tribune Company: Revisited" (Evanston, IL: Kellogg School of Management, 2006).

3. This distinction between willingness and ability was first made by Morten Hansen and Nitin Nohria, "How To Build Collaborative Advantage," *MIT Sloan Management Review* 46, no. 1 (2004): 22–30.

4. A rich body of research on the dynamic capabilities of firms focuses primarily on organization-level processes that enable firm success. For a key article in this domain, please see David J. Teece, Gary Pisano, and Amy Shuen, "Dynamic Capabilities and Strategic Management," *Strategic Management Journal* 18, no. 7 (1997): 509–533. My focus here is less on such organizational capabilities and more on those capabilities resident within a firm's employees.

5. David Krackhardt and Jeffrey R. Hanson, "Informal Networks: The Company Behind the Charts," *Harvard Business Review*, July–August 1993, 104–111.

6. Rob Cross, Nitin Nohria, and Andrew Parker, "Six Myths About Informal Networks—And How to Overcome Them," *MIT Sloan Management Review* 43, no. 3 (2002): 67.

7. Krackhardt and Hanson, "Informal Networks," 104, suggest that while the formal organization is designed to handle typical issues, the informal organization is crucial for dealing with unexpected problems; however, most managers lack key information about the informal networks of their firms.

8. Brian Uzzi and Shannon Dunlap, "How to Build Your Network," *Harvard Business Review*, December 2005, 58, discuss numerous benefits of shared activities, arguing that activities that "evoke passion in participants, necessitate interdependence, and have something at stake" are more likely to produce higher-value informal networks.

9. See Rob Cross and Lawrence Prusak, "The People Who Make Organizations Go—Or Stop," *Harvard Business Review*, June 2002, 110, for a discussion of how such boundary spanners play a key role in driving integration within organizations.

10. See Uzzi and Dunlap, "How to Build Your Network," for a review of the concept of information brokers, including how it relates to Paul Revere.

11. Krackhardt and Hanson, "Informal Networks," discuss in detail the benefits of analyzing internal networks, along with specific practical steps in network analysis.

12. Ronald Burt, *Structural Holes* (Cambridge, MA: Harvard University Press, 1992), presents a detailed account of the implications of brokers within organizations.

13. Matthew Guthridge, Asmus Komm, and Emily Lawson, "The People Problem in Talent Management," *McKinsey Quarterly*, no. 2 (2006): 6.

14. Lowell L. Bryan, Claudia L. Joyce, and Leigh M. Weiss, "Making a Market in Talent," *McKinsey Quarterly*, no. 2 (2006): 98.

15. Ibid., 99.

Chapter 6

1. David Kletter and I (Ranjay Gulati and David Kletter, "Shrinking Core-Expanding Periphery: The Relational Architecture of High-Performing Organizations," *California Management Review* 47, no. 1 [Fall 2004]: 77–104) asked senior executives responding to our survey about the primary organizational challenges and imperatives they perceived regarding customer-focused partnerships; then we stratified their companies into quartiles based on total returns to shareholders over the five-year period preceding the survey. Among the other findings of our study were (1) 88 percent of total respondents expected to increase their level of information sharing with suppliers, indicating the universal perceived importance of close supplier relationships; (2) 75 percent of top-quartile performers intended to increase the duration and strength of supplier relationships, compared to 55 percent of their bottom-quartile peers; and (3) 75 percent of top performers expected to increase the involvement of alliance partners in product development, versus only 59 percent of bottom-quartile firms. Thus, not only are firms across industries placing major emphasis on external integration as a key component of providing solutions, but winning companies are already ahead of their peers in forging and deepening relationships with suppliers and allies. The survey results also provide a preview of the means by which firms are enhancing external relationships (e.g., sharing information and entering into longer-term relationships with suppliers) to improve customer focus and, ultimately, top- and bottom-line growth.

2. For a detailed discussion of these concepts, see Ranjay Gulati and David Kletter, "Shrinking Core, Expanding Periphery," *California Management Review* 47, no. 3 (2005): 77–104.

3. Pete Engardio, Michael Arndt, and Dean Foust, "The Future of Outsourcing," *BusinessWeek*, January 30, 2006, 50–58.

4. Ibid.

5. Jeffrey H. Dyer, *Collaborative Advantage: Winning Through Extended Supplier Partnerships* (Oxford: Oxford University Press, 2000).

6. Patricia Panchak, "Suppliers Provide Competitive Edge," *IndustryWeek*, September 2004, 9.

7. Quote from Daniel Marovitz, technology managing director for Deutsche Bank's global businesses, in Engardio, Arndt, and Foust, "The Future of Outsourcing."

8. Kerry A. Dolan, "Speed, the New X Factor," *Forbes*, December 26, 2005, 74–77.

9. Arik Hesseldahl, "Unpeeling Apple's Nano," *BusinessWeek Online*, September 22, 2005.

10. C. K. Prahalad and Gary Hamel, "The Core Competence of the Corporation," *Harvard Business Review*, May–June 1990, 79–91, provide an extensive discussion of the core competence concept.

11. Mark Gottfredson, Rudy Puryear, and Stephan Phillips, "Strategic Sourcing: From Periphery to the Core," *Harvard Business Review*, February 2005, 132–139, discuss how strategic sourcing has made 7-Eleven an industry leader, along with presenting more details of Pfizer's and American Express's sourcing decisions.

12. For example, in 1992 American Express spun off its transaction-processing business, one of its core skills, using the new business, First Data, as a supplier. Gottfredson, Puryear, and Phillips, "Strategic Sourcing."

13. Rick Mullin, "The Partnership Push," *Chemical & Engineering News*, March 6, 2006, 21–27, discusses why pharmaceutical companies engage in alliances with biotechnology firms and provides numerous examples of successful partnerships.

14. Michael McCoy, "Merck Taps India for New Drug," *Chemical & Engineering News*, October 23, 2006, 14.

15. This description draws heavily on the following research: F. Asis Martinez-Jerez and V. G. Narayanan, "Strategic Outsourcing at Bharti Airtel Limited," Case 9-107-003 (Boston: Harvard Business School, 2006); and F. Asis Martinez-Jerez and V. G. Narayanan, "Strategic Outsourcing at Bharti Airtel Limited, One Year Later," Case 9-107-004 (Boston: Harvard Business School, 2006). Clay Chandler, "Wireless Wonder," *Fortune*, January 22, 2007, 130–136.

16. Chandler, "Wireless Wonder"; and Martinez-Jerez and Narayanan, "Strategic Outsourcing at Bharti Airtel Limited. One Year Later."

17. Chandler, "Wireless Wonder."

18. Martinez-Jerez and Narayanan, "Strategic Outsourcing at Bharti Airtel Limited."

19. Chandler, "Wireless Wonder."

20. Martinez-Jerez and Narayanan, "Strategic Outsourcing at Bharti Airtel Limited."

21. Martinez-Jerez and Narayanan, "Strategic Outsourcing at Bharti Airtel Limited. One Year Later."

22. Gulati and Kletter, "Shrinking Core, Expanding Periphery," discuss ladders of relationship integration between firms and their suppliers, allies, and customers.

23. For a discussion of the advantages that ensue from a collaborative supply chain see: Jeffrey H. Dyer, *Collaborative Advantage: Winning Through Extended Enterprise Supplier Networks*, (Oxford: Oxford University Press, 2000); and Edward W. Davis and Robert E. Spekman, *The Extended Enterprise: Gaining Competitive Advantage Through Collaborative Supply Chains*, (Upper Saddle River, NJ: Prentice Hall, 2004).

24. Information on Starbucks and all quotations of executives in this chapter are taken from author interviews and the following cases and articles unless otherwise noted: Ranjay Gulati, Sarah Huffman, and Gary Neilson, "The Barista Principle," Strategy + Business, third quarter 2002; Ranjay Gulati, Suzanne Carpenter, and Sarah Huffman, "Starbucks: Shrinking the Core, Expanding the Periphery," (Evanston, IL: Kellogg School of Management, 2002); and Gulati and Kletter, "Shrinking Core, Expanding Periphery," *California Management Review* 47, no. 3 (2005): 77–104.

25. John Carlin, "25 million of us buy his skinny lattes every week," *The Observer* online, July 13, 2003. (http://www.guardian.co.uk/lifestyle/2003/jul/13/foodanddrink.features.

26. "Starbucks Corporation," Hoovers Company Factsheet, http://www.hoovers.com/starbucks/—ID__15745—/free-co-factsheet.xhtml.

27. "Solo Cup Company—Company History," Solo Cup Company, http://www.solocup.com/soloabout/aboutHistory.html.

28. As of this writing, Starbucks—faced with significant competition, stagnation of stock value, innovation fatigue, and slowing domestic growth—has begun to rethink its expansion at the periphery, focus or prune away some partnership activities, and work to revitalize and stay closer to its core.

29. For expedience, I will refer to partners offering complementary products and services as "allies."

30. Jeffrey H. Dyer, Prashant Kale, and Harbir Singh, "How to Make Strategic Alliances Work," *MIT Sloan Management Review* 42, no. 4 (2001): 37–43.

31. *Electronic News*, "Sanyo, Quanta Form Flat Panel Joint Venture," March 17, 2006, http://www.edn.com/article/CA6316753.html?text=sanyo%2C+quanta+form+flat+p.

32. Gottfredson, Puryear, and Phillips, "Strategic Sourcing."

33. Harvard Business School Working Knowledge, "Capability Sourcing at 7-Eleven," March 28, 2005, http:hbswk.edu/archive/4719.html.

34. Michael Goul, "Teradata Reborn," September 22, 2009. Available at SSRN: http://ssrn.com/abstract=1477025.

35. Gulati and Kletter, "Shrinking Core, Expanding Periphery."

36. Jim Beam Global, "Starbucks Coffee Company and Jim Beam Brands Co. Expand Spirits Offering with New Starbucks Cream Liqueur," news release, October 19, 2005, http://www.beamglobal.com/jbbw/pr/SBUXCreamRelease.pdf.

37. Richard Hurst, "Proof Positive," *Progressive Grocer*, August 1, 2006, 54–58.

38. Jim Beam Global, "Starbucks Coffee Company."

39. Susan Dominus, "The Starbucks Aesthetic," *New York Times*, October 22, 2006.

40. Barbara Kiviat, "The Big Gulp at Starbucks," *Time*, December 18, 2006, 124–126.

41. Dominus, "The Starbucks Aesthetic."

42. Kiviat, "The Big Gulp at Starbucks."

43. Dominus, "The Starbucks Aesthetic."

44. EDS information is from Andrew Park and Jay Greene, "EDS Turbocharges Its Teamwork," *BusinessWeek*, February 28, 2005, 66–68, unless otherwise noted.

45. Ibid.

46. Ibid.

47. Ibid.

48. EDS, "Coca-Cola FEMSA Extends Relationship with EDS," news release, April 30, 2007, http://www.eds.com/news/releases/3691/.

49. JLL information is from author interviews and Ranjay Gulati and Alberto Gastelum, "Jones Lang LaSalle: 2001–2005" (Evanston, IL: Kellogg School of Management, 2006).

50. Bernard Levine, "Solectron Buying IBM Repair Unit," *Electronic News*, December 11, 2000.

51. Dyer, Kale, and Singh, "How to Make Strategic Alliances Work."

52. Dyer, Kale, and Singh, "How to Make Strategic Alliances Work," discuss multiple firms that have forged successful partnerships using a dedicated alliance-management function.

53. Ibid.

54. Ibid.

55. Kumar, "The Power of Trust."

56. Aron and Singh, "Getting Offshoring Right."

57. Kumar, "The Power of Trust."

58. Aron and Singh, "Getting Offshoring Right."

59. Goodwyn, "Risk and Reward in Vendorville."

60. Jeffrey Liker and Thomas Choi, "Building Deep Supplier Relationships," *Harvard Business Review*, December 2004, 104–113, discuss how Japanese automakers have developed deep and successful relationships with North American suppliers.

61. In the context of discussing trust between manufacturers and retailers, Kumar, "The Power of Trust," presents multiple issues related to distributive justice, procedural justice, bilateral communication, and others.

62. Gulati, Khanna, and Nohria, "Unilateral Commitments and the Importance of Process."

63. Gulati and Sytch, "Dependence Asymmetry and Joint Dependence."

64. Ranjay Gulati, "Does Familiarity Breed Trust? The Implications of Repeated Ties for Contractual Choice in Alliances," *Academy of Management Journal* 38, no. 1 (1995): 85–112; Kumar, "The Power of Trust"; and Brian Uzzi, "Social Structure and Competition in Interfirm Networks: The Paradox of Embeddedness," *Administrative Science Quarterly* 42, no. 1 (1997): 35–67, discuss extensively the benefits of trust in interorganizational partnerships.

65. Dyer, *Collaborative Advantage*, presents this and other statistics in an account of how Toyota and DaimlerChrysler have outpaced rivals in building supplier networks.

66. Ranjay Gulati, *Managing Network Resources: Alliances, Affiliations, and Other Relational Assets* (Oxford: Oxford University Press, 2007), discusses multiple dimensions of *network resources*, or the assets held within the connections among firms.

Conclusion

1. Francois M. Jacques, "Even Commodities Have Customers," *Harvard Business Review*, May 2007, 1.

2. Information on Lafarge and all quotations of executives in this chapter are taken from author interviews and the following cases unless otherwise noted: Ranjay Gulati and Alberto Gastelum, "Lafarge North America" (Evanston, IL: Kellogg School of Management, 2006).

3. My model isn't the only one encompassing how a firm becomes more customer or market focused. For example, Gary Gebhardt, Gregory Carpenter, and John Sherry, "Creating a Market Orientation: A Longitudinal, Multifirm, Grounded Analysis of Cultural Transformation," *Journal of Marketing* 70 (October 2006): 37–55, provide an empirically based four-stage model of how firms become more market oriented, largely through the promulgation of organizationally shared market understandings. Their four stages include initiation, reconstitution, institutionalization, and maintenance.

4. Gebhardt, Carpenter, and Sherry, "Creating a Market Orientation," 4, point out that getting business unit managers more involved in marketing efforts led to their taking significant ownership of these efforts. Evidence: by late 2005, marketing took up one-third of Lafarge's annual conference for cement executives, but almost none of the presenters were marketers.

5. A prescient account of this shift toward a broader understanding of customer needs can be found in David A. Garvin, "Competing on the Eight Dimensions of Quality," *Harvard Business Review*, November–December 1987, 101–109.

6. Jacques, "Even Commodities Have Customers," 7.

7. Ibid., 6.

8. Ibid., 7.

9. Ibid., 9.

10. Ibid.

11. Ibid.

12. Ibid., 1.

13. Ranjay Gulati and David Kletter, "Shrinking Core, Expanding Periphery," *California Management Review* 47, no. 3 (2005): 96, note that while many studies reveal a high failure rate for alliances, some companies consistently enjoy high returns from partnerships, while others have a much poorer track record.

14. Apple-related information in this chapter is from Peter Burrows, Arik Hesseldahl, and Roger Crockett, "Welcome to Apple World," *BusinessWeek*, July 9, 2007, 89–92, unless otherwise noted.

Bibliography

"A la Carte Outsourcing; The Emerging Model for Pharma." *Chemical Week*, May 28, 2003, p. 41.

Aron, Ravi, and Jitendra Singh. "Getting Offshoring Right." *Harvard Business Review*, December 2005, pp. 135–143.

Arussy, Lior. *Passionate and Profitable: Why Customer Strategies Fail and 10 Steps to Do Them Right!* Hoboken, NJ: Wiley, 2005.

Barnard, Chester I. *The Functions of the Executive*. Cambridge, MA: Harvard University Press, 1938.

Bartlett, Christopher. "GE's Growth Strategy: The Immelt Initiative." Harvard Business School Case no. 9-306-087. Boston: Harvard Business School, 2006.

Bartlett, Christopher, and Sumantra Ghoshal. *Managing Across Borders: The Transnational Solution*. Boston: Harvard Business School Press, 1989.

Basch, Michael. *Customer Culture: How FedEx and Other Great Companies Put the Customer First Every Day*. Upper Saddle River, NJ: Prentice Hall, 2002.

Bechky, Beth. "Sharing Meaning Across Occupational Communities: The Transformation of Understanding on a Production Floor." *Organization Science* 14 (2003): 312–330.

Berger, Peter, and Thomas Luckmann. *The Social Construction of Reality*. New York: Doubleday, 1966.

Bilger, Burkhard. "Salad Days." *The New Yorker*, September 6, 2004, p. 136.

Bossidy, Larry, and Ram Charan. *Confronting Reality: Doing What Matters to Get Things Right*. New York: Crown Publishing, 2004.

Brady, Diane. "The Immelt Revolution." *BusinessWeek Online*, March 28, 2005. (http://www.businessweek.com/magazine/content/05_13/b3926088_mz056.htm.).

Bryan, Lowell, Claudia Joyce, and Leigh Weiss. "Making a Market in Talent." *McKinsey Quarterly*, no. 2 (2006) reprint.

Burns, Tom, and G. M. Stalker, *The Management of Innovation*. London: Tavistock, 1961.

Burrows, Peter, Arik Hesseldahl, and Roger Crockett. "Welcome to Apple World." *BusinessWeek*, July 9, 2007.

Burt, Ronald. *Structural Holes: The Social Structure of Competition*. Cambridge: Harvard University Press, 1992.

Chandler, Clay. "Wireless Wonder." *Fortune*, January 22, 2007, pp. 130–136.

Chang, Julia. "Team Player: EDS Partners for Profit." *Sales and Marketing Management*, October 31, 2006.

Chatman, Jennifer, and Sandra Cha. "Leading by Leveraging Culture." *California Management Review* 45, no. 4, 2003, pp. 20–34.

Chidi, George. "Analysis: Cisco's Reorganization Cannot Unpop the Bubble." *InfoWorld*, August 24, 2001, http://www.infoworld.com/articles/hn/xml/01/08/24/010824hnciscofollow.html.

Christensen, Clayton M. *The Innovators Dilemma: When New Technologies Cause Great Firms to Fail*. Boston: Harvard Business School Press, 1997.

"Coca-Cola FEMSA Extends Relationship with EDS." EDS press release, April 30, 2007. (http://www.eds.com/news/releases/3691/.

Cross, Rob, and Lawrence Prusak. "The People Who Make Organizations Go—or Stop." *Harvard Business Review*, June 2002, p. 110.

Cross, Rob, Nitin Nohria, and Andrew Parker. "Six Myths About Informal Networks—and How to Overcome Them." *MIT Sloan Management Review* 43, no. 3 (2002): 67.

Davis, Edward, and Robert Spekman. *The Extended Enterprise: Gaining Competitive Advantage Through Collaborative Supply Chains*. Upper Saddle River, NJ: Prentice Hall, 2004.

Day, George S. *Market Driven Strategy: Process for Creating Value*. New York: Free Press, 1990.

———. *The Market-Driven Organization: Understanding, Attracting, and Keeping Valuable Customers*. New York: Free Press, 1999.

Deal, Terrance, and Allen Kennedy. *Corporate Cultures: The Rites and Rituals of Corporate Life*. Reading, MA: Addison-Wesley, 1982.

Delong, Thomas, and Vineeta Vijayaraghava. "Harrah's Entertainment, Inc.: Rewarding our People." Harvard Business School Case no. 9-403-008. Boston: Harvard Business School, 2003.

Deshpande, Rohit, ed. *Developing a Market Orientation*. Thousand Oaks, CA: Sage Publications, 1999.

DiMaggio, Paul, ed. *The Twenty-First-Century Firm: Changing Economic Organization in International Perspective*. Princeton, NJ: Princeton University Press, 2001.

Dolan, Kerry. "Speed, the New X Factor." *Forbes*, December 26, 2005, pp. 74–77.

Dominus, Susan. "The Starbucks Aesthetic." *New York Times*, October 22, 2006.

Dougherty, Deborah. "Interpretive Barriers to Successful Product Innovation in Large Firms." *Organization Science* 3, no. 2 (1992): 179–202.

Doz, Yves, and Gary Hamel. *Alliance Advantage: The Art of Creating Value Through Partnering*. Boston: Harvard Business School Press, 1998.

Drucker, Peter F. "There's More Than One Kind of Team." *Wall Street Journal*, February 1, 1992.

———. *The Concept of the Corporation*. New York: New American Library, 1946.

Dyer, Jeffrey. *Collaborative Advantage: Winning Through Extended Enterprise Supplier Networks*. Oxford: Oxford University Press, 2000.

Dyer, Jeffrey, and Kentaro Nobeoka. "Creating and Managing a High-Performance Knowledge-Sharing Network: The Toyota Case." *Strategic Management Journal* 21, no. 3 (2000): 345–367.

Dyer, Jeffrey, Prashant Kale, and Harbir Singh. "How to Make Strategic Alliances Work." *MIT Sloan Management Review* 42, no. 4 (2001): 37–43.

———. "When to Ally and When to Acquire." *Harvard Business Review*, July 2004, pp. 109–115.

"EDS Agility Alliance Publication, synnovation, Awarded for Debut Issue." EDS press release, August 24, 2006., http://www.eds.com/news/releases/3184/.

Ellsworth, Richard. *Leading with Purpose: The New Corporate Realities*. Stanford, CA: Stanford Business Books, 2002.

Engardio, Peter, Michael Arndt, and Dean Foust. "The Future of Outsourcing." *BusinessWeek*, January 30, 2006, pp. 50–58.

Engardio, Peter, Bruce Einhorn, Manjeet Kripalani, Andy Reinhardt, Bruce Nussbaum, and Peter Burrows. "Outsourcing Innovation." *BusinessWeek*, March 21, 2005, pp. 84–94.

"European Biotechnology Industry Shows Double Digit Growth." Ernst and Young, http://www.ey.com/global/content.nsf/UK/Media_-_07_04_16_DC_-_European_biotech_industry_shows_double_digit_revenue_growth.

Ewing, Jack, and Arik Hesseldahl. "The iPhone's German Accent." *BusinessWeek*, April 16, 2007, p. 38.

Fonda, Daren. "Has Sony Got Game?" *Time*, November 13, 2006, pp. 42–43.

Galbraith, Jay. *Designing Complex Organizations*. Boston, MA: Addison-Wesley Longman Publishing Co., 1973.

———. *Organization Design*. Reading, MA: Addison-Wesley, 1977.

———. *Designing the Customer-Centric Organization: A Guide to Strategy, Structure, and Process*. San Francisco: Jossey-Bass, 2005.

"Gannett, McClatchy and Tribune Reach Ownership Agreement on CareerBuilder, ShopLocal.com and Topix.net," M2PressWire, August 2, 2006.

Garvin, David A. "Competing on the Eight Dimensions of Quality." *Harvard Business Review*, November–December 1987, pp. 101–109.

———. *General Management: Processes and Action*. New York: McGraw-Hill, 2002.

———. "The Processes of Organization and Management." *MIT Sloan Management Review* 39, no. 4 (1998): 33–50.

Garvin, David A., and Lynn Levesque. "The Multiunit Enterprise." *Harvard Business Review*, June 2008, pp. 106–117.

Garvin, David A., and Michael Roberto. "Change Through Persuasion." *Harvard Business Review*, February 2005, pp. 104–112.

General Electric Company, *Annual Report*, 2006.

GE Imagination at Work Web site, 2007, http://cwcdn. geimaginationatwork.com/@v=092520050111@/imaginationatwork/flash.html.

Gebhardt, Gary, Gregory Carpenter, and John Sherry. "Creating a Market Orientation: A Longitudinal, Multifirm, Grounded Analysis of Cultural Transformation." *Journal of Marketing* 70 (October 2006): 37–55.

Geertz, Clifford. *The Interpretation of Cultures*. New York: Basic Books, 1973.

Goodwyn,Wayne. "Risk and Reward in Vendorville." Radio report. *Morning Edition*, June 2003.

Gottfredson, Mark, Rudy Puryear, and Stephan Phillips. "Strategic Sourcing: From Periphery to the Core." *Harvard Business Review*, February 2005, pp. 132–139.

Goul, Michael. "Teradata Reborn." September 22, 2009. Available at SSRN: http://ssrn.com/abstract=1477025.

Gulati, Ranjay. "Does Familiarity Breed Trust? The Implications of Repeated Ties for Contractual Choice in Alliances." *Academy of Management Journal* 38, no. 1 (February 1995): 85–112.

———. "Harley-Davidson." Evanston, IL: Kellogg School of Management, 2003.

———. *Managing Network Resources: Alliances, Affiliations, and Other Relational Assets.* Oxford: Oxford University Press, 2007.

Gulati, Ranjay, Suzanne Carpenter, and Sarah Huffman. "Starbucks." Evanston, IL: Kellogg School of Management, 2002.

Gulati, Ranjay. "Silo Busting: How to Execute on the Promise of Customer Focus." *Harvard Business Review* (May 2007): 98–108.

Gulati, Ranjay, and Alberto Gastelum. "Best Buy Company, Inc." Evanston, IL: Kellogg School of Management, 2006.

———. "GE Healthcare." Evanston, IL: Kellogg School of Management, 2006.

———. "Lafarge North America." Evanston, IL: Kellogg School of Management, 2006.

Gulati, Ranjay, Alberto Gastelum, and Melissa D'Arabian. "The Tribune Company: Revisted." Evanston, IL: Kellogg School of Management, 2006.

Gulati, Ranjay, Sarah Huffman, Abbas Khan, James Oldroyd, and Stephanie Pfeffer. "The Tribune Company: Redefining Sales." Evanston, IL: Kellogg School of Management, 2002.

Gulati, Ranjay, Sarah Huffman, and Gary Neilson. "The Barista Principle: Starbucks and the Rise of Relational Capital." *Strategy and Business* (Fall 2002): 1–12.

Gulati, Ranjay, and David Kletter. "Shrinking Core, Expanding Periphery." *California Management Review* 47, no. 3 (2005): 77–104.

Gulati, Ranjay, Tarun Khanna, and Nitin Nohria. "Unilateral Commitments and the Importance of Process in Alliances." *MIT Sloan Management Review* (Spring 1994): 61–69.

Gulati, Ranjay, and Lucia Marshall. "Cisco Business Councils: Unifying a Functional Enterprise with an Internal Governance System." Harvard Business School Case no. 9-409-062. Boston: Harvard Business School, 2009.

Gulati, Ranjay, and Lucia Marshall. "Cisco Systems: Building and Sustaining a Customer-Centric Culture." Harvard Business School Case no. 409–061. Boston: Harvard Business School, 2009.

———. "Corporate Solutions at Jones Lang LaSalle." Harvard Business School Case no. 9-409-111. Boston: Harvard Business School, 2009.

Gulati, Ranjay and Lucia Marshall. "Jones Lang LaSalle: Reorganizing around the Customer." Harvard Business School Case no. 410-007. Harvard Business School, 2010.

Gulati, Ranjay, and Nitin Nohria. "Thrive or Survive? Breakaway Strategies for Success in Turbulent Markets." Working paper, Harvard Business School, 2009.

Gulati, Ranjay, and James Oldroyd. "Coordinating Centralized Infor-
    mation and Decentralized Decision-Making." Working paper,
    Harvard Business School, 2009.

——. "The Quest for Customer Focus." *Harvard Business Review*, April
    2005, pp. 92–101.

Gulati, Ranjay and Lisa Khan-Kapadia. "Best Buy 2006–2007."
    Evanston, IL: Kellogg School of Management, 2007.

Gulati, Ranjay, James Oldroyd, Suzanne Carpenter, and Abbas Khan.
    "GE Medical Systems." Evanston, IL: Kellogg School of Manage-
    ment, 2002.

Gulati, Ranjay, and Phanish Puranam. "Renewal Through Reorganiza-
    tion: The Value of Inconsistencies Between Formal and Informal
    Organization." *Organization Science* 20, no. 3 (2009): 422–440.

Gulati, Ranjay, and Maxim Sytch. "Dependence Asymmetry and Joint
    Dependence in Interorganizational Relationships: Effects of
    Embeddedness on a Manufacturer's Performance in Procurement
    Relationships." *Administrative Science Quarterly* 52, no. 3 (September
    2007): 32–69.

——. "Does Familiarity Breed Trust? Revisiting the Antecedents of
    Trust." *Managerial and Decision Economics* 29, no. 2–3 (March–April
    2008): 165–190.

Gupta, Anil K., and Vijay Govindarajan. "Knowledge Flows within
    Multinational Corporations." *Strategic Management Journal* 21, no.
    4 (2000): 473–496.

Guthridge, Matthew, Asmus Komm, and Emily Lawson. "The People
    Problem in Talent Management." *McKinsey Quarterly*, no. 2 (2006):
    6–8.

Hall, Brian, "Incentive Strategy Within Organizations." Harvard Business
    School Case no. 9-902-131. Boston: Harvard Business School, 2002.

Hammer, Michael, and James Champy. *Reengineering the Corporation*.
    New York: HarperCollins, 2001.

Hansen, Morten T., and Nitin Nohria. "How to Build Collaborative
    Advantage." *MIT Sloan Management Review* 46, no. 1 (2004): 22–30.

Harley-Davidson home page. http://www.harley-davidson.com/wcm/
    Content/Pages/Company/company.jsp?locale=en_US.

Harvard Business School Working Knowledge, "Capability Sourcing at
    7-Eleven," March 28, 2005, http:hbswk.edu/archive/4719.html.

Heckscher, Charles, and Anne Donnellon, eds. *The Post-Bureaucratic
    Organization: New Perspectives on Organizational Change*. Thousand
    Oaks, CA: Sage Publications, 1994.

Helm, Burt. "Saving Starbucks' Soul." *BusinessWeek*, April 9, 2007, pp. 56–61.

Hesseldahl, Arik. "Unpeeling Apple's Nano." *BusinessWeek Online*, September 22, 2005.

Hill, Linda. "Power Dynamics in Organizations." Harvard Business School Teaching Note 9-494-083. Boston: Harvard Business School, 1995.

———. "What It Really Means to Manage: Exercising Power and Influence." Harvard Business School Teaching Note 9-400-041. Boston: Harvard Business School, 2000.

Hirsch, Paul. "From Ambushes to Golden Parachutes: Corporate Takeovers as an Instance of Cultural Framing and Institutional Integration." *American Journal of Sociology* 91, no. 4 (1986): 800–837.

Hurst, Richard. "Proof Positive." *Progressive Grocer*, August 1, 2006, pp. 54–58.

"IBM Will Rule Services, Says Gerstner." *IT World*, May 11, 2001. http://www.itworld.com/Man/3918/ITW010511ibm/.

Jacques, Francois. "Even Commodities Have Customers." *Harvard Business Review*, May 2007, pp. 1–10.

Kafka, Franz. *The Castle*. 1922; reprinted New York: Schocken, 1974.

Kasler, Dale. "Tribune Forced to Confront Breakup, as Knight-Ridder Did." *Sacramento Bee*, September 28, 2006.

Khanna, Tarun, Ranjay Gulati, and Nitin Nohria. "The Dynamics of Learning Alliances: Competition, Cooperation, and Relative Scope." *Strategic Management Journal* 19, no. 3 (1998): 193–210.

———. "The Economic Modeling of Strategy Process: 'Clean Models' and 'Dirty Hands'." *Strategic Management Journal* 20, no. 7 (2000): 781–790.

Kiviat, Barbara. "The Big Gulp at Starbucks." *Time*, December 18, 2006, pp. 124–126.

Kotter, John P., and James Heskett. *Corporate Culture and Performance*. New York: Free Press, 1992.

Krackhardt, David, and Jeffrey Hanson. "Informal Networks: The Company Behind the Charts." *Harvard Business Review*, July–August 1993, pp. 104–111.

Kreps, David. "Intrinsic Motivation and Extrinsic Incentives." *American Economic Review* 87, no. 2, 1997, pp. 359–364.

Kumar, Nirmalya. "The Power of Trust in Manufacturer-Retailer Relationships." *Harvard Business Review*, November–December 1996, pp. 92–106.

Larsen DeCarlo, Amy, and Kate Gerwig. "Synergy or Stupidity? Rejiggered Cisco Targets the Telecom Market by Way of the Enterprise." *Call Center Magazine*, September 5, 2001. http://www.callcentermagazine.com/shared/article/showArticle.jhtml?articleID=8709945.

Lawrence, Paul, and Jay Lorsch. *Organizations and Environment: Managing Differentiation and Integration*. Boston: Harvard Business School Press, 1967.

Leonard-Barton, Dorothy, and Walter Swap. *When Sparks Fly: Igniting Creativity in Groups*. Boston: Harvard Business School Press 1999.

Levine, Bernard. "Solectron Buying IBM Repair Unit." *Electronic News*, December 11, 2000.

Liker, Jeffrey, and Thomas Choi. "Building Deep Supplier Relationships." *Harvard Business Review*, December 2004, pp. 104–113.

Loveman, Gary. "Diamonds in the Data Mine." *Harvard Business Review*, May 2003, pp. 109–113.

March, James, and Herbert Simon. *Organizations*. New York, John Wiley, 1958.

Martin, Jeffrey, and Kathleen Eisenhardt. "Cross-business Collaborations." Working paper, University of Texas at Austin, Austin, TX, 2005.

Martinez-Jerez, F. Asis, and V. G. Narayanan. "Strategic Outsourcing at Bharti Airtel Limited." Harvard Business School Case no. 9-107-003. Boston: Harvard Business School, 2006.

———. "Strategic Outsourcing at Bharti Airtel Limited, One Year Later." Harvard Business School Case no. 9-107-004. Boston: Harvard Business School, 2006.

McCoy, Michael. "Merck Taps India for New Drug." *Chemical & Engineering News*, October 23, 2006, p.14.

Mintzberg, Henry. *The Structuring of Organizations*. Englewood Cliffs, NJ: Prentice Hall, 1979.

Mullin, Rick. "The Partnership Push." *Chemical & Engineering News*, March 6, 2006, pp. 21–27.

Nadler, David, and Michael Tushman. *Competing by Design: The Power of Organizational Architecture*. New York: Oxford University Press, 1997.

Nohria, Nitin, and Sumantra Ghoshal. *The Differentiated Network: Organizing Multinational Corporations for Value Creation*. San Francisco: Jossey-Bass, 1997.

O'Reilly, Charles. "Cooperation, Culture, and Commitment: Motivation and Social Control in Organizations." *California Management Review* 31, no. 4 (1989): 9–25.

O'Reilly, Charles, and Michael Tushman. "The Ambidextrous Organization." *Harvard Business Review*, April 2004, pp. 74–81.

Ostroff, Frank. *The Horizontal Organization: What the Organization of the Future Actually Looks Like and How It Delivers Value to Customers*. New York: Oxford University Press, 1999.

Panchak, Patricia. "Suppliers Provide Competitive Edge." *IndustryWeek*, September 2004, p.9.

Park, Andrew, and Jay Greene. "EDS Turbocharges Its Teamwork." *BusinessWeek*, Februrary 28, 2005, pp. 66–68.

Pasternack, Bruce, and Albert Viscio. *The Centerless Corporation: A New Model for Transforming Your Organization for Growth and Prosperity*. New York: Simon & Schuster, 1998.

Pereira Lima, Edvaldo. "Winning Cultures." *Air Transport World*, February 2006, pp. 54–57.

Pfeffer, Jeffrey. *Managing with Power: Politics and Influence in Organizations*. Boston: Harvard Business School Press, 1992.

———. "Six Dangerous Myths About Pay." *Harvard Business Review*, May 1998, pp. 109–119.

Pick, Adam. "The Rise and Rise of ODM Handset Manufacturing." *Electronics Manufacturing Asia Online*, November 16, 2006. http://www.emasiamag.com/article.asp?id=76.

Porac, Joseph F., and Howard Thomas. "Cognitive Categorization and Subjective Rivalry Among Retailers in a Small City." *Journal of Applied Psychology* 79, no. 1 (1994): 54–66.

Prahalad, C. K., and Gary Hamel. "The Core Competence of the Corporation." *Harvard Business Review*, March–April 1990, pp. 79–91.

Prasannarajan, S. "Power Pyramid." *India Today*, March 26, 2007, p.4.

Roberts, John. *The Modern Firm: Organizational Design for Performance and Growth*. New York: Oxford University Press, 2004.

Rosen, Corey, John Case, and Martin Staubus. "Every Employee an Owner. Really." *Harvard Business Review*, June 2005, pp. 122–130.

"Sanyo, Quanta Form Flat Panel Joint Venture." *Electronic News*, March 20, 2006. http://www.edn.com/article/CA6316753.html?text=sanyo%2C+quanta+form+flat+p.

Schein, Edgar. *Organizational Culture and Leadership*, 3rd edition. San Francisco: Jossey-Bass, 2004.

Simon, Herbert. *Administrative Behavior: A Study of Decision-making Processes in Administrative Organizations*. New York: Macmillan, 1945.

Simons, Robert. *Levers of Organization Design: How Managers Use Accountability Systems for Greater Performance and Commitment*. Boston: Harvard Business School Press, 2005.

Snook, Scott. *Friendly Fire: The Accidental Shootdown of U.S. Black Hawks Over Northern Iraq*. Princeton, NJ: Princeton University Press, 2000.

Solo Cup Company. Solo Cup Web site. 2005–2007. http://www.solocup.com/soloabout/aboutHistory.html.

"Starbucks Coffee Company and Jim Beam Brands Co. Expand Spirits Offering with New Starbucks Cream Liqueur." Press release, Jim Beam Global, October 19, 2005. http://www.beamglobal.com/jbbw/pr/SBUXCreamRelease.pdf.

Starbucks Corporation. 2007. http://www.hoovers.com/starbucks/—ID__15745—/free-co-factsheet.xhtml.

Stewart, Thomas. "Growth as a Process." *Harvard Business Review,* June 2006, pp. 60–70.

Sullivan, Carl. "CareerBuilder: Three's Company." *Editor and Publisher*, October 7, 2002, p. 8.

Taylor, Colleen. "Samsung, Infineon, big players in iPhone." *Electronic News*, July 3, 2007. http://www.edn.com/index.asp?layout=articlePrint&articleID=CA6457031.

Teece, David, Gary Pisano, and Amy Shuen. "Dynamic Capabilities and Strategic Management." *Strategic Management Journal* 18, no. 7 (1997): 509–533.

Thompson, Harvey. *The Customer-Centered Enterprise: How IBM and Other World-Class Companies Achieve Extraordinary Results by Putting Customers First*. New York: McGraw-Hill, 2000.

Thompson, James. *Organizations in Action: Social Science Bases of Administrative Theory*. New York: McGraw-Hill, 1967.

Tichy, Noel. *Control Your Destiny or Someone Else Will*. New York: Harper-Collins, 1994.

Tushman, Michael, and Charles O'Reilly. *Winning Through Innovation*. Boston: Harvard Business School Press, 2002.

Tushman, Michael, and David Nadler. "Information Processing as an Integrating Concept in Organizational Design." *Academy of Management Review* 3, no. 3 (1978): 613.

Useem, Michael. "America's Most Admired Companies." *Fortune*, March 7, 2005.

Uzzi, Brian. "Social Structure and Competition in Interfirm Networks: The Paradox of Embeddedness." *Administrative Science Quarterly* 42, no. 1 (1997): 35–67.

Uzzi, Brian, and Shannon Dunlap. "How to Build Your Network." *Harvard Business Review*, December 2005, pp. 53–60.

Van Maanen, John, and Edgar Schein. "Toward a Theory of Organiza-
    tional Socialization." In *Research in Organizational Behavior*, vol. 1,
    edited by Barry Staw. Greenwich, CT: JAI Press, 1979, pp. 209–269.
Van Rossum, Bram, and Jan de Witt. "Multiplying Development Capac-
    ity: A New Model." *Applied Clinical Trials* 15, no. 3 (2006): 50–54.
Vogelstein, Fred. "The Untold Story: How the iPhone Blew Up the Wire-
    less Industry." *Wired*, January 9, 2008.
Weick, Karl. *Sensemaking in Organizations*. Thousand Oaks, CA: Sage,
    1995.
Welch, Jack, and John Byrne. *Jack: Straight from the Gut*. New York:
    Warner Business Books, 2001.
Wenger, Etienne. *Communities of Practice: Learning, Meaning, and Iden-
    tity*. Cambridge: Cambridge University Press, 1998.
Whiteley, Richard. *The Customer-Driven Company: Moving from Talk to
    Action*. Cambridge, MA: Persus, 1991.

Acknowledgments

This book has been anything but a solitary affair. My community of collaborators who have inspired, guided, and assisted me in this journey is large.

I am grateful to the executives of the companies I researched for this book for allowing me the opportunity to document their journey over the last decade. Their willingness to share their experiences and insights were critical for this project. A number of colleagues gave me valuable feedback on this manuscript and include: Peter Barge, Mike Beer, Robin Ely, David Garvin, Boris Groysberg, Linda Hill, Rajiv Lal, Paul Lawrence, Nitin Nohria, Phanish Puranam, Jan Rivkin, and Michael Tushman. I also want to thank the following individuals for valuable discussions that shaped my thinking on the topic: James Anderson, Steve Burnett, Greg Carpenter, Tom DeLong, Bob Eccles, Jack Gabarro, Vijay Govindrajan, Dipak Jain, Phil Kotler, Das Narayandas, Peter Olsen, Mark Warren, and Ed Zajac.

I was fortunate to have a number of able research associates, assistants, and doctoral students over the years who worked tirelessly on tasks ranging from intellectual work to the mundane. Some of them helped me with drafting the cases, others on ensuring that all the quotes and information reported in this book were accurate, and some read and commented on earlier drafts of this book. I would like to acknowledge the valuable assistance of: Alyssa Bittner-Gibbs, Patrick Cullen, Bret Fund, Alberto Gastelum, Sarah Huffman, John Joseph, Lisa Khan-Kapadia, James Oldroyd, Bart Vanneste, and Franz Wohlgezogen. I would also like to thank John Butman, Stuart Cranier, Monica Jainschigg, Lucy McCaulay,

Howard Means, Jeff Strabone, Sachin Waiker, and Karl Weber for input on various chapters of this book that improved the clarity of my message.

I am indebted to the two institutions where I have been on the faculty that have both generously supported my research efforts: the Kellogg School of Management and the Harvard Business School. I am also grateful to the Teradata Corporation and SAP for research grants to support this research. They were all brave enough to believe in my vague ideas and supported this project from the exploratory phase.

Finally, I am grateful to my family, who tolerated my prolonged pursuit of this book.

Index

Note: Numbers followed by an *n* refer to note entries and numbers followed by a *b* refer to bibliography entries.

About the Author

Ranjay Gulati is the Jaime and Josefina Chua Tiampo Professor at the Harvard Business School. He is an expert on leadership, strategy, and organizational issues in firms. His recent work explores leadership and strategic challenges for building high-growth organizations in turbulent markets. Some of his prior work has looked at both when and how firms should leverage greater connectivity within and across their boundaries to enhance performance.

Professor Gulati has received numerous scholarly awards. He was ranked as one of the top ten most cited scholars in Economics and Business over a decade by ISI-Incite. The Economist Intelligence Unit has listed him among the top handful of business school scholars whose work is most relevant to management practice. He has been a Harvard MacArthur Fellow and a Sloan Foundation Fellow. He has published three books, including most recently *Managing Network Resources: Alliances, Affiliations, and other Relational Assets* (Oxford University Press, 2007). His research has been published in leading journals such as *American Journal of Sociology*, *Strategic Management Journal*, *Administrative Science Quarterly*, *Harvard Business Review*, *Sloan Management Review*, *Academy of Management Journal*, and *Organization Science*. He has also written for the *Wall Street Journal*, *Forbes*, *strategy+business*, and the *Financial Times*. Professor Gulati sits on the editorial board of several leading journals including *Administrative Science Quarterly* and *Strategic Management Journal*. He is the past President of the Business Policy and Strategy Division at the Academy of Management and an elected fellow of the Strategic Management Society.

Professor Gulati teaches courses in Harvard Business School's MBA and Executive Education programs. He has directed several executive programs and is also active in custom executive education. He has received a number of awards for his teaching, including the Best Professor Award for his teaching in the MBA and executive MBA programs at the Kellogg School, where he was on the faculty prior to joining Harvard.

Professor Gulati advises and speaks to corporations large and small around the globe. Some of his representative speaking and consulting clients include: GE, SAP, Bank of China, Sanofi Aventis, Novartis, Caterpillar, Allergan, Metlife, Target, Honda, Qualcomm, Aetna, Future Brands, Ford, Seyfarth Shaw, SAP, McGraw-Hill, Rockwell Collins, Lafarge, Merck, General Mills, Abbott Laboratories, Baxter, Credit Suisse, and Microsoft. He has served on the advisory boards of several startup companies and has appeared as an expert witness in business litigations.

He is a frequent guest on CNBC and has been a panelist on several of their series on topics that include the business of innovation, collaboration, and leadership vision. He has also been interviewed by such media as *Businessweek*, the *Los Angeles Times*, and *Chicago Tribune*.

Professor Gulati holds a PhD from Harvard University, a Master's Degree in Management from MIT's Sloan School of Management, and bachelor's degrees in Computer Science, from Washington State University, and Economics, from St. Stephens College, New Delhi.